IMAGES
of America

COLFAX TOWNSHIP

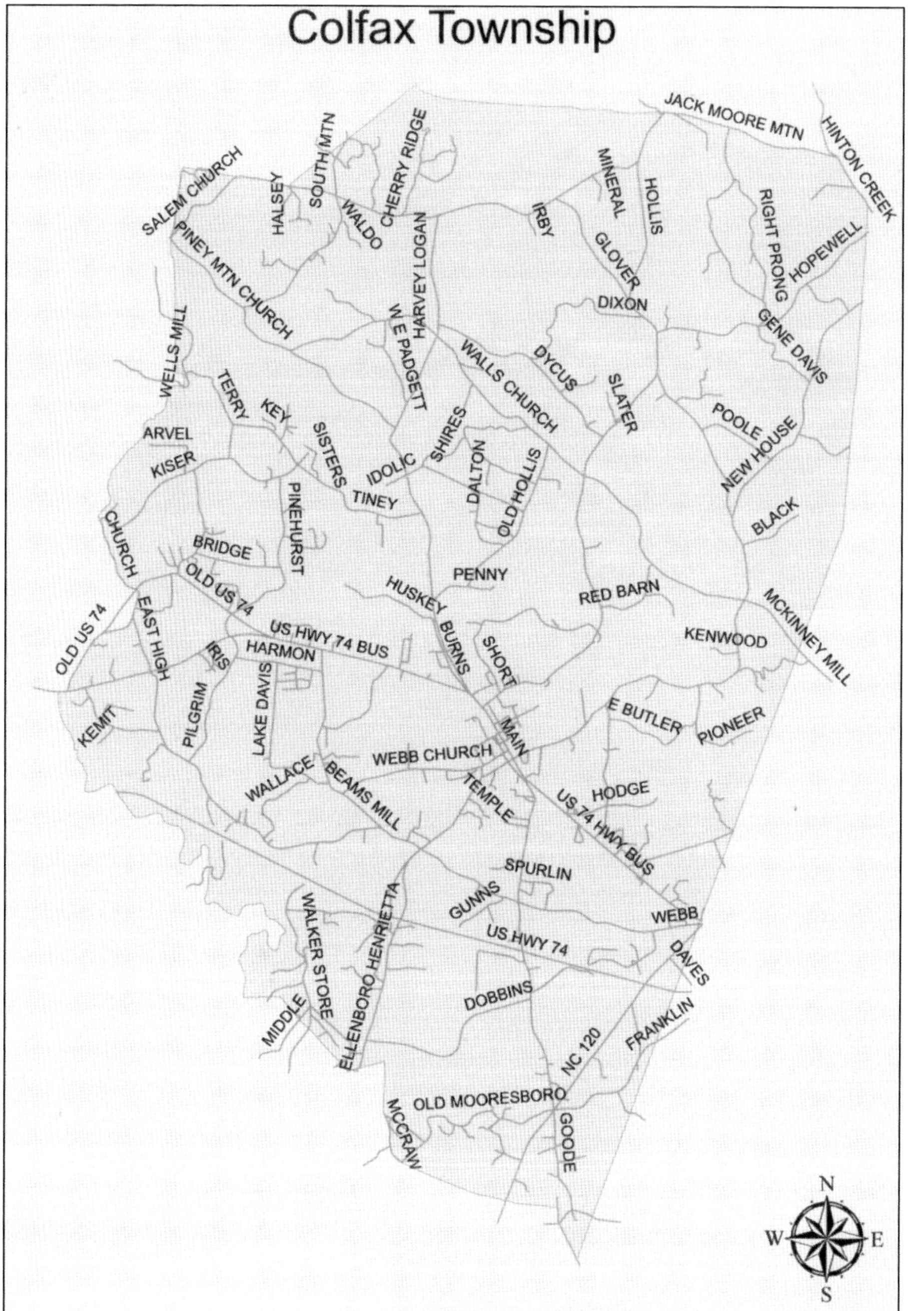

Above is a map of Colfax Township. Jack Moore Mountain is in the north, the state line is in the south, Cleveland County is to the east, and Cool Springs Township lies to the west. (Courtesy of Rutherford County Board of Elections and Debbie Bedford, director.)

On the Cover: The cover image from 1930 shows the Cherry Mountain Service Station, originally on Highway 74 Business and owned by J. L. Wilson. Shown from left to right are an unidentified customer, proprietor J. L. Wilson, and Guy Edwards. (Courtesy of Wilbur Wright.)

IMAGES
of America

COLFAX TOWNSHIP

Anita Price Davis, Mike Rhyne,
and Scott Withrow

ARCADIA
PUBLISHING

ISBN 978-0-7385-8691-5

Published by Arcadia Publishing
Charleston, South Carolina

Printed in the United States of America

Library of Congress Control Number: 2010933586

For all general information, please contact Arcadia Publishing:
Telephone 843-853-2070
Fax 843-853-0044
E-mail sales@arcadiapublishing.com
For customer service and orders:
Toll-Free 1-888-313-2665

Visit us on the Internet at www.arcadiapublishing.com

The authors dedicate Images of America: Colfax Township *to the memory of James M. Walker (1949–2008), professional railroad historian, photographer, and friend.*

Contents

ACKNOWLEDGMENTS

The authors wish to acknowledge all the people who so willingly shared their memories, their memorabilia, and their photographs. It is impossible to recognize them all by name. We especially thank our spouses for their encouragement. Pat Rhyne was always hospitable and helpful, her food was delicious, and her photographs were always professional. Ann Withrow worked hard to help us collect information and achieve the final product. Buren Davis carried computers, unloaded vehicles, and drove from Spartanburg to Ellenboro on many occasions. Collectively, we have spent 101 (mostly good) years with our three partners—and look forward to 101 more. Thank you!

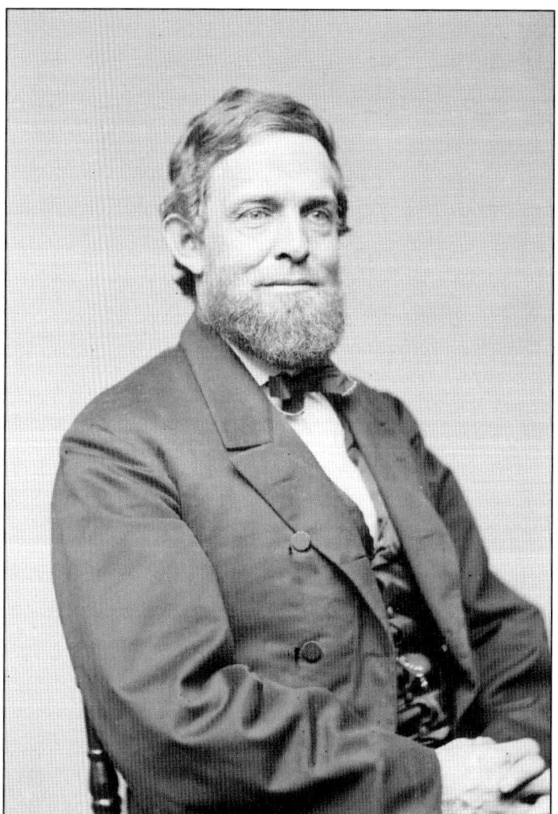

Schuyler Colfax (1823–1885) was the 17th vice president (1869–1873) of the United States. Colfax Township took its name from him. "Smiler" Colfax served under Pres. Ulysses Grant, former general-in-chief of the Union army. (Courtesy of the Library of Congress.)

Introduction

The book Images of America: *Colfax Township* begins with an apology: the authors could not include every person in Colfax Township and the many important facts relevant to each resident and each family. Other people may have been vital to the integrity and the growth of the township; the authors simply used a sampling of people and events.

The population of Colfax Township in 2010 was 7,680 (one percent urban, 99 percent rural), and its land area was 53.1 square miles. Colfax Township residents are primarily those who have lived here for more than five years. Colfax citizens have a strong sense of community; they attend—by the hundreds—such regular celebrations as Big Day, the Christmas parade, the Fourth of July parade, the fiddler's convention, and the Colfax Free Fair (a five-day annual fall event). The recent establishment of the Colfax Museum in the 1882 Ellenboro Depot serves to house a collection of memorabilia of Colfax Township—further evidence of the pride the township has in its past and present. Regular contributions of materials and frequent visitors to the museum indicate the residents' interest in the area; interest in the landmark by regional curators and historians attests to its quality.

The center of local government in most Southern states is the county, but North Carolina is an exception. The North Carolina Constitution of 1868 mandated the division of every county in the state into townships, which would share in governmental responsibilities.

Townships remain a way of determining and dividing up geographic areas for administrative purposes, such as collecting county taxes, determining fire and school districts, registering voters, establishing polling places, and categorizing land deeds. Each township has its own unique name.

Colfax Township took its name from Schuyler Colfax (1823–1885), the 17th vice president (1869–1873) of the United States. Because "Smiler" Colfax served under Pres. Ulysses Grant, who had been general-in-chief of the Union army, it may seem strange that a Carolina township chose Colfax as its name—until one considers voter registration in Rutherford County in 1868. In *The History of Old Tryon and Rutherford Counties* (1937), Clarence W. Griffin notes that in 1856 there were 560 Democrats and 407 Whigs who had registered as voters. By 1868, there were 688 Democrats and 1,297 Republicans; of these additional voters, at least 83 percent were African American. The reason for the choice of Colfax as the name of the township becomes more apparent when one looks at these Reconstruction facts.

The population of the entire county was 56,918 in 1990; by 2008, the population had increased more than eight percent to 63,424. This book, however, will address the largest voter precinct in Rutherford County: Colfax Township. Historical and current images will help tell the story of this unique area.

Many people, communities, churches, schools, and businesses make up Colfax Township, which is rich in veterans from all wars and with memories of those who did not return. Colfax has a long, intense history of patriotism. Because the township is primarily rural, most people live in the country and not in town limits. Both Colfax Township and Rutherford County are made up of decent, hardworking people who value each other, their country, their community, their work, education, and their churches.

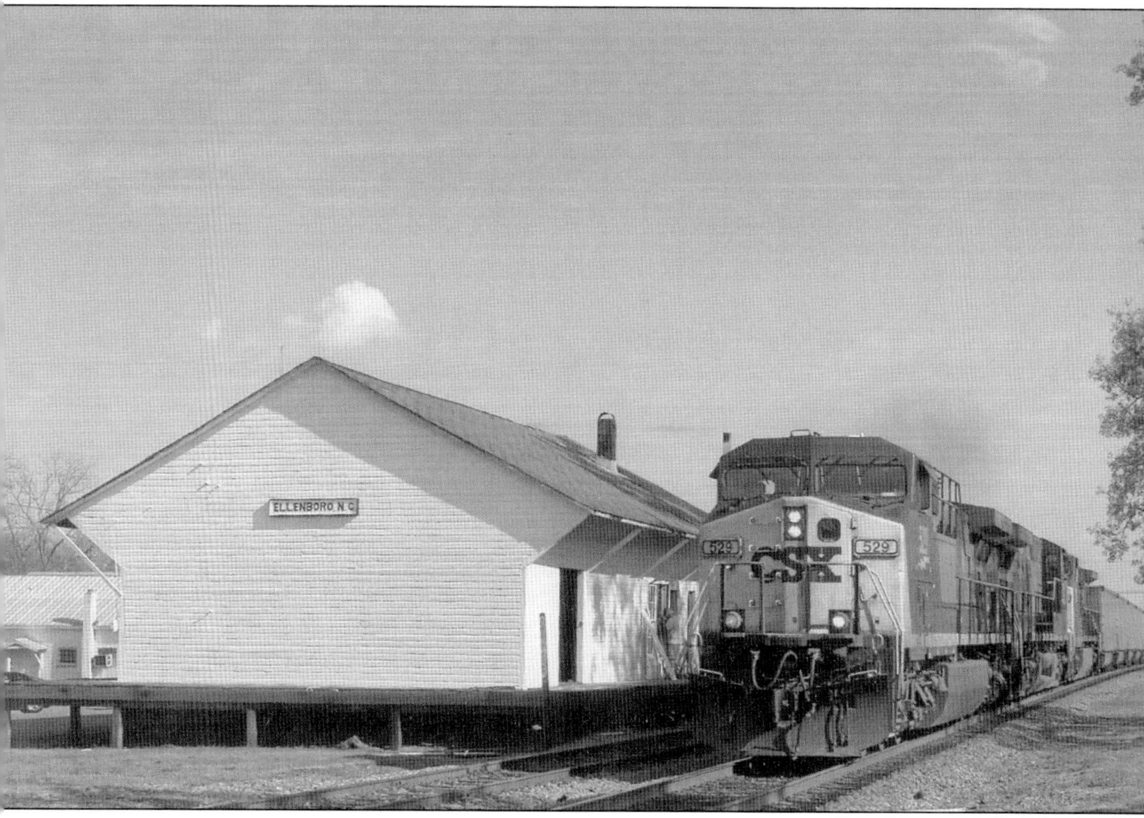

The Ellenboro Depot and Museum houses photographs and material culture from Colfax Township. James M. Walker (1949–2008), professional railroad historian, photographer, and friend, captured the scene above. (Courtesy of the Ellenboro Depot and Colfax Museum.)

One

Churches

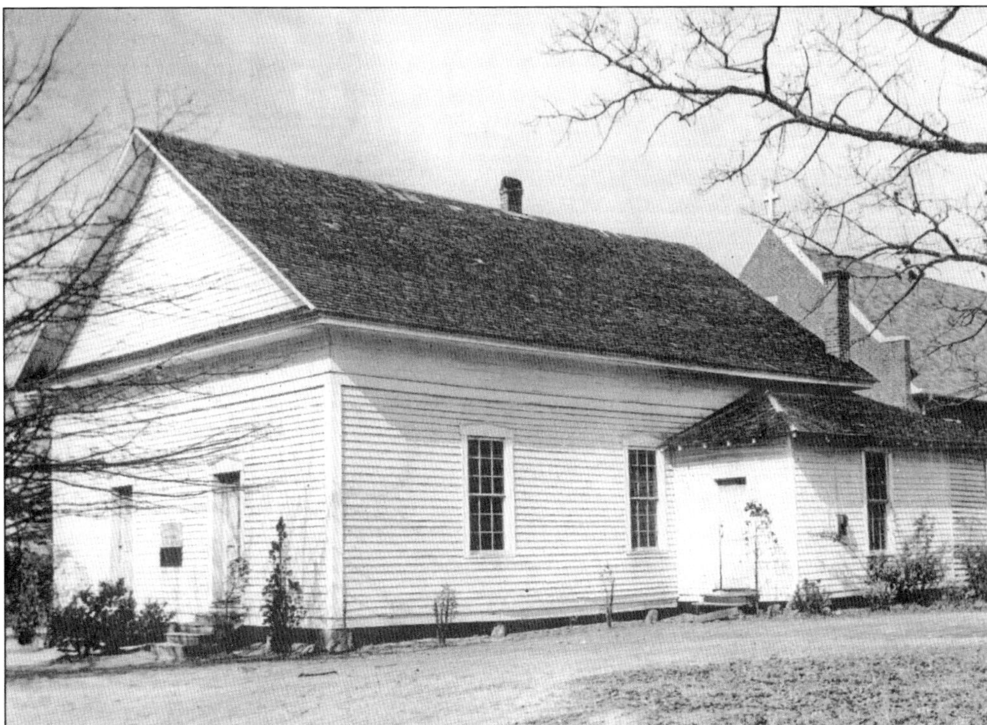

After the American Revolution, the area that is now Colfax grew materially and spiritually. Circuit riders, home meetings, and brush arbors ensured worship opportunities. Numerous small churches of various denominations sprang up in many parts of the area because travel was difficult. Later tent revivals came in vogue, and traveling evangelists drew many people to the services. Church founder Jeremiah Blanton organized a house-raising in 1792 for Oak Grove Methodist Church, the first actual church building in what is now Colfax Township. A wooden structure replaced the first building. This frame building for Oak Grove Methodist Church dates from 1885. (Courtesy of Jo Ann Martin.)

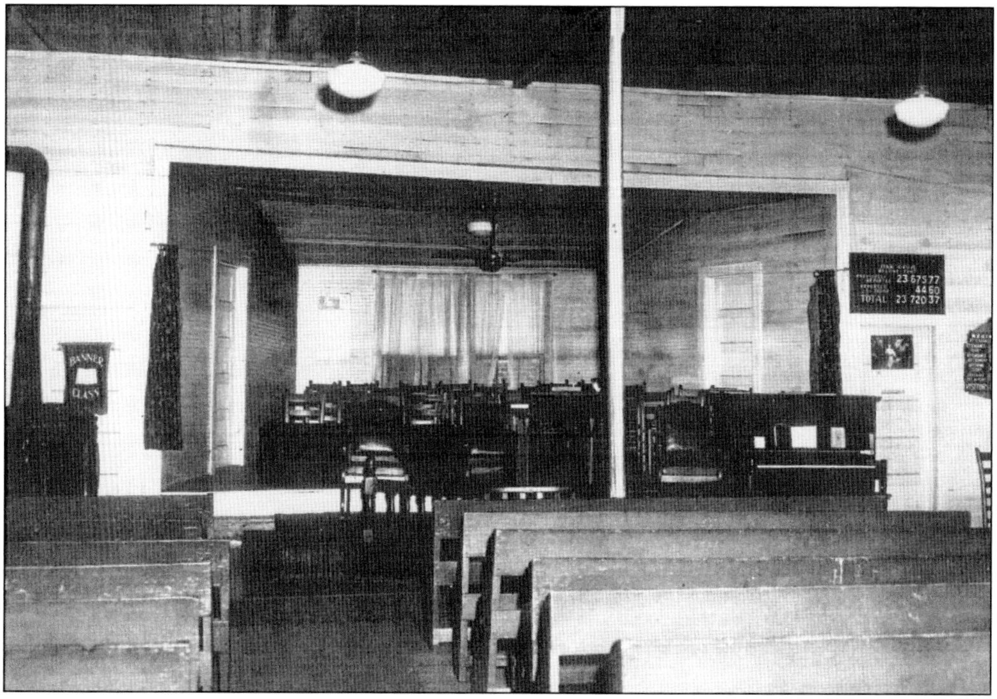

This interior of the 1885 Oak Grove Church shows the potbellied stove and the wooden pews in use at the time. At the right side of the photograph, the wooden register shows the attendance and the offering. (Courtesy of Jo Ann Martin.)

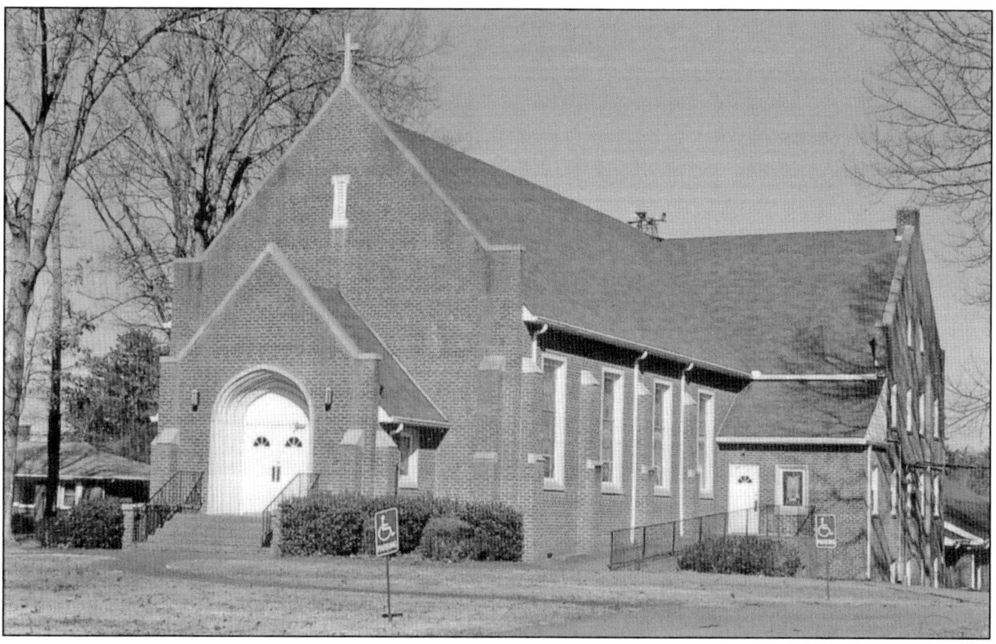

A brick building replaced the frame structure of Oak Grove Methodist Church. The congregation held its first service in the current brick Oak Grove Church on Memorial Day in 1950. The building is still in use. The church is now Oak Grove United Methodist Church. (Courtesy of Jo Ann Martin.)

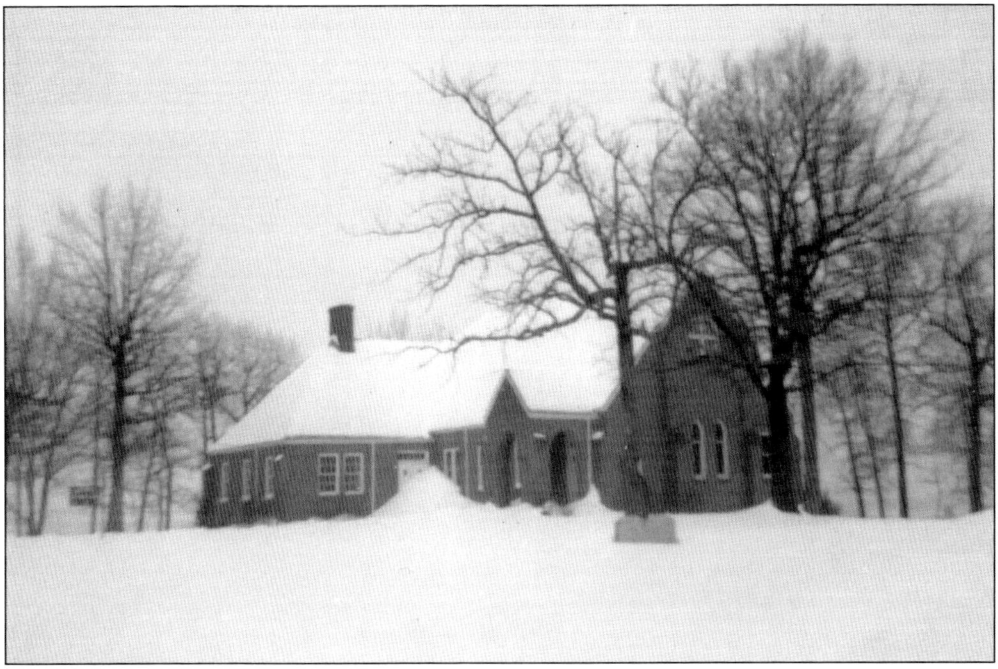

The second Methodist church established in Colfax Township was Hopewell Methodist Church (1800). The first structure was a log building that was 1 mile east of the current church. The second facility was in the old Robbins School building, which was on the present church property. A wooden frame structure dates from 1893. The building seen here was complete by 1946; fire destroyed it in January 1961. (Courtesy of Joyce McFarland and Brenda McFarland Toney.)

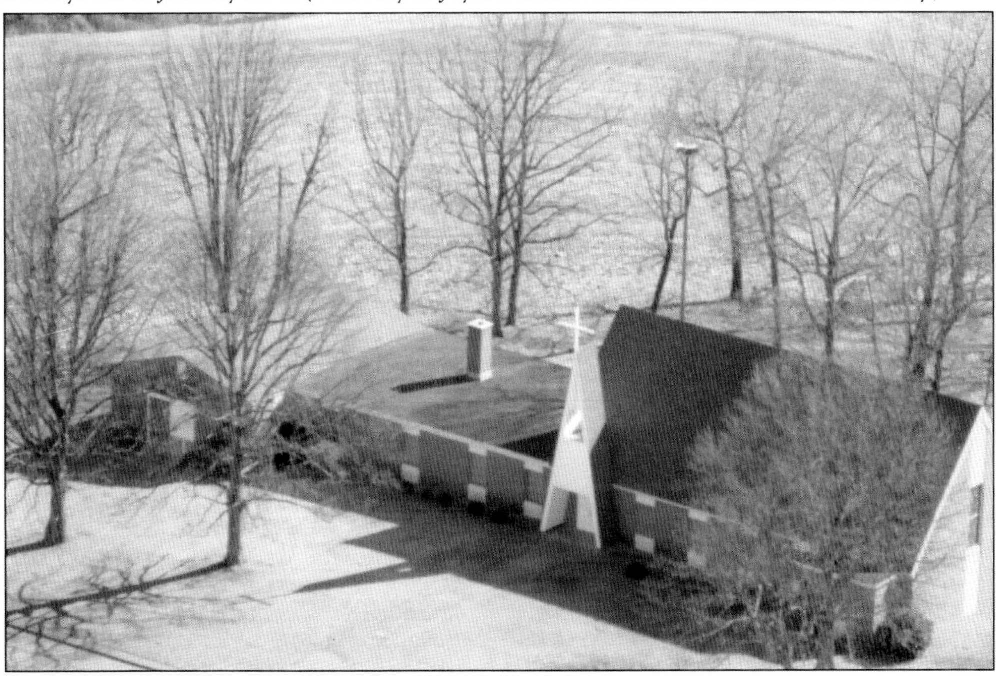

In April 1962, members held the first worship service in the current sanctuary of the Hopewell United Methodist Church. (Courtesy of Joyce McFarland and Brenda McFarland Toney.)

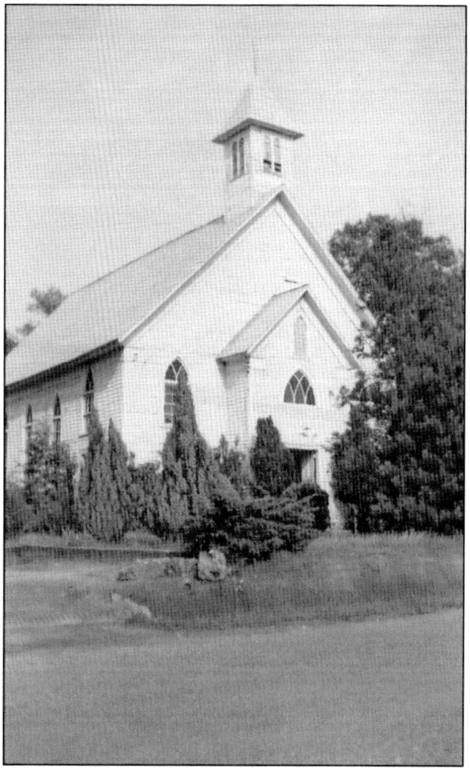

Concord Baptist Church was organized in 1804. Thirty-one members were on the original roster, which reportedly included Nancy Hanks, Abraham Lincoln's mother. The rebuilt church in 1961 was in a slightly different location in Colfax Township. (Courtesy of Kim Jones.)

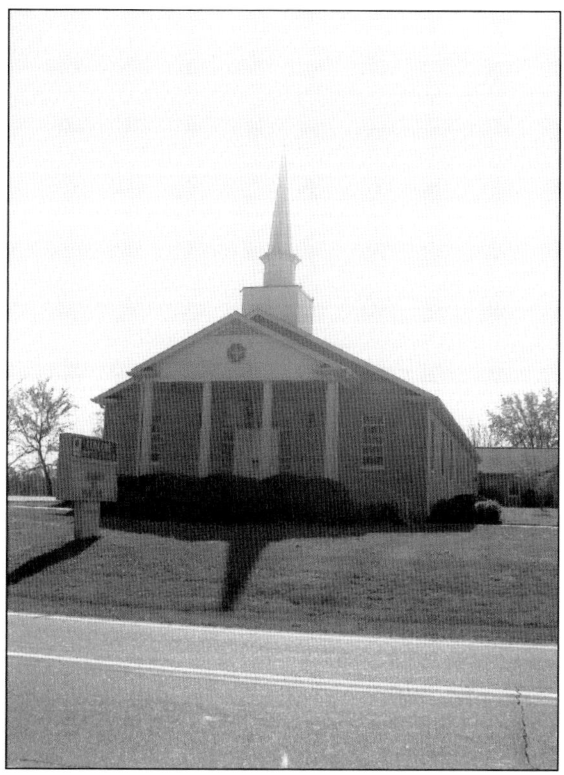

The new sanctuary of the current Concord Baptist Church dates from 1974. (Courtesy of Pat Rhyne.)

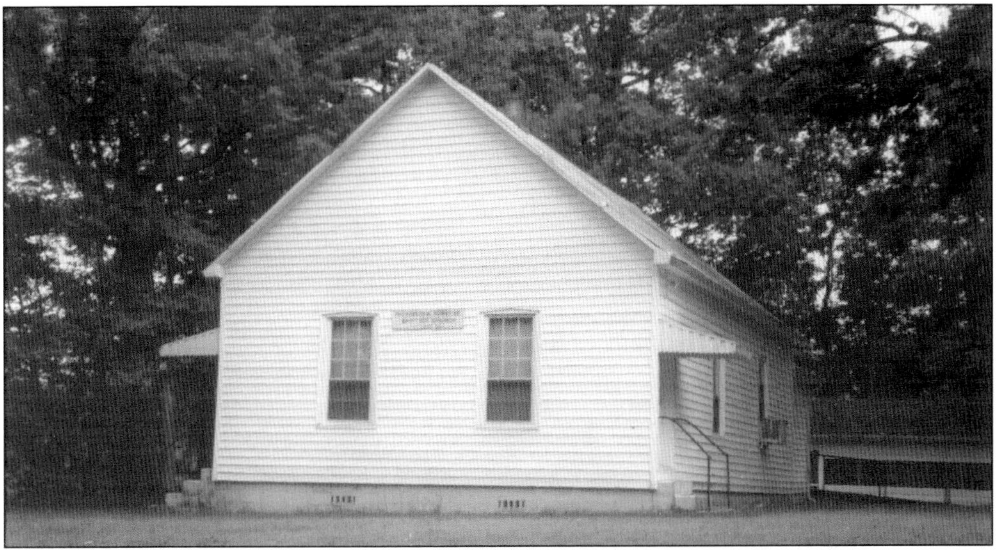

John Edwards donated the land for Philadelphia Primitive Baptist Church in 1850, the same year the church was organized. The church observes the rite of foot washing to demonstrate humility and service. This photograph of Philadelphia Primitive Baptist Church shows the white frame structure. (Courtesy of Ivey Ray Mauney.)

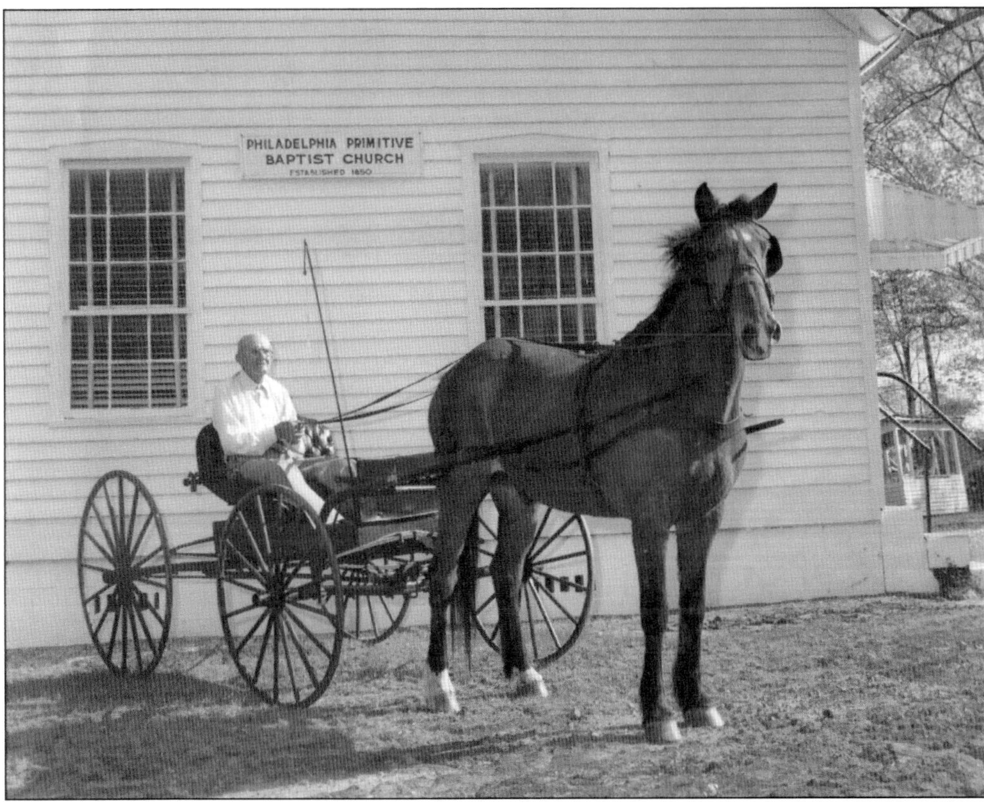

This photograph shows Vaughn Beam in front of the wood-frame Philadelphia Primitive Baptist Church. (Courtesy of Beth Beam King and Dan King.)

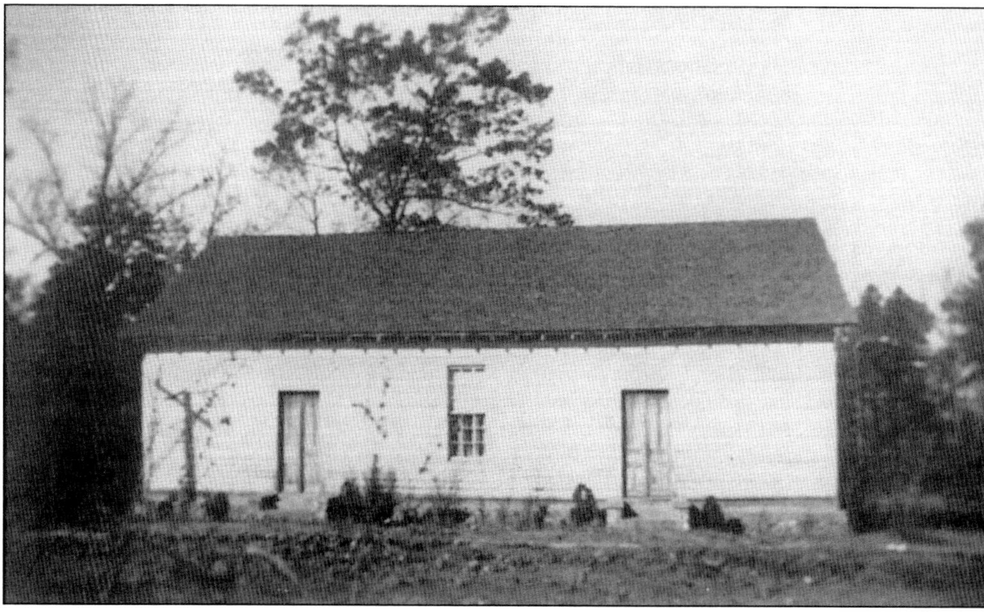

The organization of Bethel Baptist Church dates from 1847. The first structure was a log building. This white, wooden building replaced the log church in 1881. (Courtesy of Colfax Museum.)

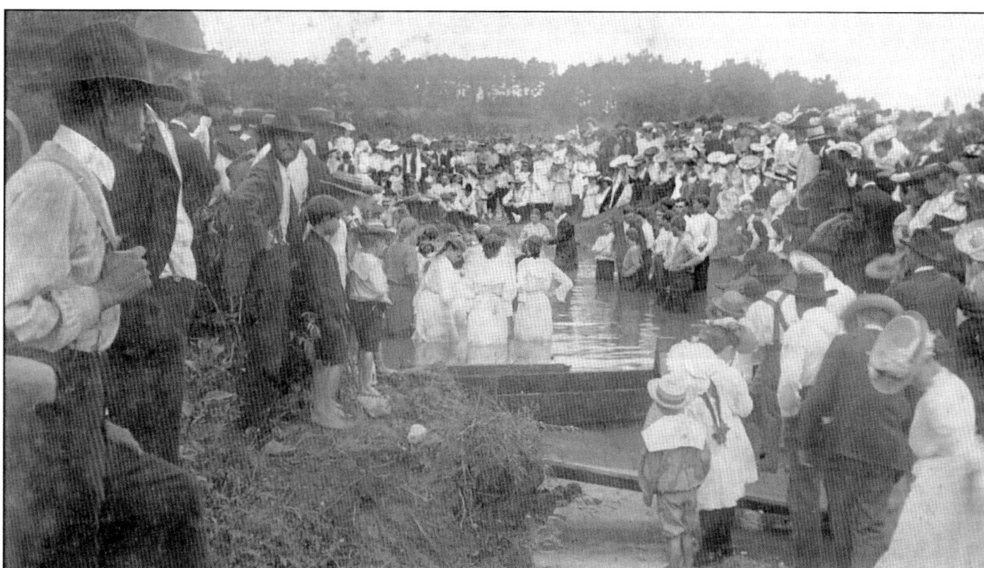

This pre-1909 scene shows a Bethel Baptist Church baptismal service in a local stream, north of the original church site. (Courtesy of Jo Ann Martin.)

The site of a newer brick building (1921) for Bethel Baptist Church was along U.S. Highway 74 Business. It was in use for 37 years. (Courtesy of Paul Price.)

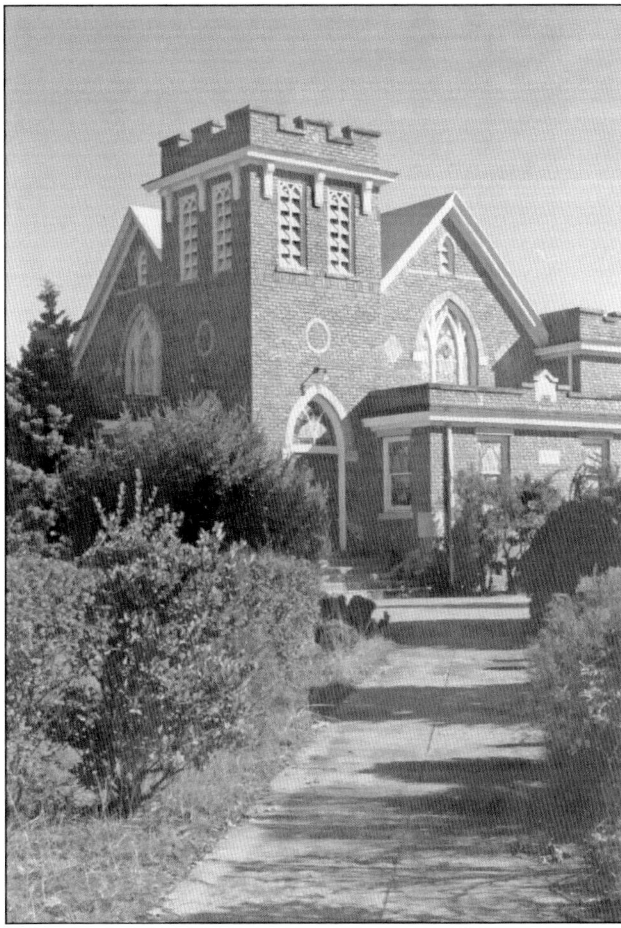

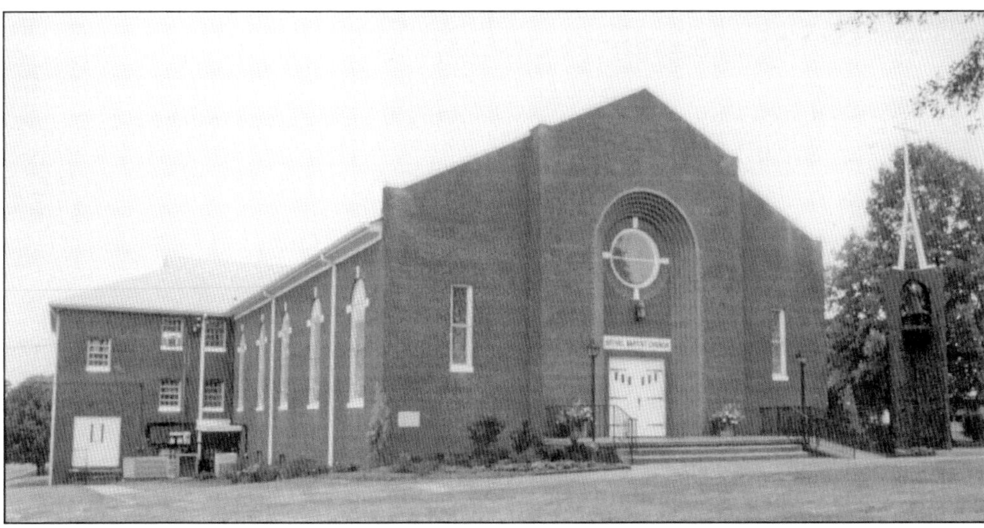

The current brick building of Bethel Baptist Church replaced the 1921 brick structure of Bethel Baptist Church. Under the leadership of Rev. Harold Brown, the new construction was complete by 1958; this photograph is the work of James M. Walker. (Courtesy of Bethel Baptist Church.)

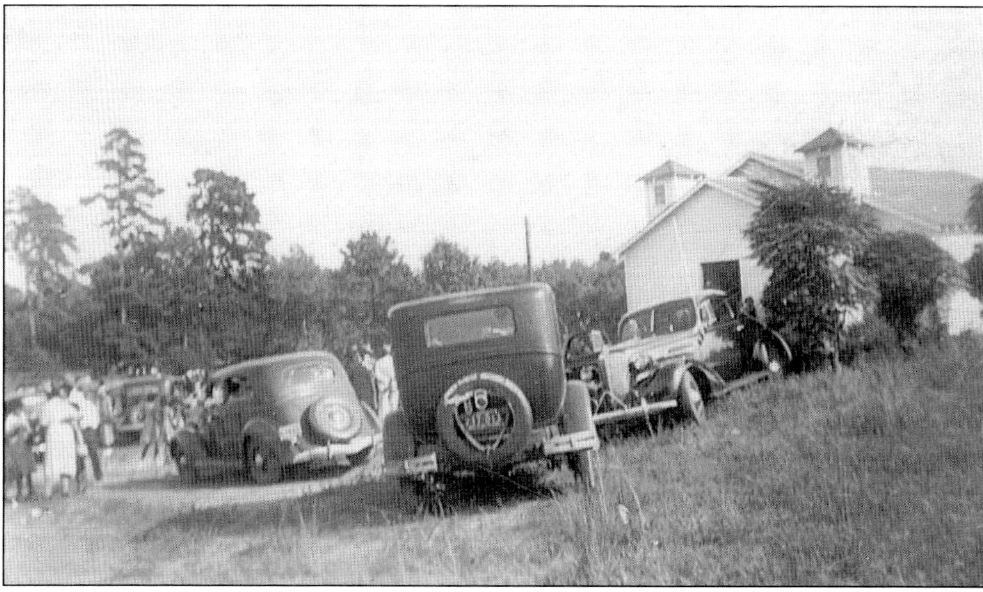

In 1867, Dave Harrill donated land 2.5 miles west of Ellenboro for Webb First Baptist Church. The first structure was a brush arbor, which later burned. The enthusiasm for worship resulted in the construction of a log church on the same plot of land. In 1935, just outside the town limits of Ellenboro, the congregation erected a wood-frame structure on Webb Church Road. (Courtesy of Hattie Logan.)

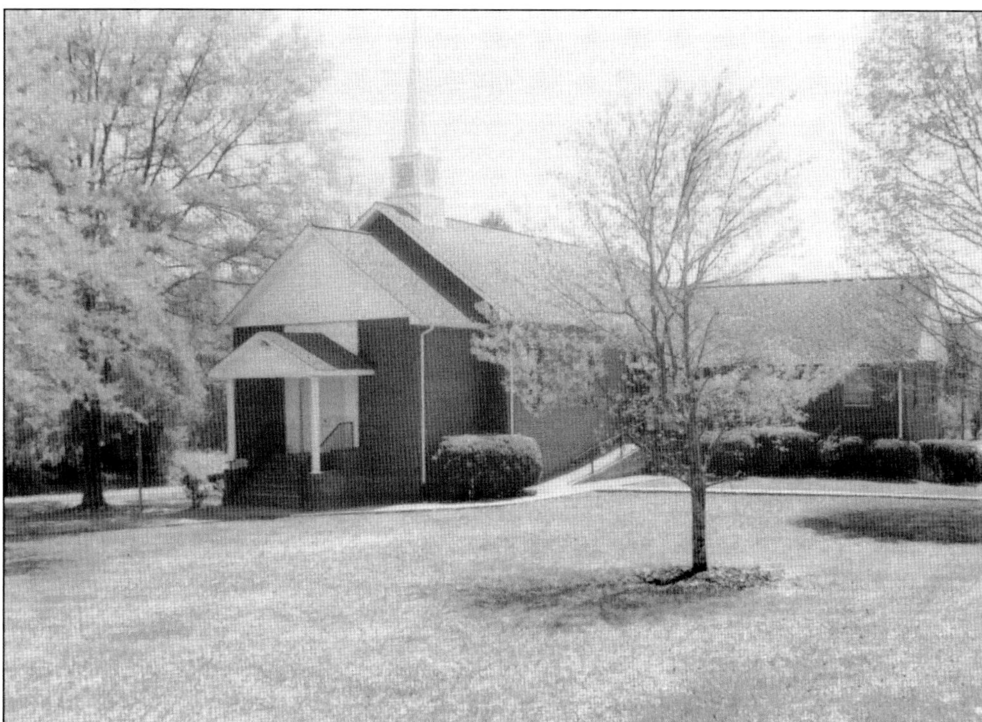

The work for the new Webb First Baptist Church facility began in 1967. Work continued in 1974; the dedication of the new building was in 1975. (Courtesy of Pat Rhyne.)

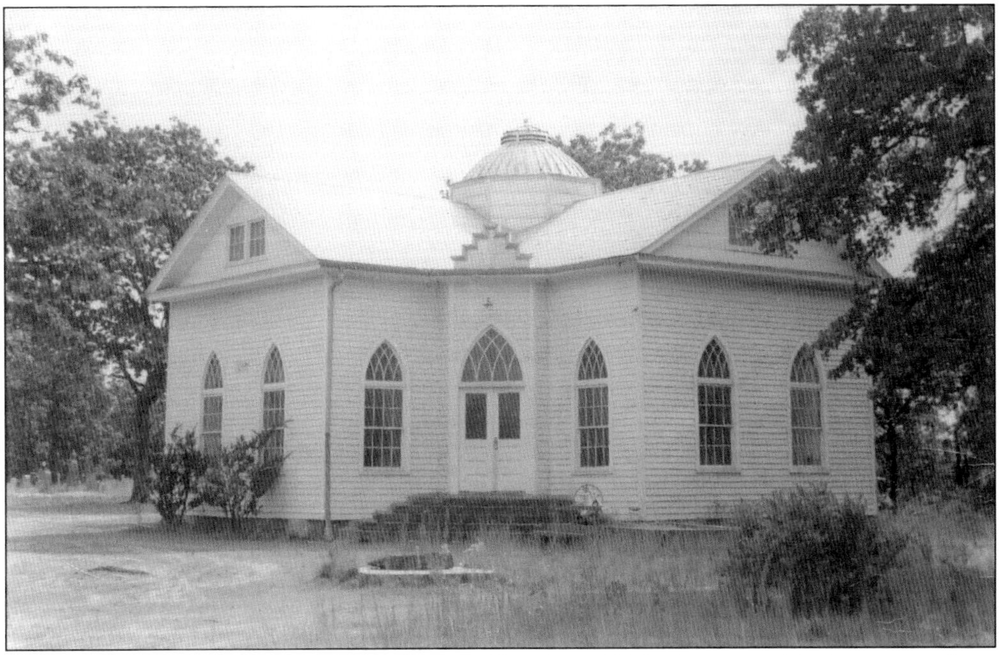

At the organization of Mount Olivet Baptist Church in 1883, there were 28 charter members. Their first meetings were in brush arbors; later the church met in a log building. The name *Mount Olivet* derives from the Olivet Sermon (Sermon on the Mount). In 1923, a white frame structure provided a gathering place for church members. (Courtesy of Bill Blanton.)

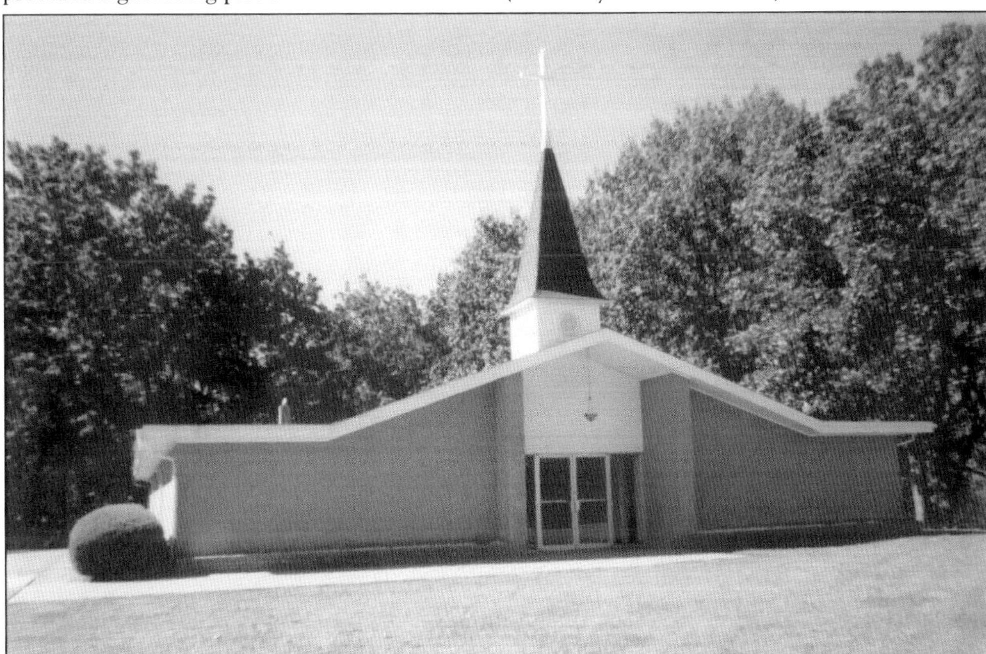

The current sanctuary and education building of Mount Olivet Baptist Church dates from 1971. The brick structure is still the place of worship and a source of pride to the congregation. (Courtesy of Bill Blanton.)

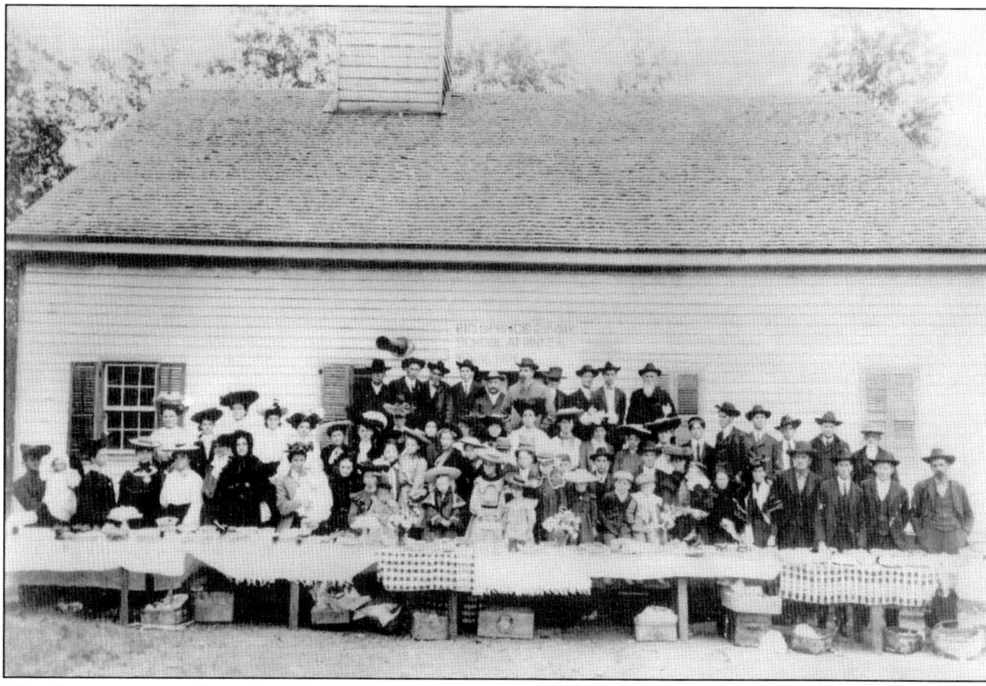

The first meeting place for Big Springs Baptist Church was constructed in 1818 in a brush arbor near Jack Moore Mountain; a log cabin followed. The next structure—this wood-frame sanctuary and education building—dates from September 10, 1870. (Courtesy of Linda Butler Bridges.)

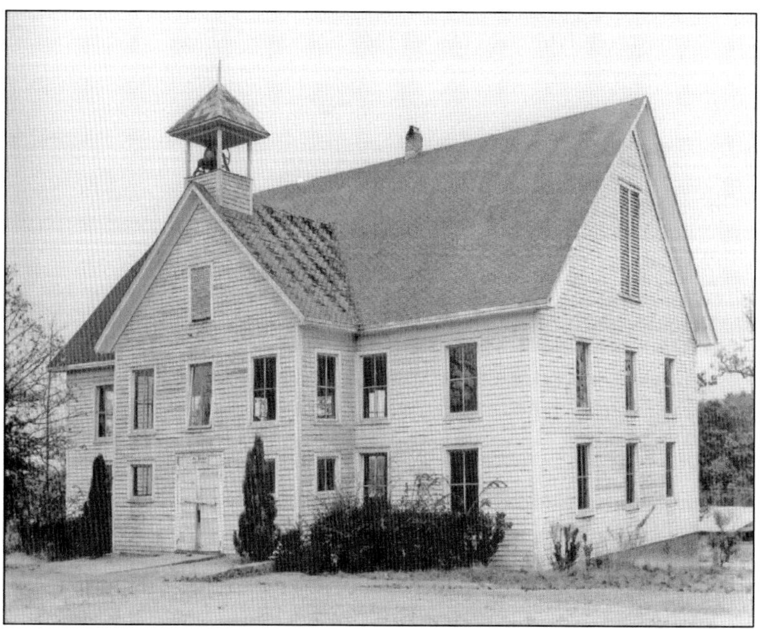

The fourth place of worship for Big Springs Baptist Church was a two-story, white frame church completed on October 10, 1908. (Courtesy of Linda Butler Bridges.)

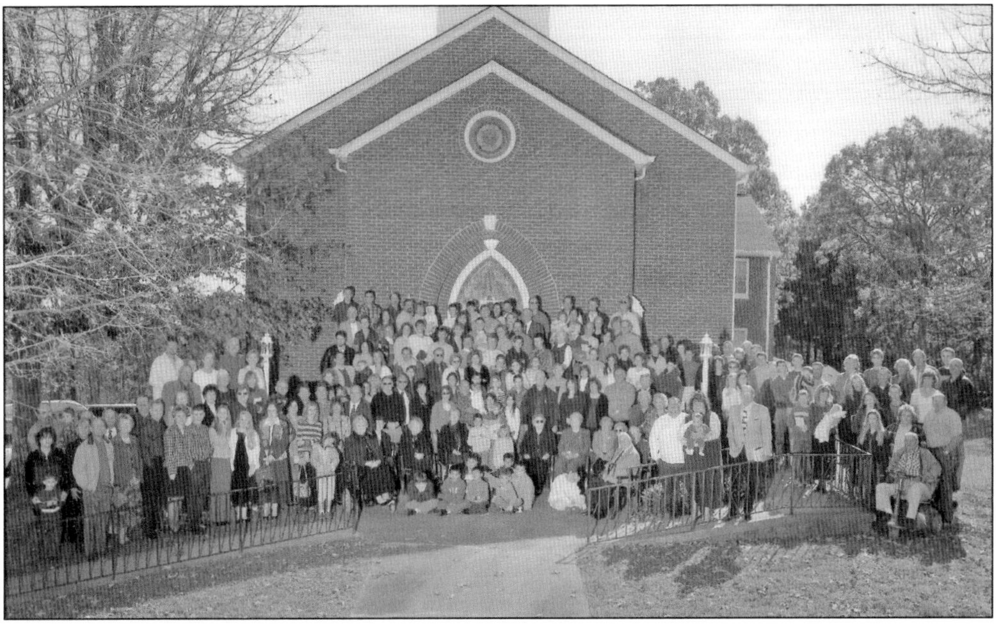

The brick building of Big Springs Baptist Church dates from January 8, 1956. The facility is still in use and is a community meeting place. (Courtesy of Linda Butler Bridges.)

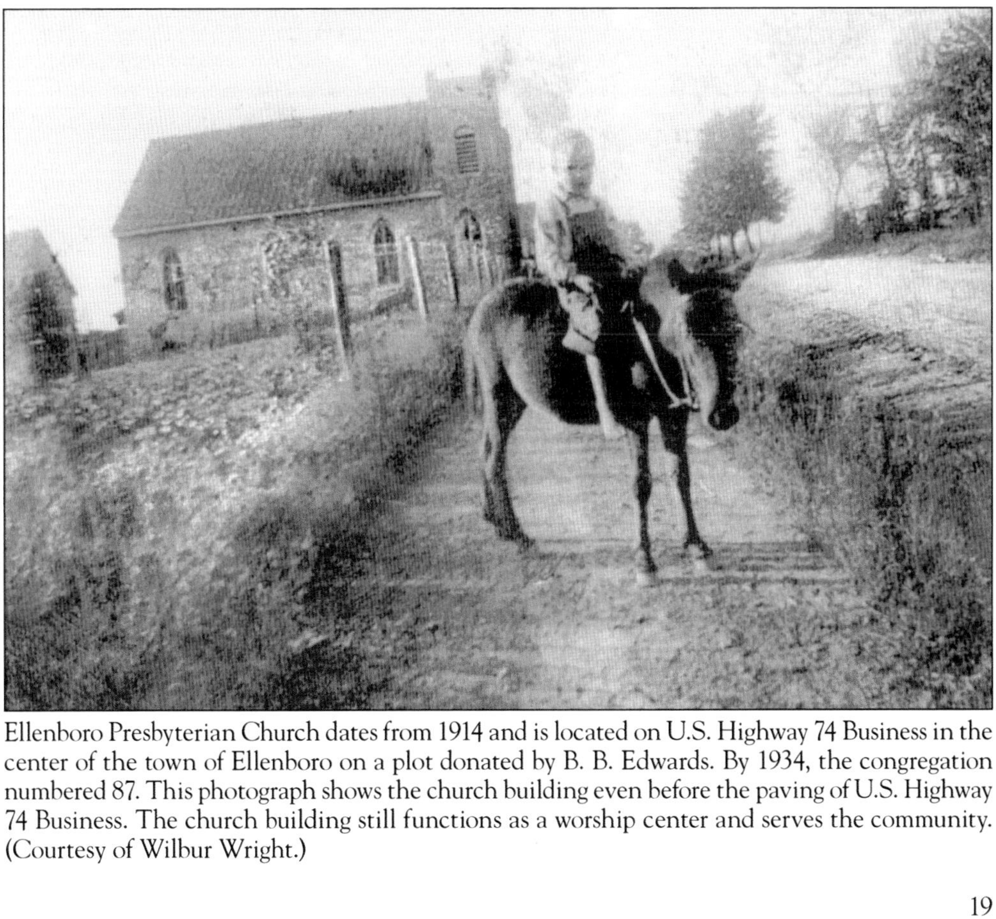

Ellenboro Presbyterian Church dates from 1914 and is located on U.S. Highway 74 Business in the center of the town of Ellenboro on a plot donated by B. B. Edwards. By 1934, the congregation numbered 87. This photograph shows the church building even before the paving of U.S. Highway 74 Business. The church building still functions as a worship center and serves the community. (Courtesy of Wilbur Wright.)

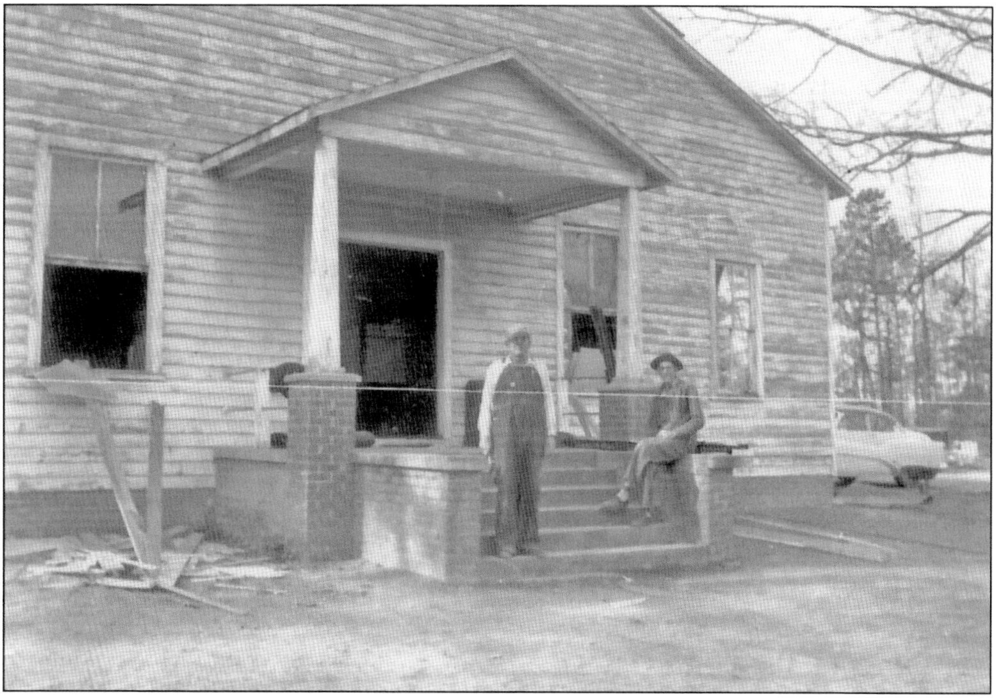

Drury Dobbins Baptist Church dates from May 9, 1918. Drury Dobbins was a well-known Baptist minister in the area. The church began as a Sunday school class in a small tenant house about a half-mile from the current structure. A brush arbor was available for worship services. The dedication of the first church building was in June 1920. Pictured are Rev. A. M. Martin (left) and Fred Doty. (Courtesy of J. T. Doty and Joe William McDaniel.)

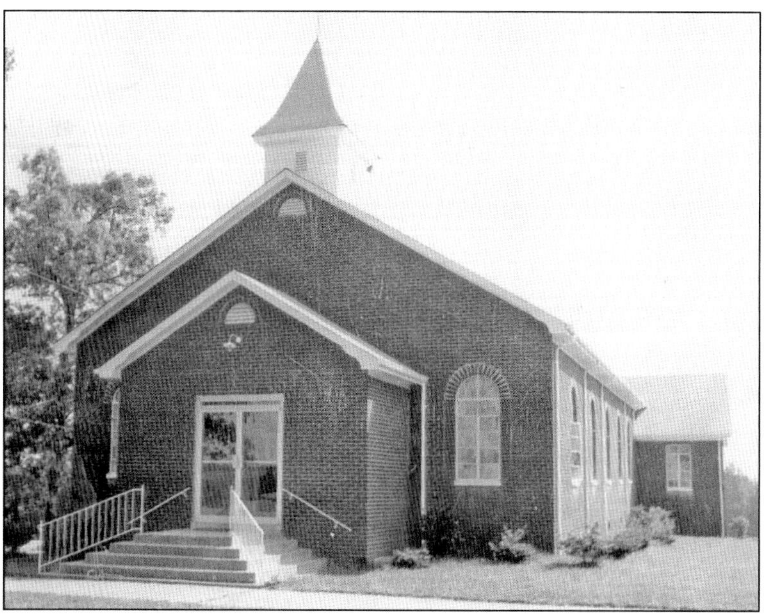

The completion of the current sanctuary of Drury Dobbins Church, pictured here, was in 1955. (Courtesy of J. T. Doty and Joe McDaniel.)

Twenty-seven founding members organized Race Path Baptist Church in 1914. Their first church building, complete with steeple, was on the site of the Old Race Path, a linear track for racing horses. (Courtesy of Race Path Baptist Church.)

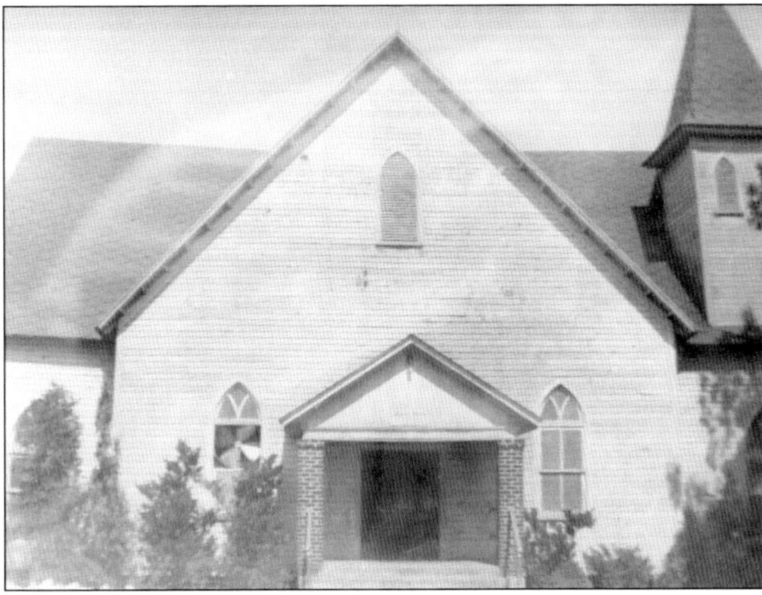

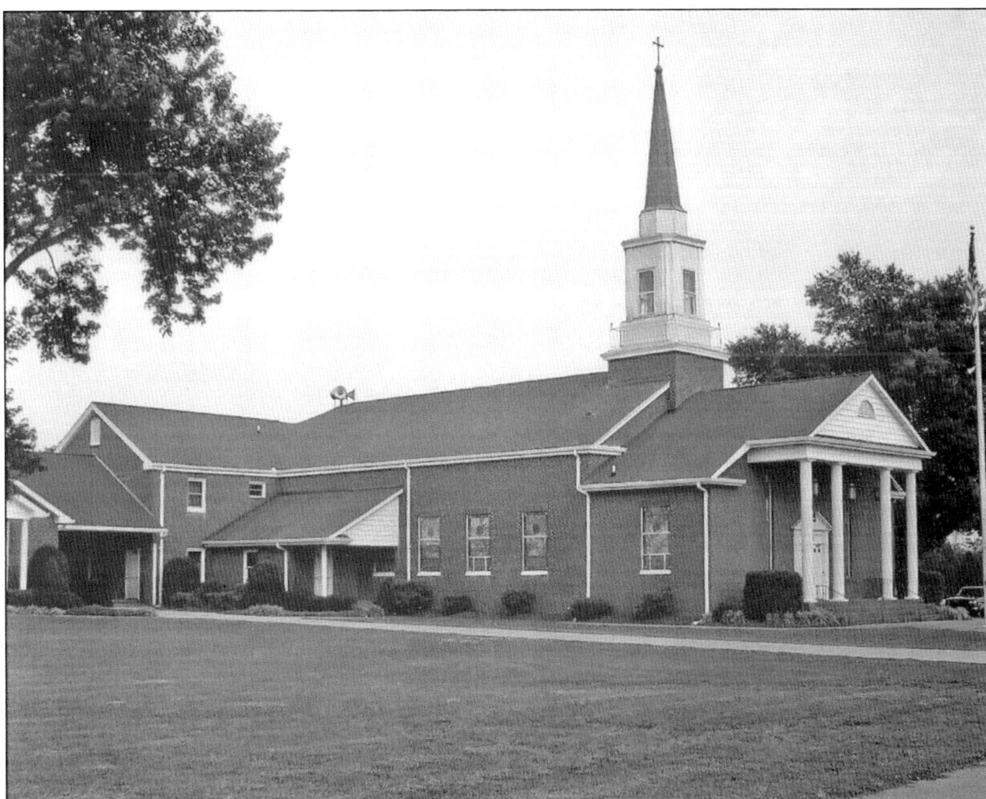

In 1952, the present Race Path Baptist Church Education Building and Sanctuary replaced the structure erected in 1916. (Courtesy of Race Path Baptist Church.)

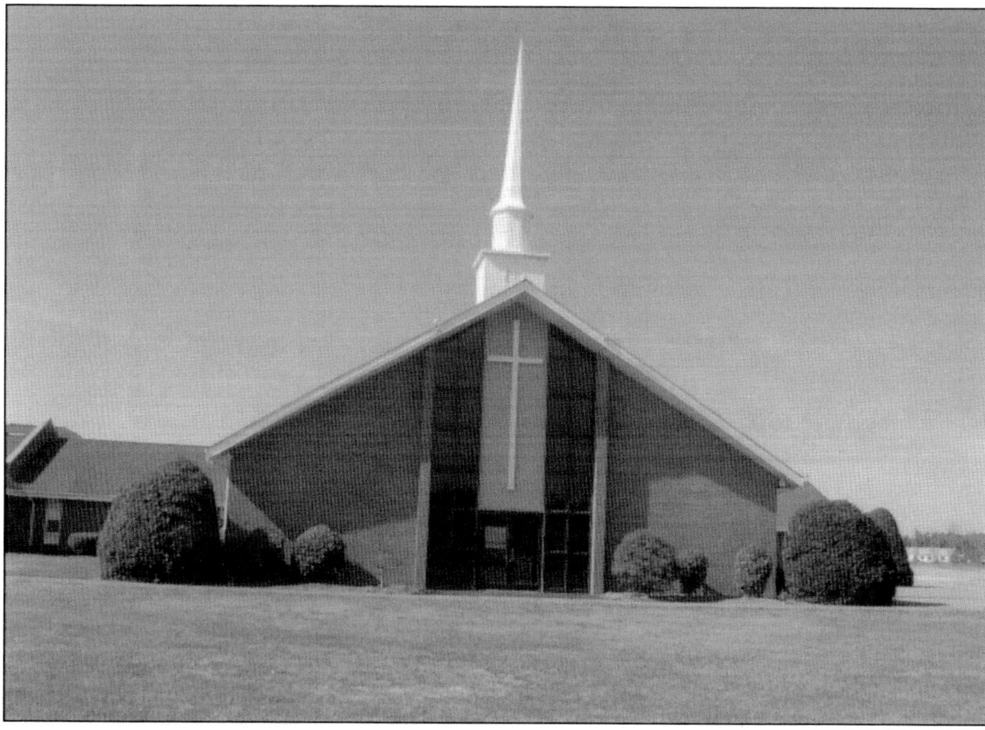

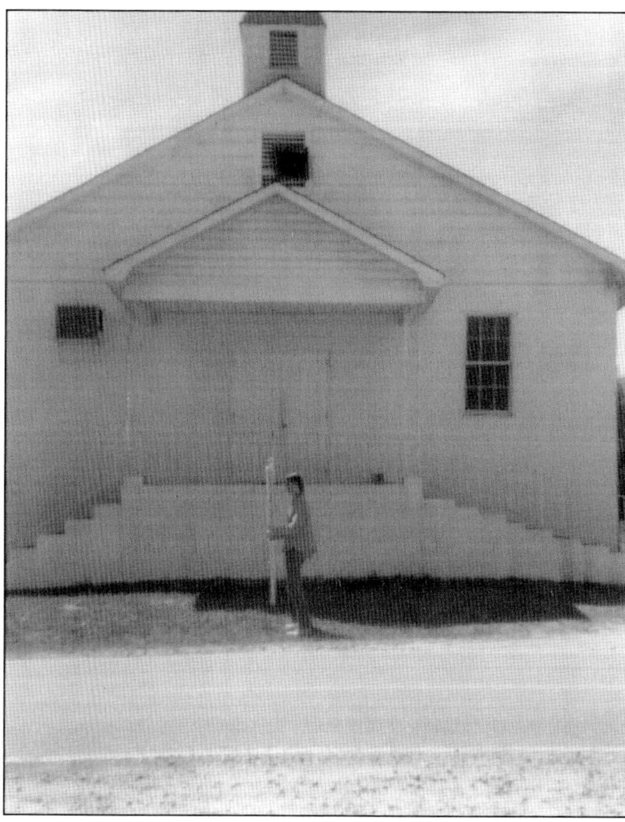

The first service of Liberty Baptist Church was on September 22, 1982, in Harrelson's Funeral Home in Henrietta, North Carolina. Because of the sale of the funeral home, the date of the last service there was July 1, 1983. Services moved to the Reid Family Store in Sandy Mush, North Carolina. On June 10, 1984, Liberty Baptist Church moved to its current building at 821 Webb Road. (Courtesy of Liberty Baptist Church.)

Piney Mountain Baptist Church dates from 1951, when people met for services in the home of Theodore Bridges. In 1952, the church purchased a lot on which to construct the original block building. (Courtesy of Diane Padgett Hewitt.)

In the mid-1960s and early 1970s, Piney Mountain Baptist Church members paid for a brick veneer to cover the block building. Many other improvements mark the progress of the building and the church itself. (Courtesy of Pat Rhyne.)

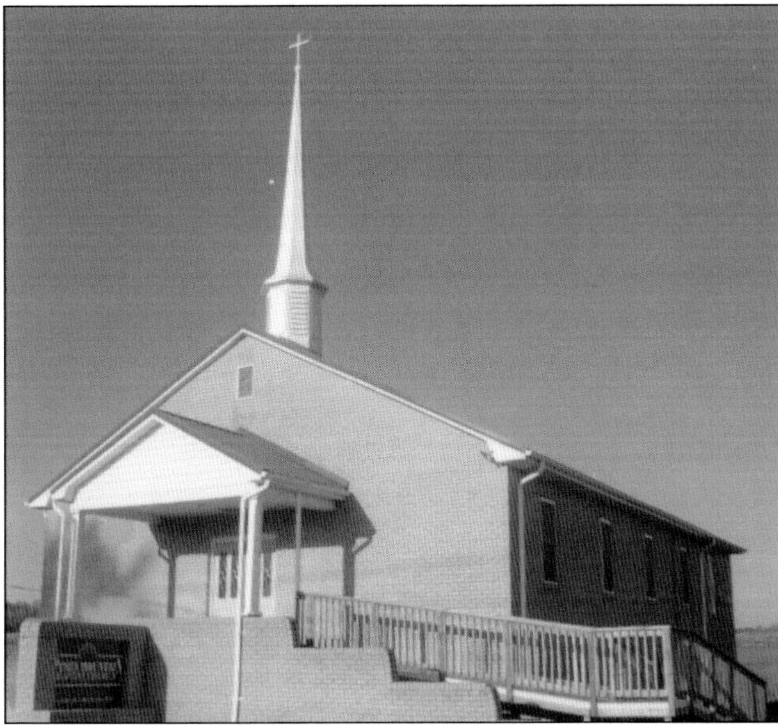

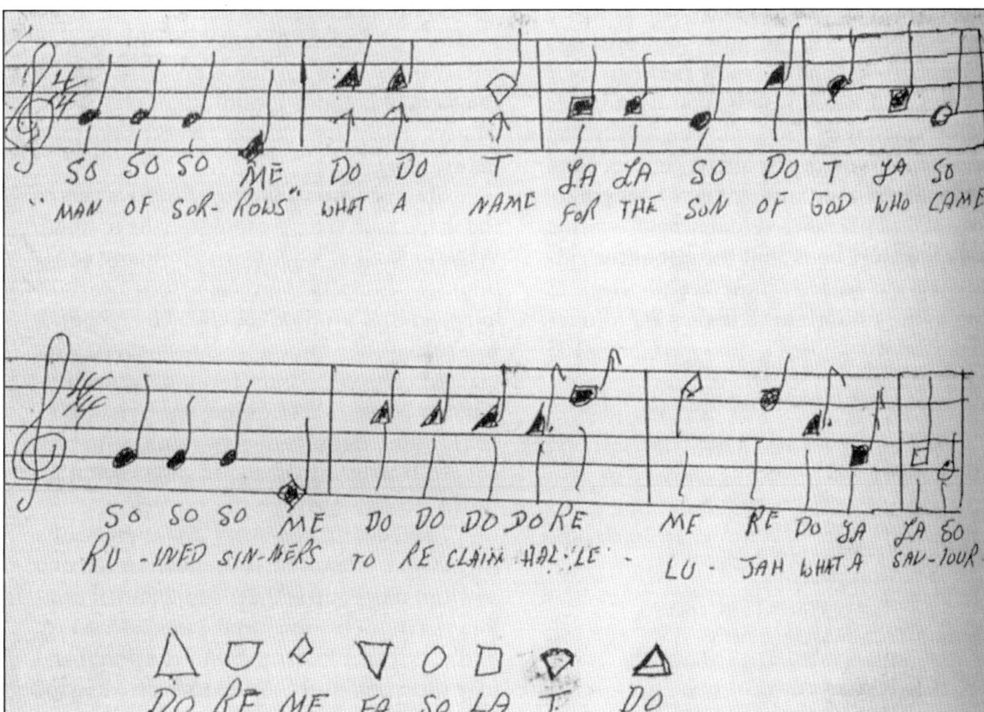

Many community churches in Colfax Township used shaped-note singing. This is a handwritten sample of shaped notes. An unidentified scholar at the local singing school provided this explanation. (Courtesy of Wayne Blackwood and the Bethel Baptist Church Files.)

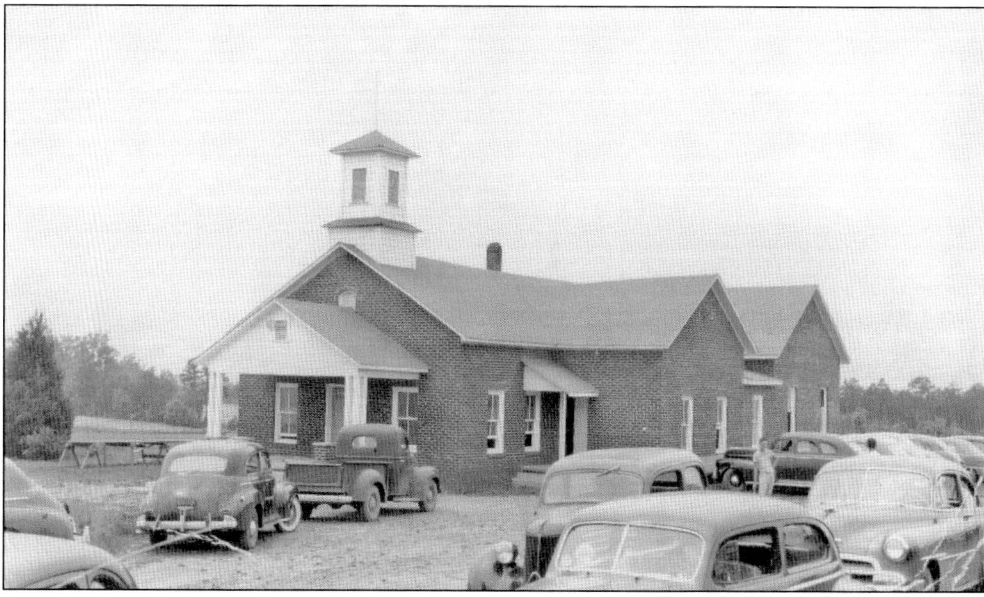

Corinth Baptist Church was established in 1932. Its original location was in the old Pinehurst School. After 1936, this brick-veneer structure served as an important meeting place. (Courtesy of Johnny Lavender.)

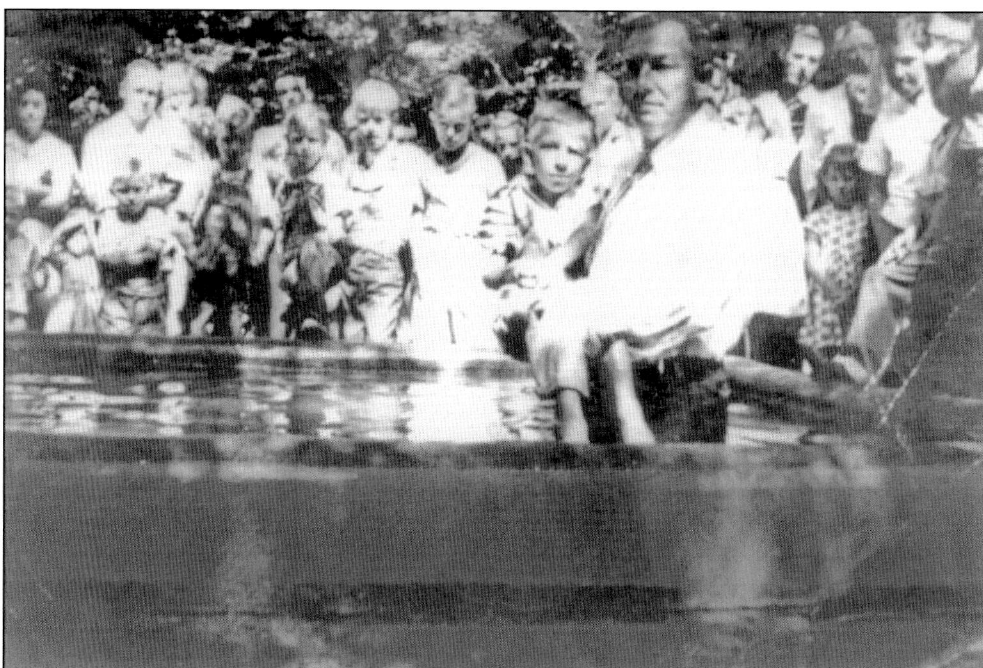

This photograph of the baptism of Lawrence Walker bears the date October 6, 1950. Rev. A. M. Martin performed the service for Corinth Baptist Church. (Courtesy of Corinth Baptist Church.)

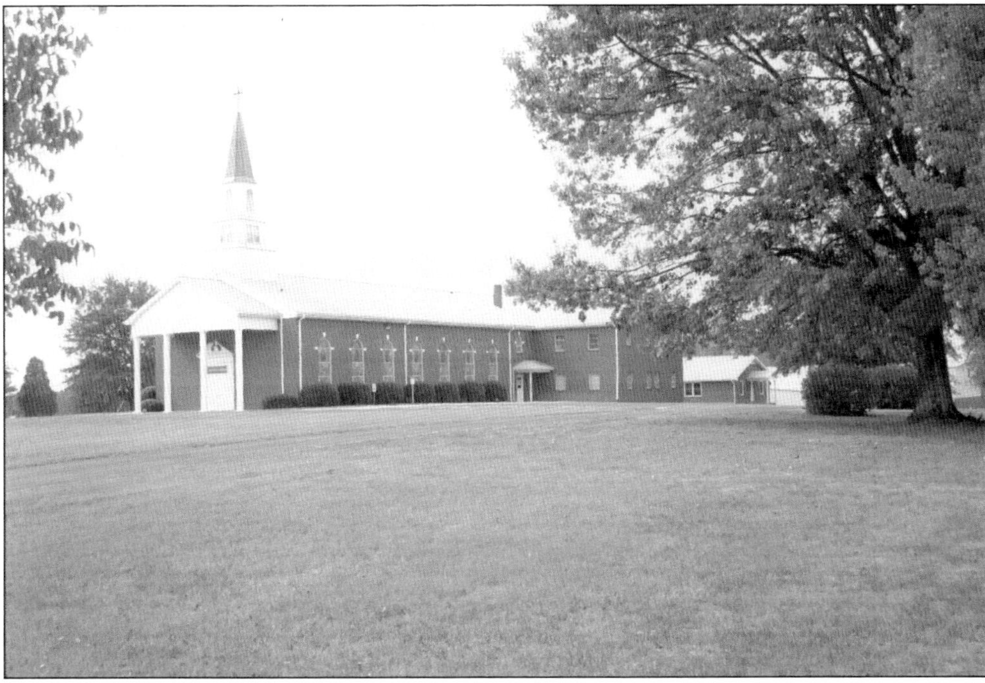

The current church building of Corinth Baptist Church was complete by January 7, 1962; the additional sanctuary dates from August 6, 1967. A year later, the congregation funded a new parsonage. (Courtesy of Pat Rhyne.)

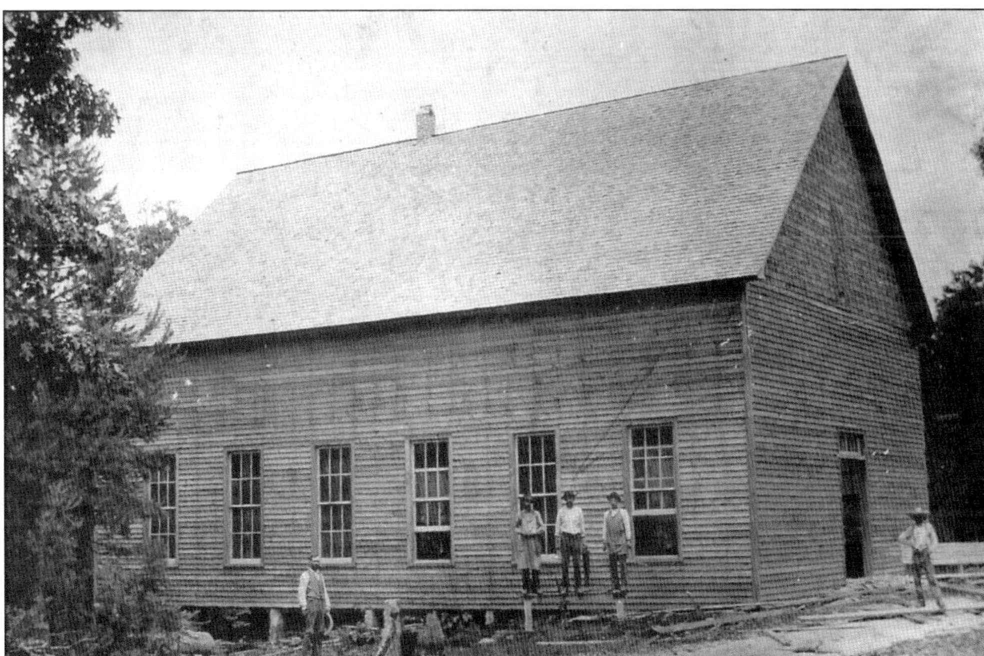

In 1831, William DePriest deeded a tract of land to four trustees of the Melton Meeting House, later Salem Church. In 1880, the church erected another church building opposite the existing cemetery; this structure remained in use until 1929. (Courtesy of Edward Washburn.)

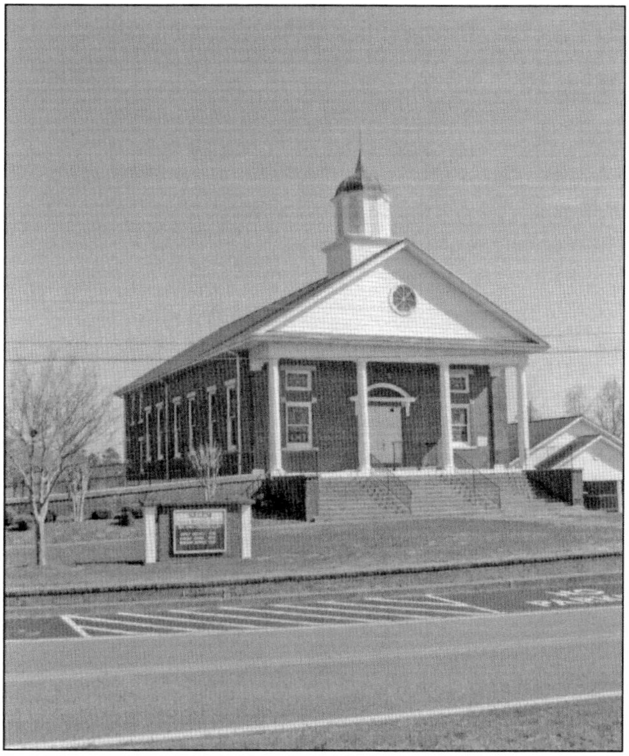

The present Salem United Methodist Church facility replaced the earlier sanctuary in 1929. (Courtesy of Edward Washburn.)

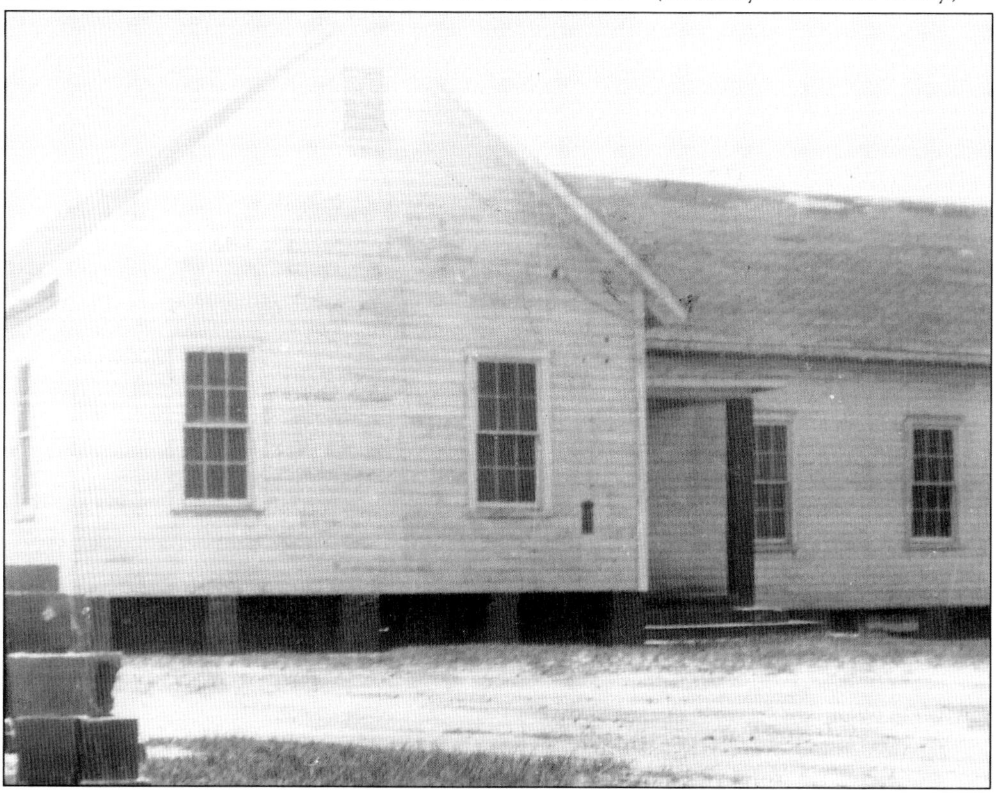

The organization of Campfield Memorial Baptist Church began in September 18, 1931. The church met in Fairview School, which members purchased from the board of education for $75. Campfield Memorial Baptist Church had 34 charter members and 13 awaiting baptism at the time. In 1934, a 30-foot-by-50-foot structure served as the church building; the cost to build it was $856.95. (Courtesy of Martina Toney.)

The present Campfield Church started with an education building in 1961; the newer auditorium dates from 1964. (Courtesy of Pat Rhyne.)

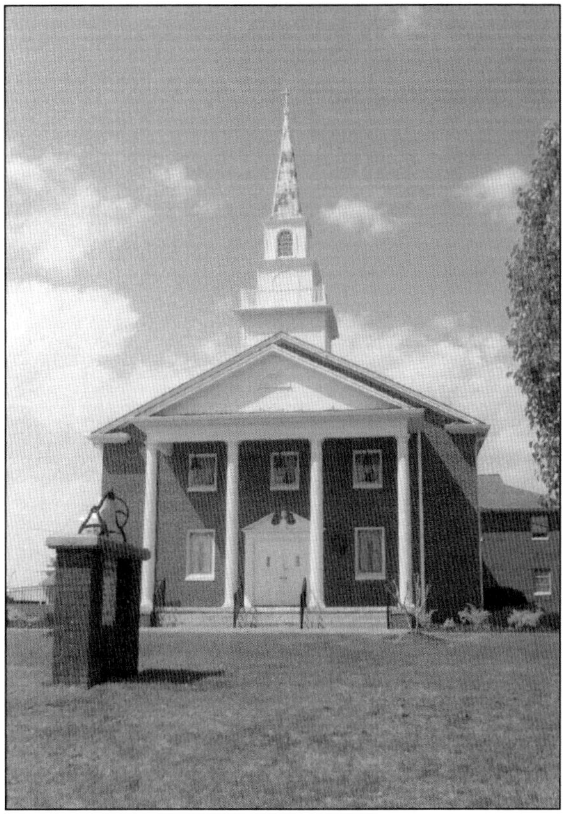

Friendship Baptist Church began in the early 1900s as an outgrowth of Webb First Baptist Church. Because of the difficulty of travel, several families began worshipping in a two-room house near the Seaboard Railroad. In 1915, the families purchased land for a church. Heaven Bound Baptist Church currently uses the Friendship Building. (Courtesy of Pat Rhyne.)

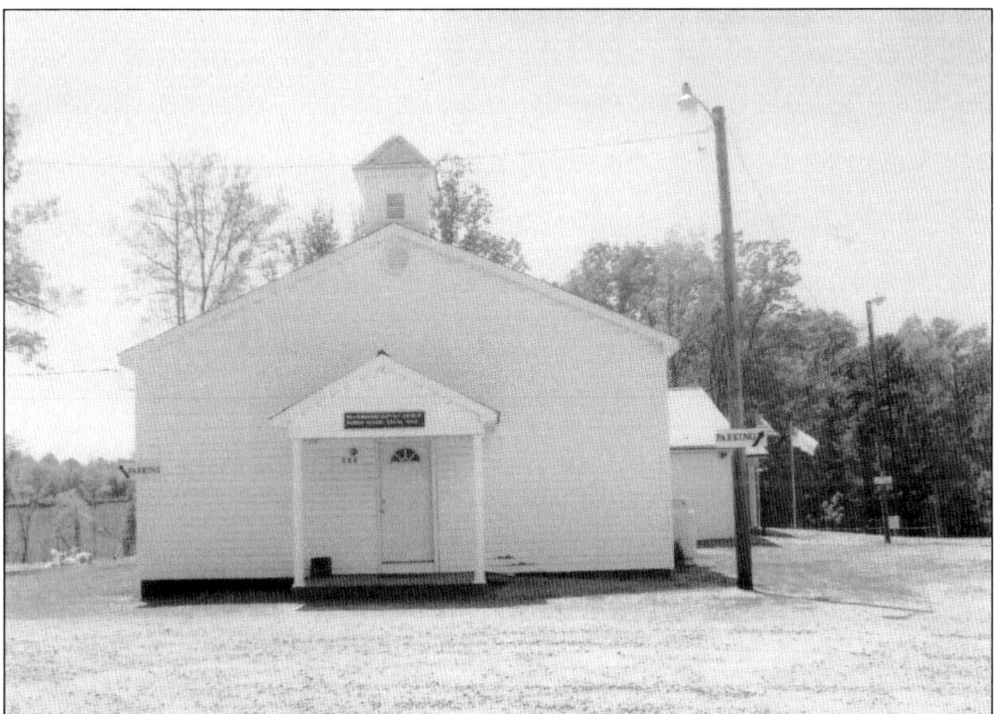

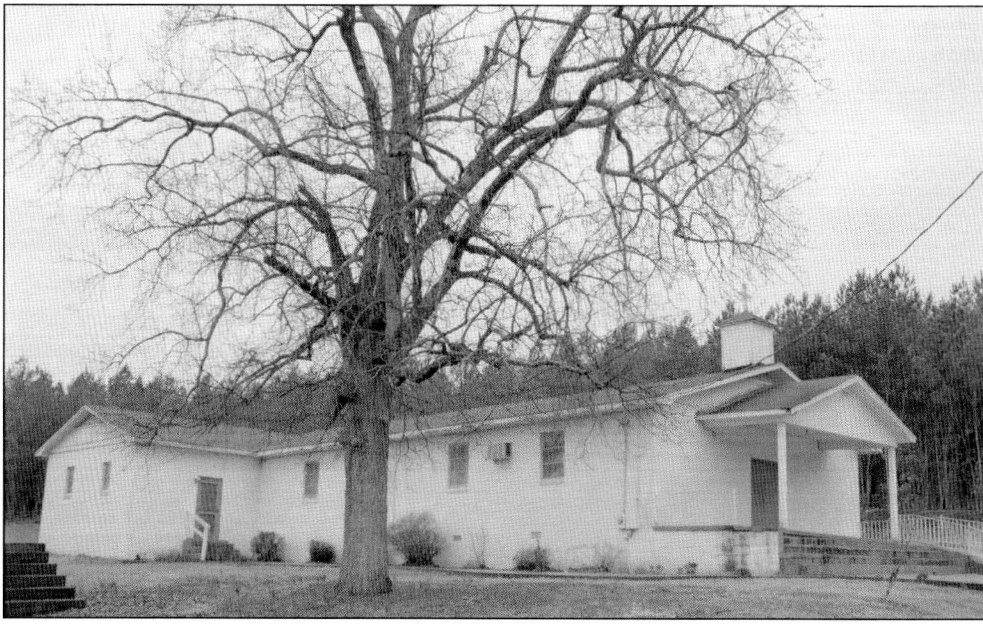

African American Baptists in the Jack Moore Mountain area erected White Oak Springs Baptist Church just off the Jack Moore Mountain Road. A cemetery beside the sanctuary dates from the early 1900s. As of 2010, this landmark church building was still in use. (Courtesy of Scott Withrow.)

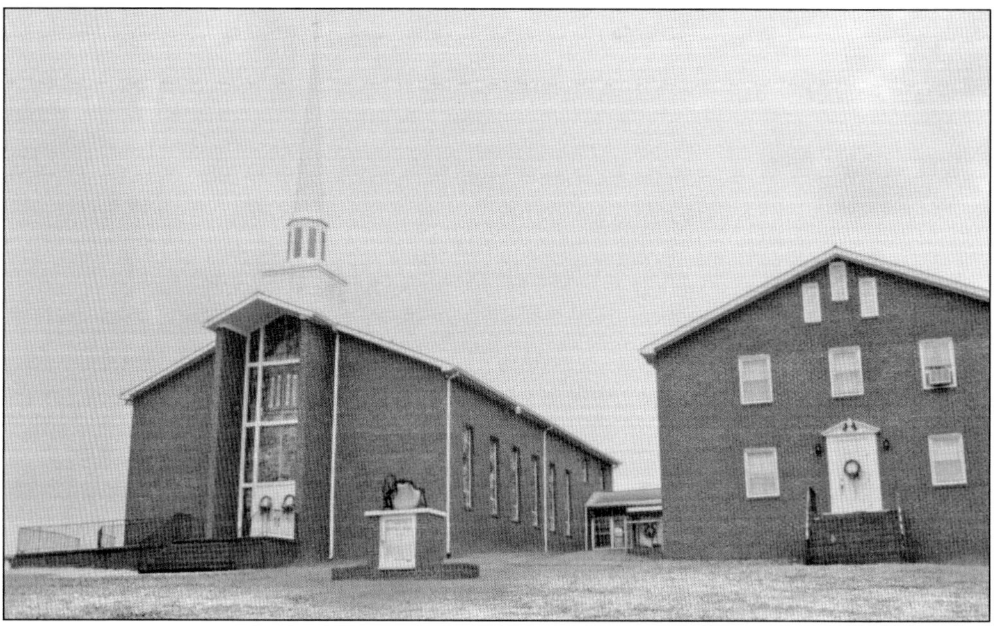

The Baptist Church of Christ at Walls (later Walls Baptist Church) dates from September 21, 1844. Several black members were a part of the original congregation; others later received baptism and membership. The first log church structure served as a school. The next building dates from 1856. In 1940 the members recommended constructing a wooden building across the road. The two current brick buildings, pictured above, date from 1966 and 1975, respectively. (Courtesy of Walls Baptist Church.)

The organization of Cherry Mountain Free Will Baptist Church dates from September 27, 1952. Sixteen charter members started the church in a one-room block building. Sunday school classes met in curtained-off areas of the room. The building has since been brick-veneered for enlarged Sunday school rooms and restrooms. Other improvements mark the progress of the church. (Courtesy of Pat Rhyne.)

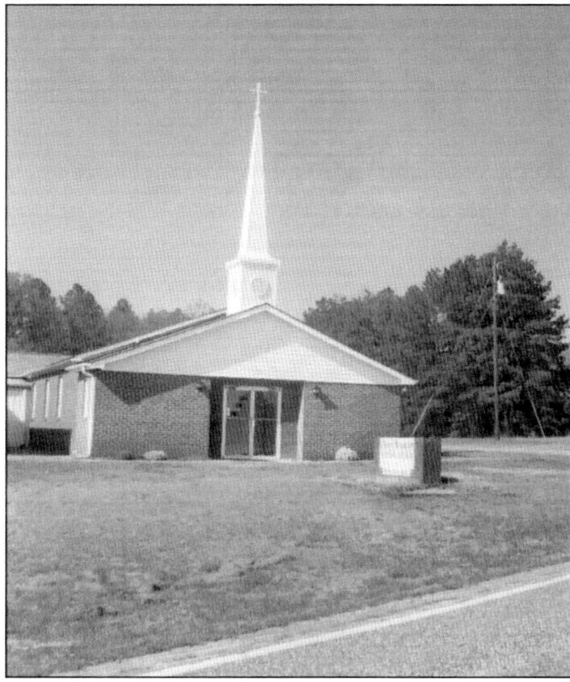

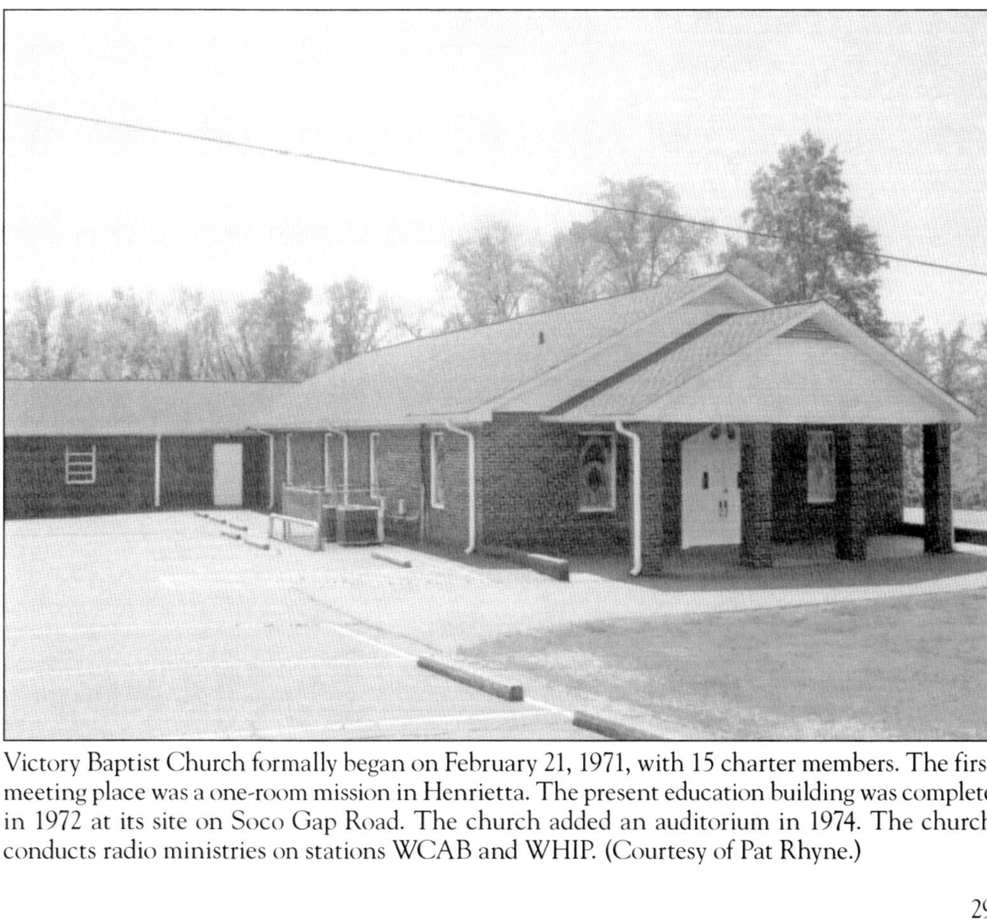

Victory Baptist Church formally began on February 21, 1971, with 15 charter members. The first meeting place was a one-room mission in Henrietta. The present education building was complete in 1972 at its site on Soco Gap Road. The church added an auditorium in 1974. The church conducts radio ministries on stations WCAB and WHIP. (Courtesy of Pat Rhyne.)

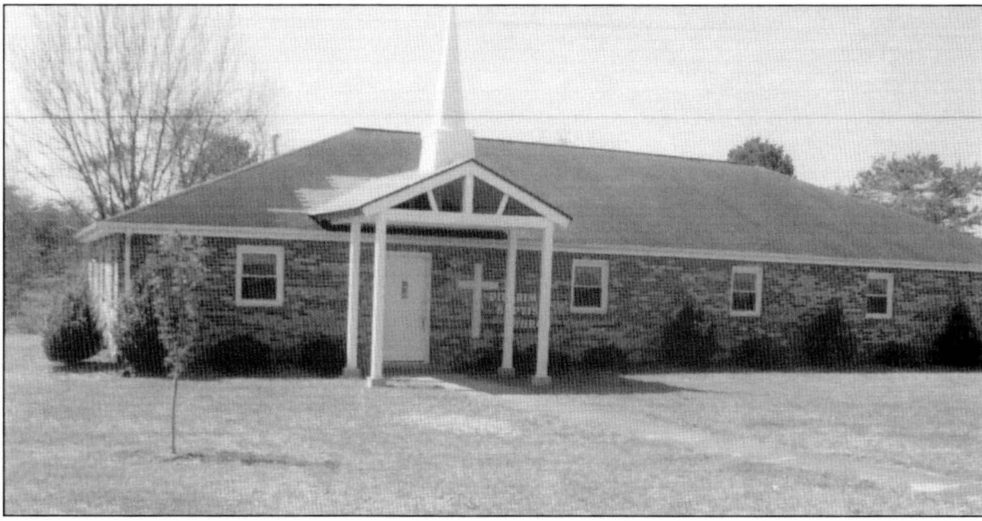

Organized on October 19, 1969, Pilgrim Baptist Church was a mission church from Mount Pleasant Baptist Church. The members first met in a one-room frame structure built as a place of prayer. In October 1970, the church purchased 1.5 acres of land and John Harmon's house, which became the new church in November 1970. The current church was erected in early 1974. (Courtesy of Pat Rhyne.)

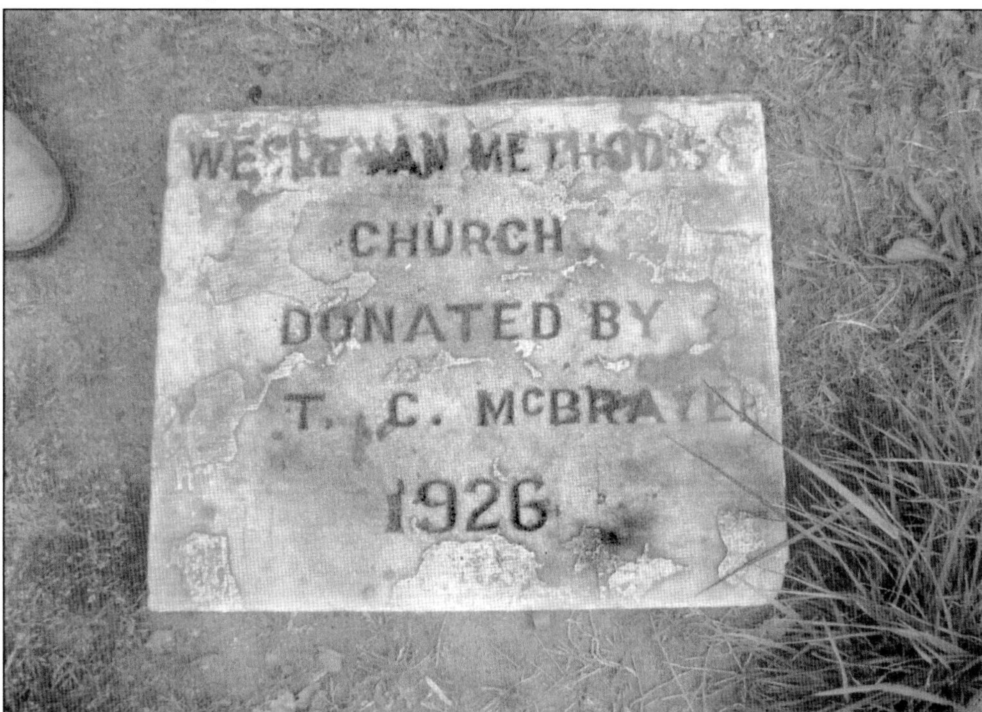

The Hopewell Wesleyan Methodist Church structure, located in Hopewell at 2467 Hollis Road, dates from the early 1920s. The bricked-up arched church windows are still evident. Russell Callahan bought the church building for a store and sold it to Bill Dycus in 1952. Kenneth Grier Plumbing Company currently uses the building. The graves in front of the structure were relocated. This photograph shows the church cornerstone. (Courtesy of Pat Rhyne.)

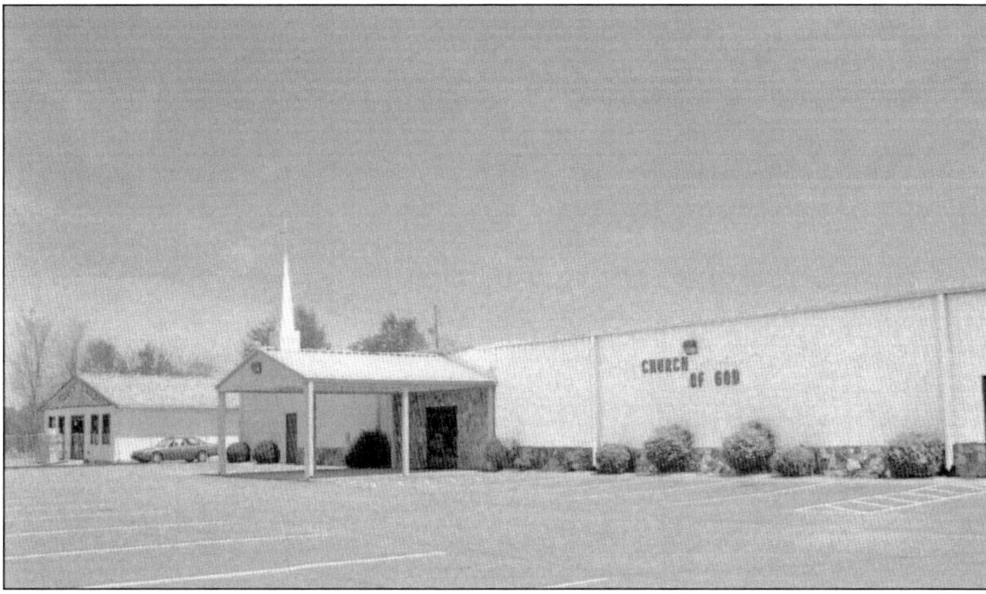

The Church of God began in Murphy, Tennessee, over a century ago. Beginning in 1980, the Church of God in Rutherford County met in the old American Legion post in Spindale. Later the church purchased an Edwards Street building and remained there for eight or nine years. In 2005, the Church of God bought the Christian Worship Center at 134 Top Avenue in Ellenboro. The current building serves 60 members. (Courtesy of Pat Rhyne.)

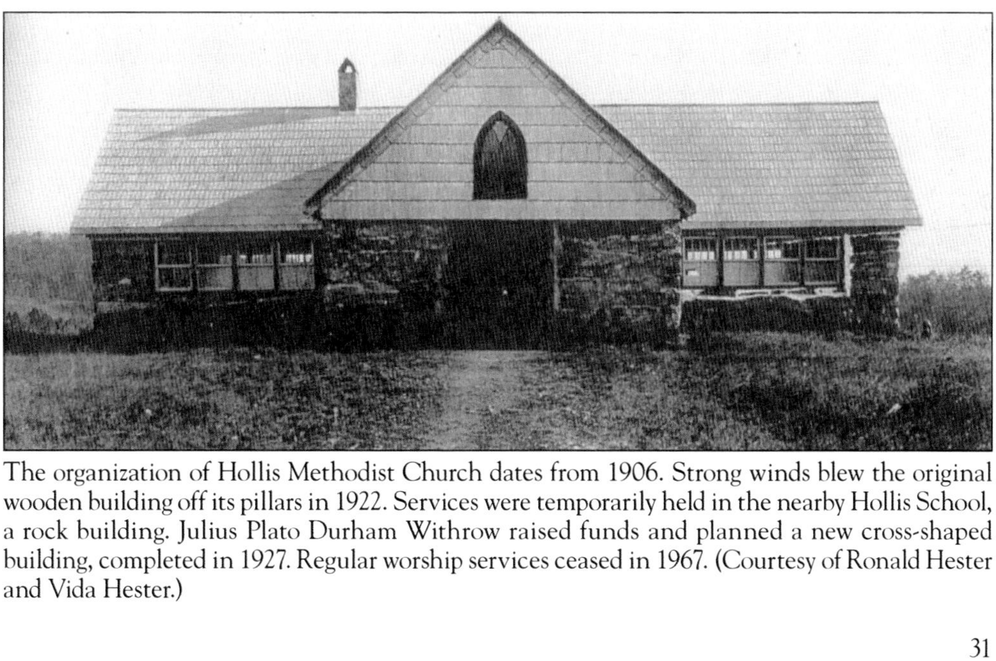

The organization of Hollis Methodist Church dates from 1906. Strong winds blew the original wooden building off its pillars in 1922. Services were temporarily held in the nearby Hollis School, a rock building. Julius Plato Durham Withrow raised funds and planned a new cross-shaped building, completed in 1927. Regular worship services ceased in 1967. (Courtesy of Ronald Hester and Vida Hester.)

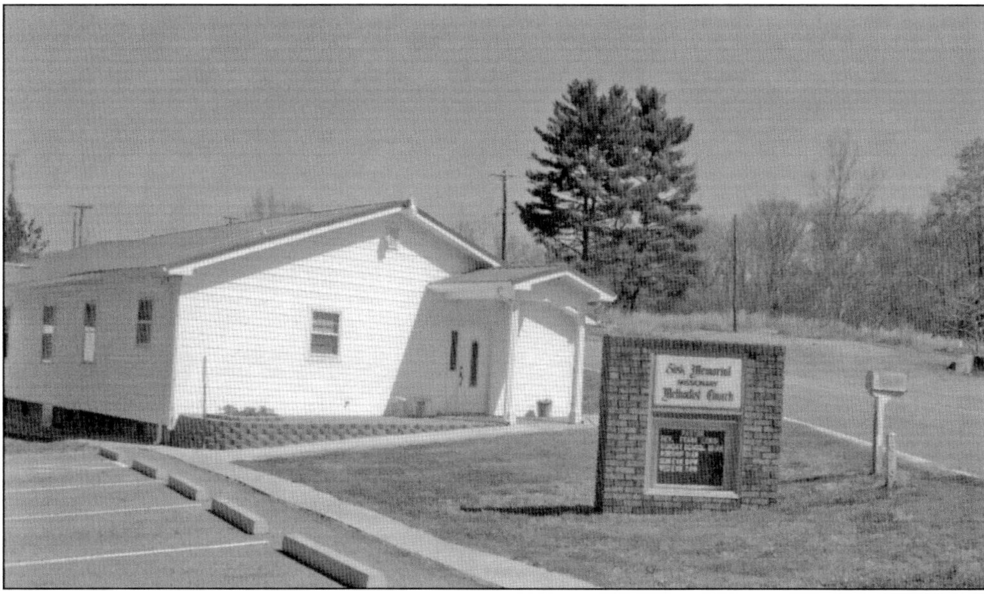

Sisk Memorial Missionary Methodist Church began as a tabernacle. Zeb Sisk and his son Thomas Julius Sisk started the church by constructing the building and benches; members named the church in their honor. Often the members who came to the services conducted the worship. Zeb was welcoming worshipers to the church in the 1950s when he suffered a stroke and died days later. (Courtesy of Pat Rhyne.)

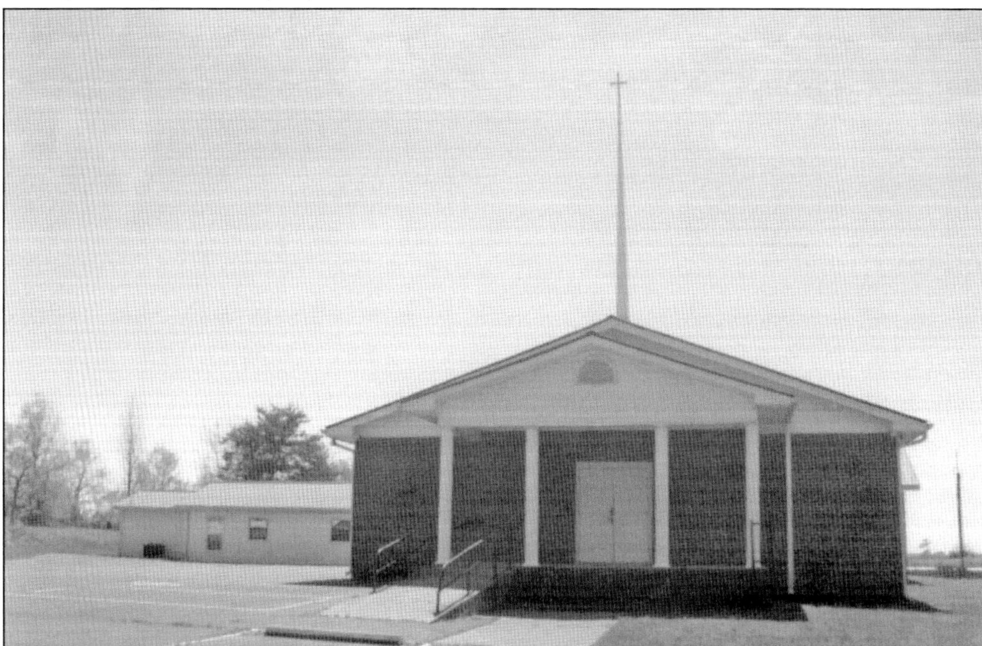

Plain View Baptist Church began as a mission of Gantts Grove Baptist Church. The first meeting place was the Reid Blackburn Store beside the old Mooresboro School in Mooresboro. In the early 1970s, members secured land on Lovelace Road near Ellenboro and built the present church. (Courtesy of Pat Rhyne.)

Traveling evangelists periodically came to Ellenboro. Emmett Hamrick and Herbert Wright often erected a tent for the audiences. Their tent was also the site for occasional moving-picture shows; cowboy features were especially popular. During the Colfax Free Fair, the tent often served as a bingo stand. (Courtesy of Paul Price.)

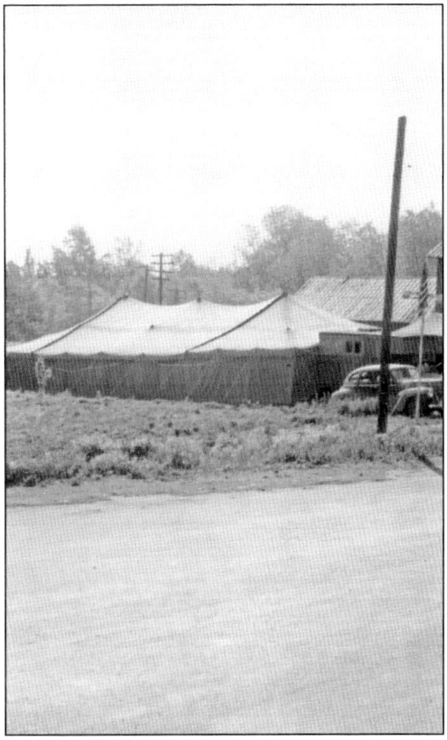

Ernest Loga (left), Jackie Miller (center), and the former "First Lady of Webb First Baptist Church" Gleenwood "Pep" Carson (right) are catching up and fraternizing in this image. (Courtesy of Hattie Logan.)

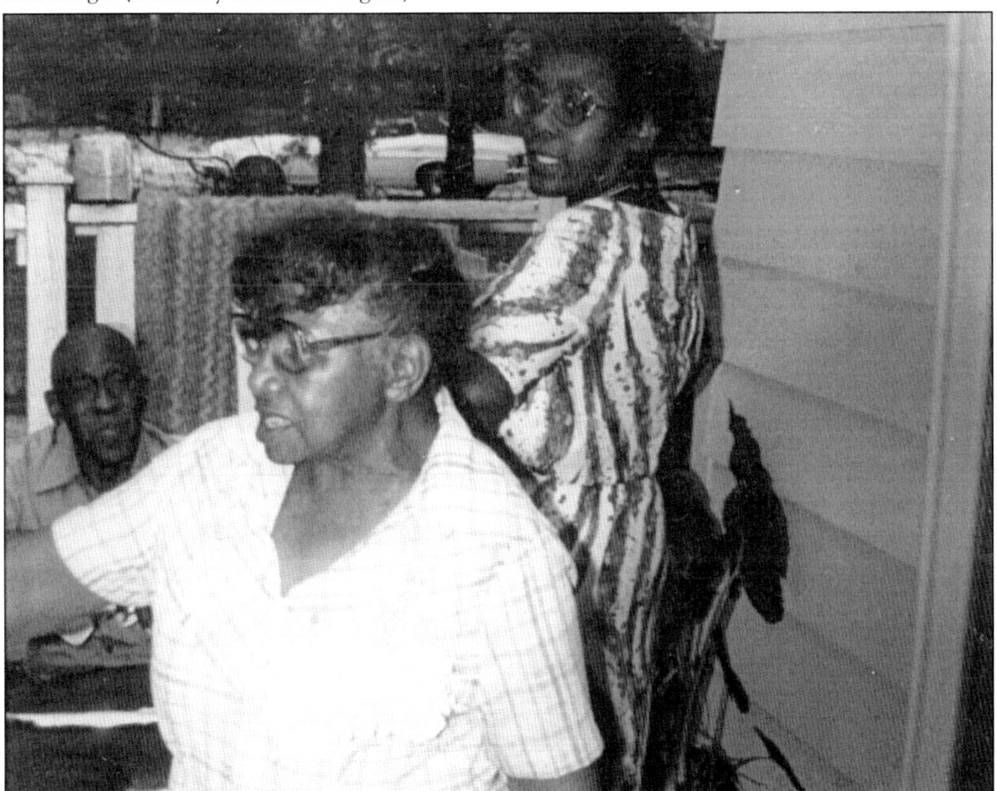

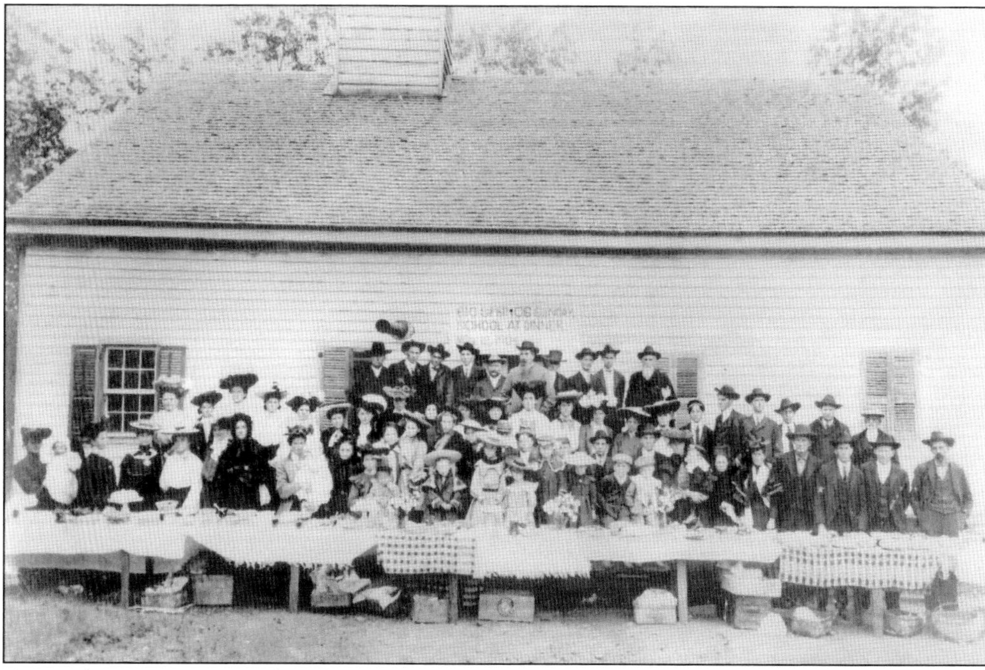

A popular event at most churches was "Dinner on the Grounds." This scene from Big Springs Baptist Church shows the Big Springs Sunday school at dinner on November 12, 1904. Notice the hats worn by most of the participants and how all were dressed in their Sunday best. (Courtesy of Linda Butler Bridges.)

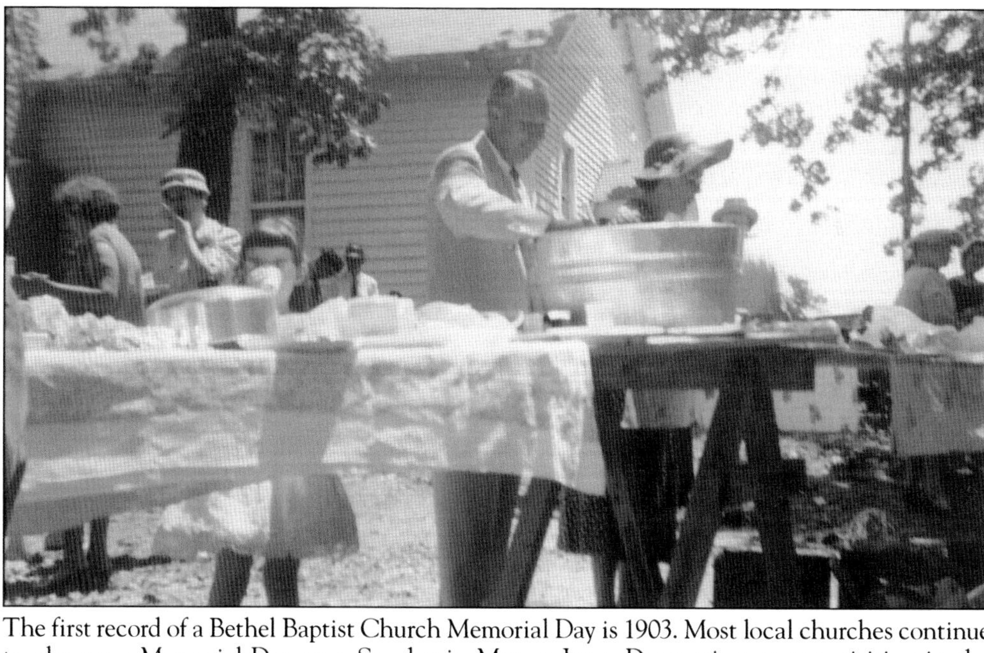

The first record of a Bethel Baptist Church Memorial Day is 1903. Most local churches continue to observe a Memorial Day on a Sunday in May or June. Decorating graves, visiting in the cemeteries, attending services, and socializing around a table of food were typical activities. In this 1959 image, Rev. Harold Brown, Bethel Baptist Church pastor (1955–1978), selects his beverage from a tub at the old Bethel Baptist Church. (Courtesy of Jo Ann Martin.)

Two

Schools

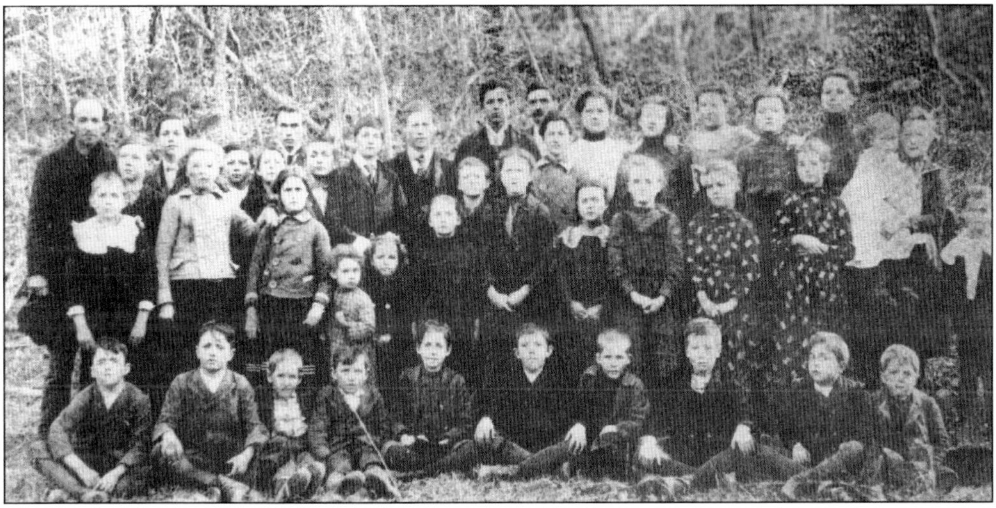

North Carolina's public school system began in 1837. By 1911, North Carolina had two systems: a six-month state school system and systems under local control. In 1931, North Carolina had 1,600 one-room schoolhouses and 6,720 schools in all. In 1940, the state's dropout rate was 75 percent, but even this was an improvement from what it had been during the days of the Great Depression when children on farms and in mill villages worked despite child labor laws. An example of a one-room school in the area that is now Colfax Township is the Smart School on Smart's Farm near Webb's Creek. The enrollment averaged 40 per year, and the school year was 16.6 weeks long. This is the class of 1900. Shown here from left to right are (first row) Sam Melton, two unidentified, Hatcher Melton, Ulysses Smart, Lotan Ledford, unidentified, Walker Smart, Jim Smart, and Humes Melton; (second row) unidentified, Ada Smart, Mary Jones , Carla Camp, Unice Lackardye, three unidentified, Mary Wright, Edna Melton, Evie Melton, and three unidentified; (third row) three unidentified, Tom Melton, Secro Toney, four unidentified, Loodie Ledford, Verdie Smart, one unidentified, Verdia Jones, and five unidentified. (Courtesy of Todd Lavender and the *Corinth Church History*.)

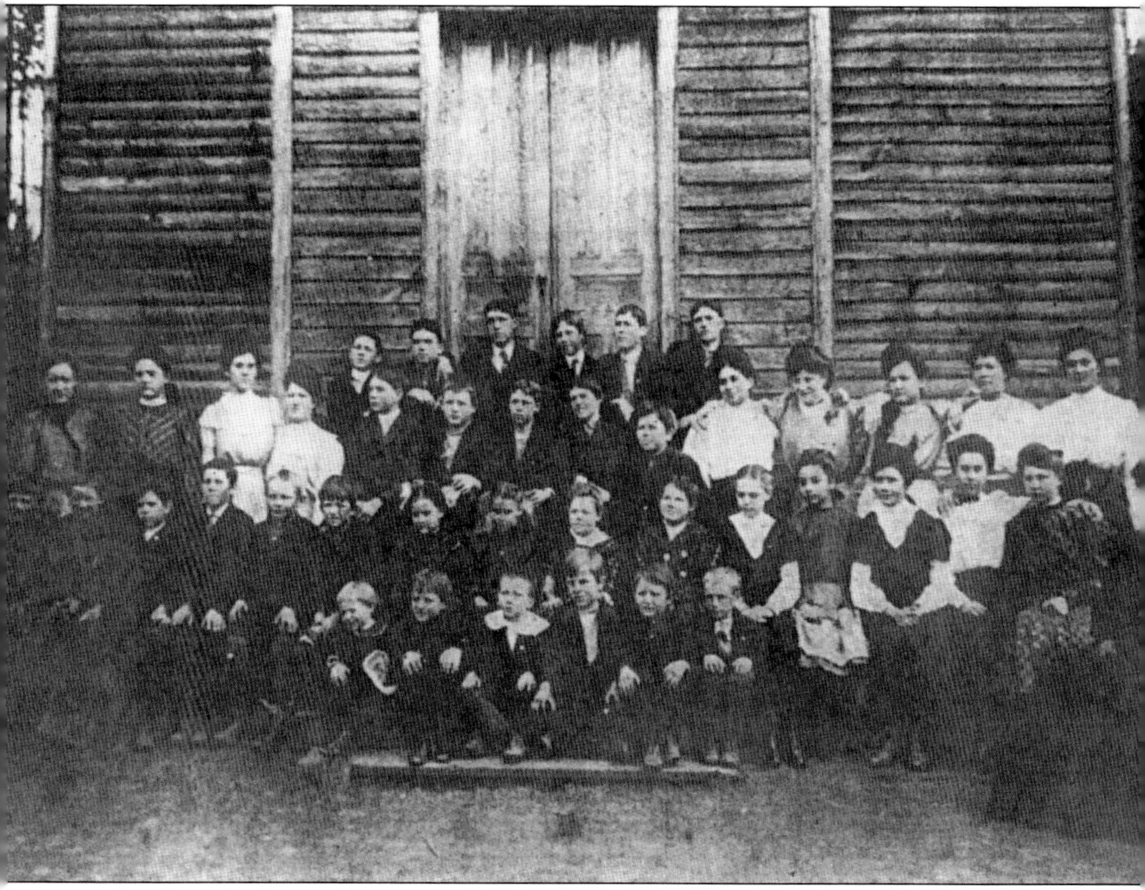

Another school opened sometime later. Affectionately called "Possum Holler," the school built on Samuel Harrill's land was formally known as either Duncan and/ or Harrill School. This 1907 class was taught by Cleo Burns (1882–1966), whose pupils included her sisters Blanche and Zina. Seen here from left to right are (first row) Lester Bailey, Coran Bailey, Leonard Bostic, Dewitt Carson, Marlin Melton, and Floyd Bostic; (second row) Hatcher Melton, Wren Randall, Laxton Burns, Paul Duncan, Bryan Randall, Gifton Melton, Selma Bright, Mae Carson, Willie McArthur, Era Duncan, Maude Smart, Estelle Bright, Maggie Bostic, Ethel Watson, Ida Butler, and teacher Cleo Burns; (third row) Ida Randall, Mamie Smart, Blanche Burns, Alda Burns, Geneva Smart, North Randall, Walker McArthur, Fletcher Melton, Willie Melton, Carl Watson, Mary Lee Butler, Brillie Randall, Dola Burns, and Zina Burns; (fourth row) Amos Duncan, Sara Melton, Henry Duncan, Fred Harrill, Yates Duncan, Bertie Melton. (Courtesy of Todd Lavender and the *Corinth Church History*.)

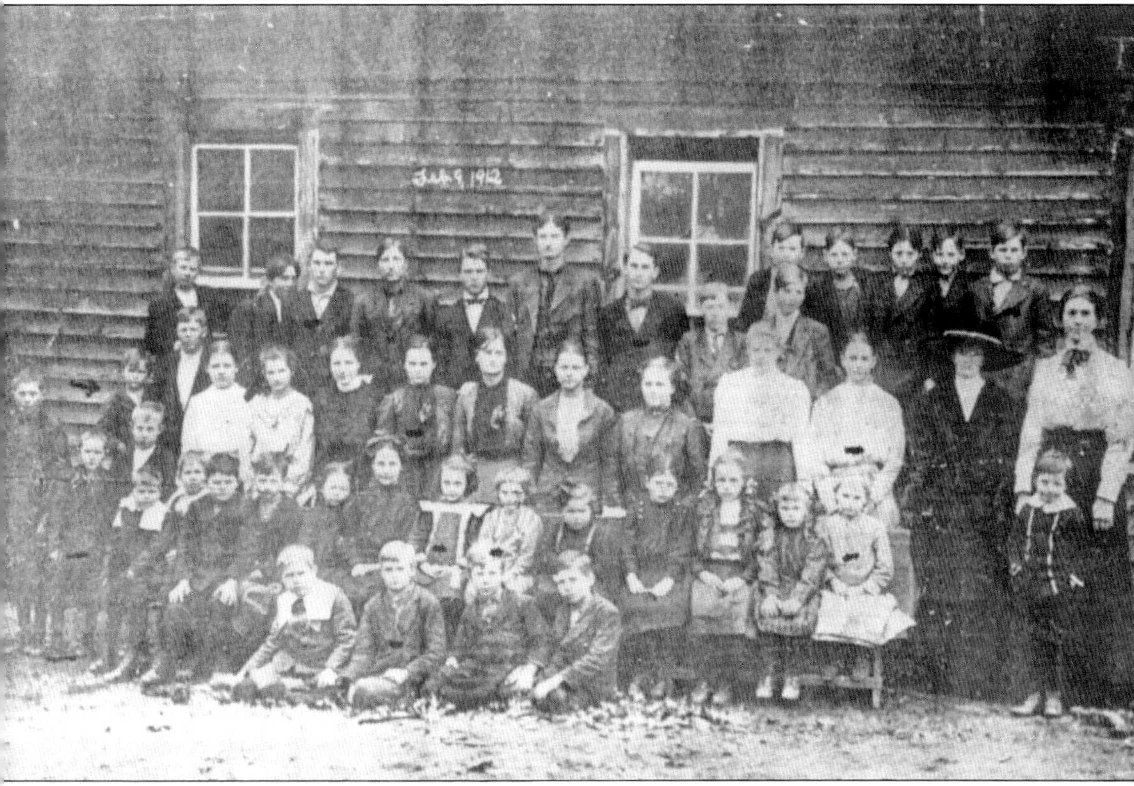

This class of Fortune School includes, from left to right, (first row) Durham Digh, Quentin Hollifield, Robert Wilson, and Edgar Padgett; (second row) Wade Digh, Edgar Digh, Guss Jackson, Gifton Black, Gurtie Black, Gurtie Hoyle, Irene Wilson, Merle Hollifield, Lillian Gurley, Mamie Digh, Ruth Padgett, Macy Lovelace, Blanche Lovelace, and Edna Hollifield; (third row) Eldridge Gurley, Leland Campbell, Willie Gurley, Ralph Callahan, Lucy Holye, Dovie DePriest, Myrtle Jackson, Buna Hollifield, Nellie "Nell" Toms, Buna Rogers, Essie Digh, Zennie Lovelace, Sudie Hollifield, Ella DePriest, and teacher Eugene Elliot; (fourth row) Kyle Hollifield, Legron Rogers, Charlie Callahan, Clyde Smawley, Clifford Hollifield, Joe Lovelace, Clarence Digh, Clifford Lovelace, Clyde Hollifield, Gene Yelton, Elon Smawley, Arthur Padgett, Russell Black, Ben Jackson, Edgar Jackson, and Omer Hollifield. (Courtesy of Todd Lavender and the *Corinth Church History*.)

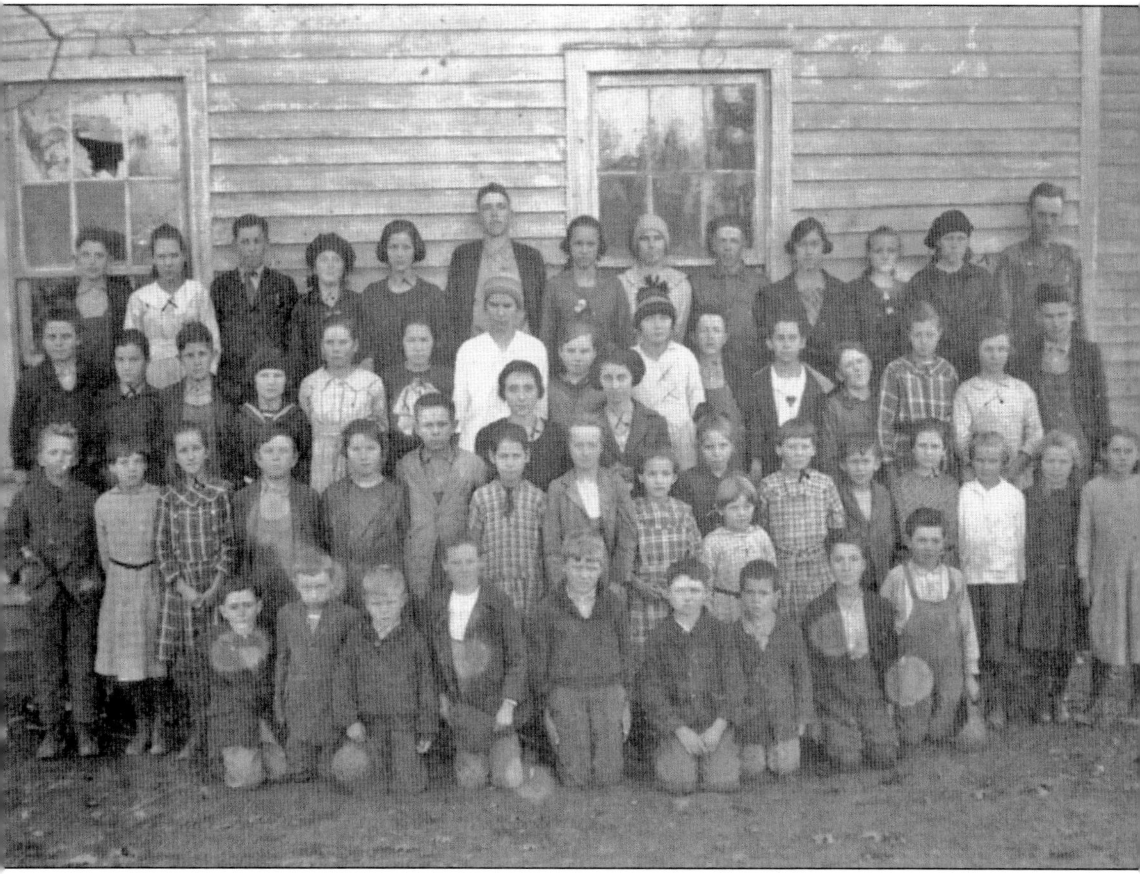

Built in the 1920s, Walls School was close to Walls Church near the Ellenboro community. It took its name from Amos Wall. Pictured from left to right are (first row) Harlen Greene, ? Owens, ? Jones, unidentified, Harlen Dycus, ? Hoyle, and an unidentified person; (second row) Coy Sparks, ? Bailey, Vernie ?, Forrest Davis, ? Greene, Loren Davis, unidentified, Vertie Jones, three unidentified persons, Vernie Davis Bridges, Vertie Padgett McCurrey, and an unidentified student; (third row) Vernon Jones, Pauline Dycus, unidentified, Clemoth Greene, Luna Padgett Bridges, Lucy Morrow, unidentified, Gertha Bowen, Iona Biggerstaff, Mary Bailey, Carl Greene, Vernie Greene, Sherrill Biggerstaff, Lona Owens, Cleo Davis, and Ray Bowen; (fourth row) Guy Greene, Mamie Morrow Dycus, Clyde Greene, Gazzie Davis, Mattie Greene Greene, Lawrence Morrow, Sarah Beam, Blanche Bowen, Lorenzo Greene, Eunice Greene, Ruby Hoyle, unidentified, Madge Greene Bridges, Lee Owens, and two more unidentified students. In the center of the picture are teachers Grace Hines Greene (left) and Lenota Daniel Phillips. (Courtesy of Delores Hill, granddaughter of teacher Grace Hines Greene.)

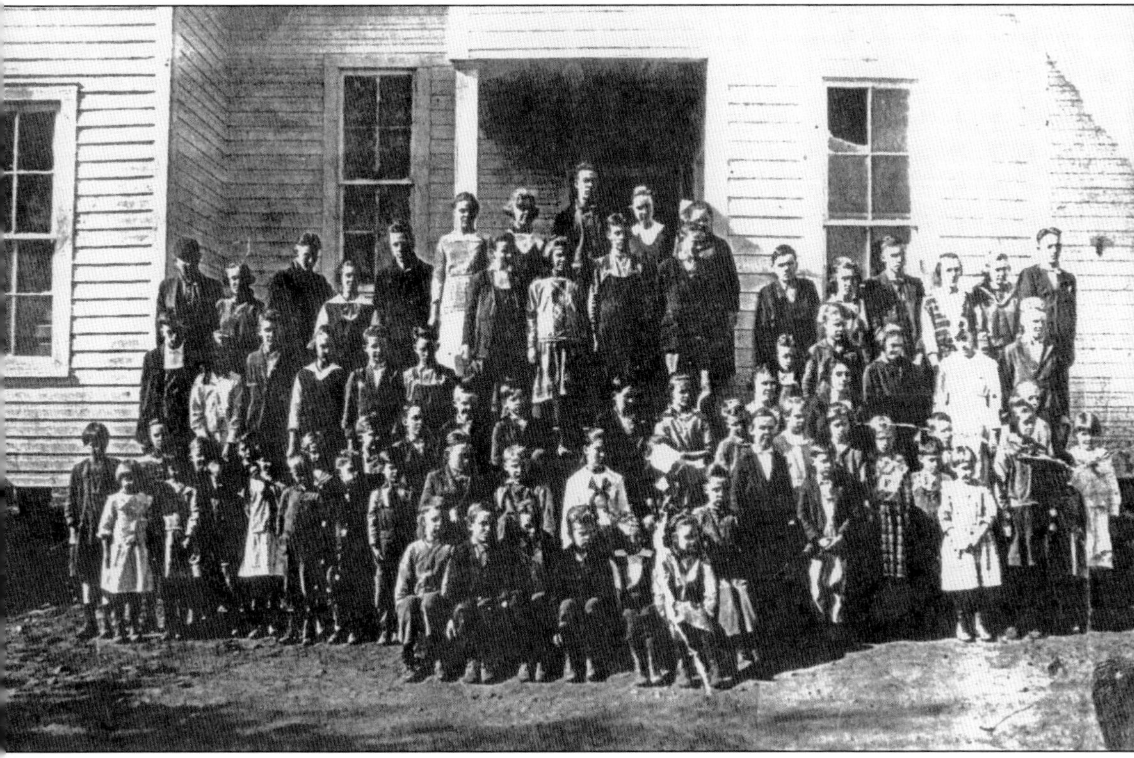

Pinehurst School opened in 1919 and was the result of consolidating Mink Den and Possum Holler Schools. The school had grades one through seven and operated until its consolidation with Ellenboro School in 1928 or 1929. The school building was just south of what is now the Corinth Church Cemetery. When Corinth Baptist Church was founded in 1932, this schoolhouse became the first church building. Pictured here is the Pinehurst School student body from around 1922. From left to right, they are (first row) Osco Walker, Robert Hensley, Norris Hensley, Thurman Wall, Xantippa Padgett, Pauline Spratt, and Lenn Smart; (second row) Ola Fortenbury, Leah Harrill, Glynn Self, Ruby Murray, Metal Self, Norris Smart, J. C. Hensley, Thomas Wall, William Martin, Argie Goforth, Beulah Philbeck Hoppes, Lee Fortenbury, and Claudius Jones; (third row) Mary Lee Philbeck Walker, Hattie Brooks, Coyt Self, Billy Walker, Mavis Smart, Marion Murray, Berry Melton, Sherman Padgett, George Melton, Claud Harrill, Wilma Bailey, teachers Docia Beam and Cora Morris, Otis Martin, Louise Smart, Alice Harrill, Hilda Smart, Glynn Brooks, Reba Philbeck Lavender, Ruth Harrill, Ola Murray, Annie Fortenbury (behind Ola), Libby Ray Smart, and Naam Melton; (fourth row) Irvin Jones, Lorenna Wall, Lester Tessenir, Minnie Lou Watson, Chivous Padgett, Thomas Nodien, Josie Bell Murray, Carl Philbeck, Ferris Bailey, Odell Jones, Bertha Martin, Ester Bailey, Bessie Walker, and Zeb Walker; (fifth row) Tommy Merck, Osteen Philbeck Walker, Guy Jones, Agnes Harrill, Brit Smart, Eula Brooks, Nora Brooks, Clyde Merck, Beth Bridges, Mable Jones, Grady Spratt, Cardie Goforth, Ernest Philbeck, Novella Melton Padgett, Darcus Jones Philbeck, and Lester Bailey. (Courtesy of Todd Lavender and the *Corinth Church History*.)

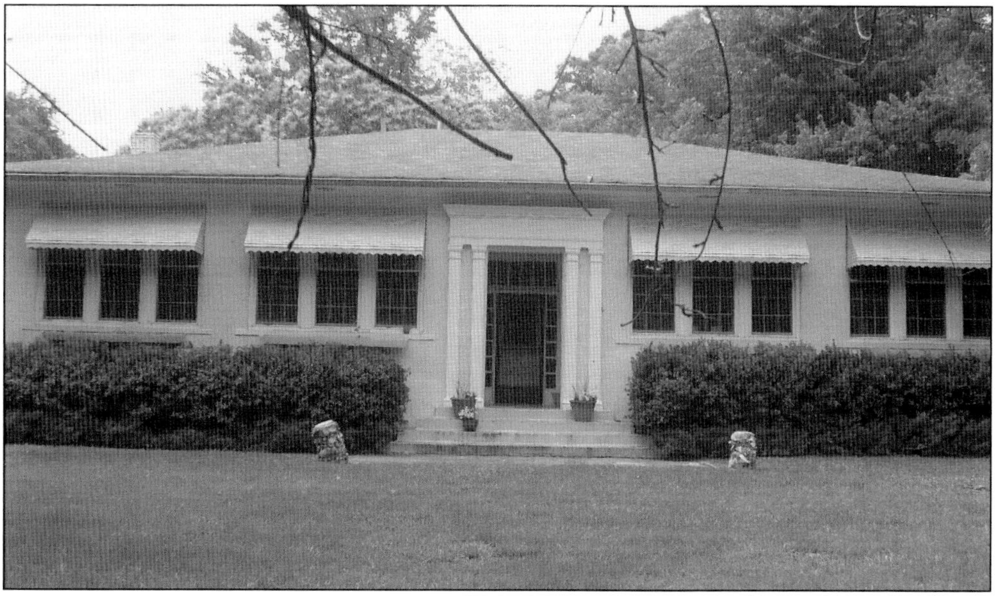

Washburn School was about 200 yards east of Salem Church, across the road. Its students started going to the Hollis, Sunshine, Ellenboro, and Bostic Schools about 1925. From the early 1930s through the early 1940s, Dr. Knight opened and ran a medical clinic in this facility. The structure is now a dwelling. (Courtesy of Pat Rhyne.)

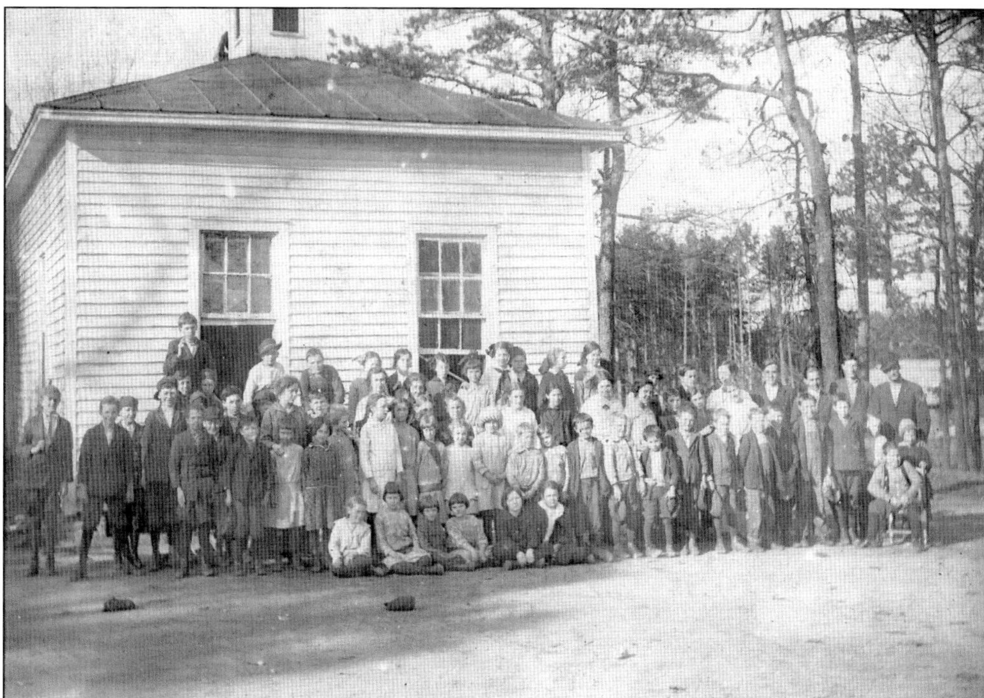

Ellenboro's three-room school housed grades 1–11 from the late 1880s until the early 1920s. Students moved into the new brick school in 1924, and the old school became a residence. A second floor was added, where Anita Price Davis's parents rented an apartment for awhile before her birth. (Courtesy of Jo Ann Martin.)

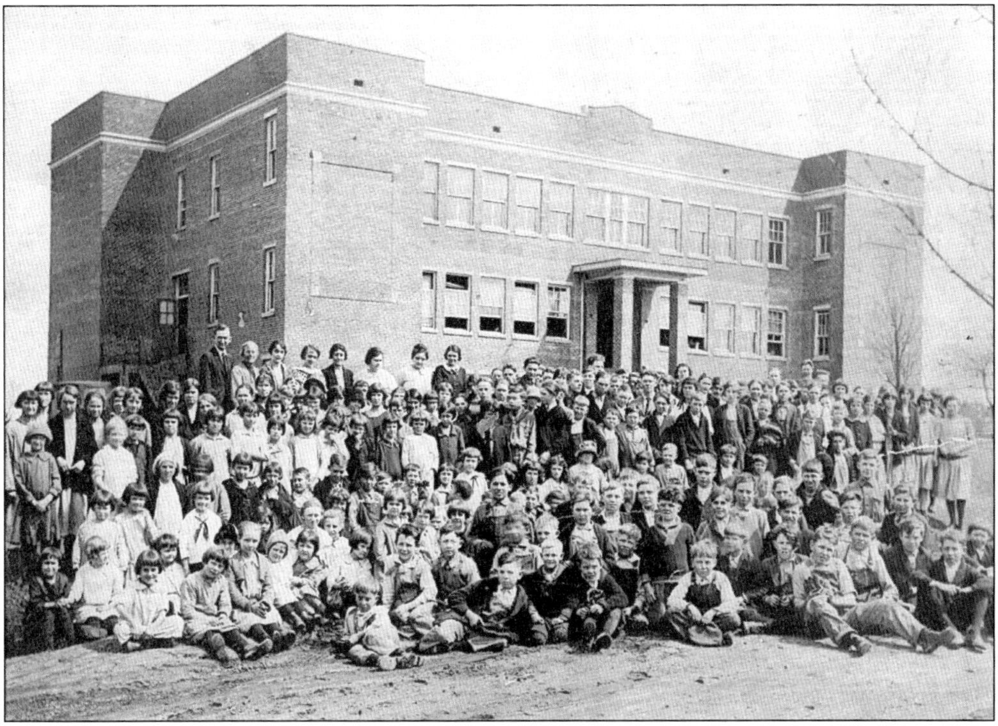

Originally constructed in 1924, the three-story brick Ellenboro School housed local students from first grade through graduation for 36 years. For more than 40 additional years, the facility served as an elementary school. (Courtesy of Mike Davis and Elizabeth Rhyne.)

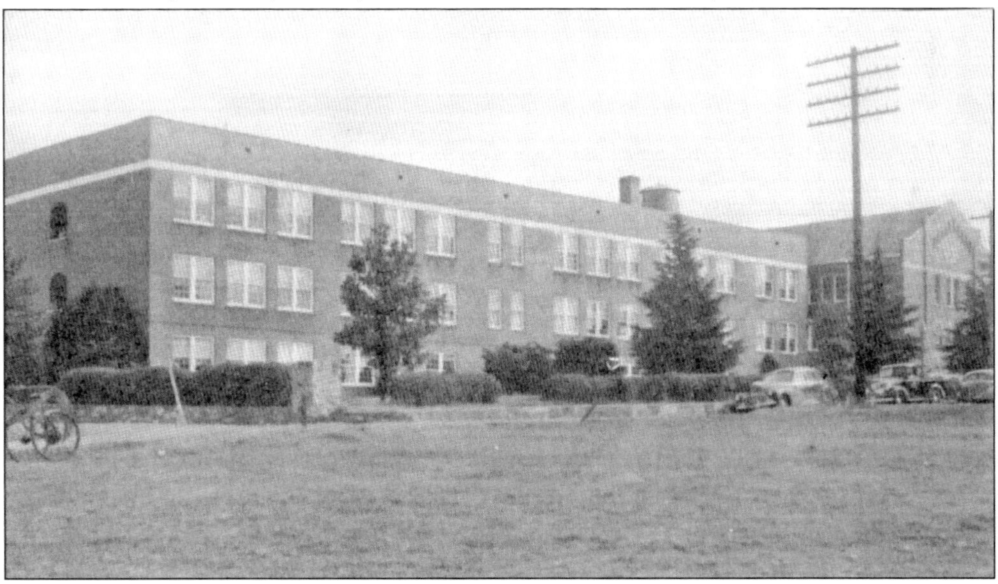

Ellenboro School received an auditorium in 1942. Several other additions helped provide the facilities that the students and community needed. The lunchroom was the site of vaccinations for the community, bazaars for local churches, and ice cream socials. In 1957, a separate, new building served as the new cafeteria. The demolition of the old Ellenboro School building was complete by 2008. (Courtesy of Mike Davis and Elizabeth Rhyne.)

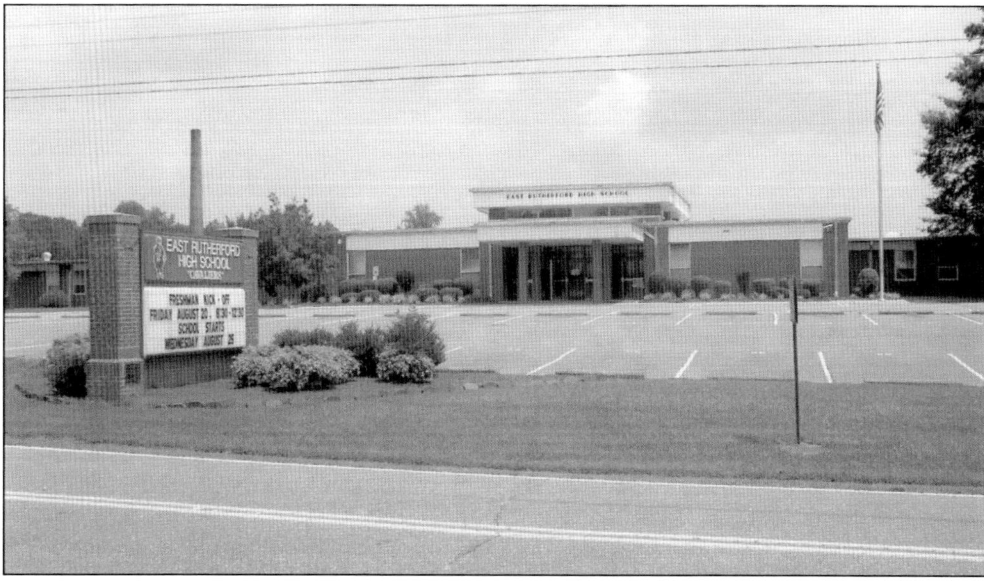

The year 1962 brought about the consolidation of Cool Springs in Forest City, Ellenboro High School, and Sunshine High School to form East Rutherford High School. The location of the new brick school stood just yards from U.S. Highway 74 Business on East High Road. (Courtesy of Donna Hensley.)

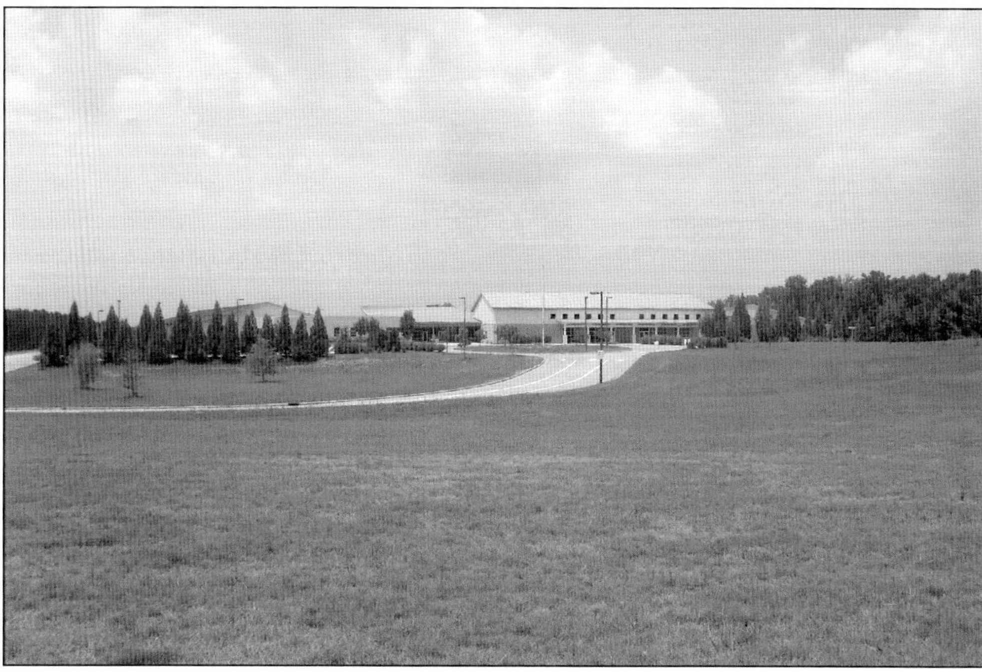

From 1962 until 2005, the Ellenboro School building housed kindergarten through eighth grade. The construction and opening of the middle school in Bostic in 1995 changed Ellenboro Elementary to a kindergarten through fifth grade school. Frank Wall was the first principal of the new Ellenboro Elementary School. In 2005, a new facility on Piney Mountain Road became the new home for the school; Bill Bass became the second principal in the new building in 2005. (Courtesy of Ellenboro Elementary School.)

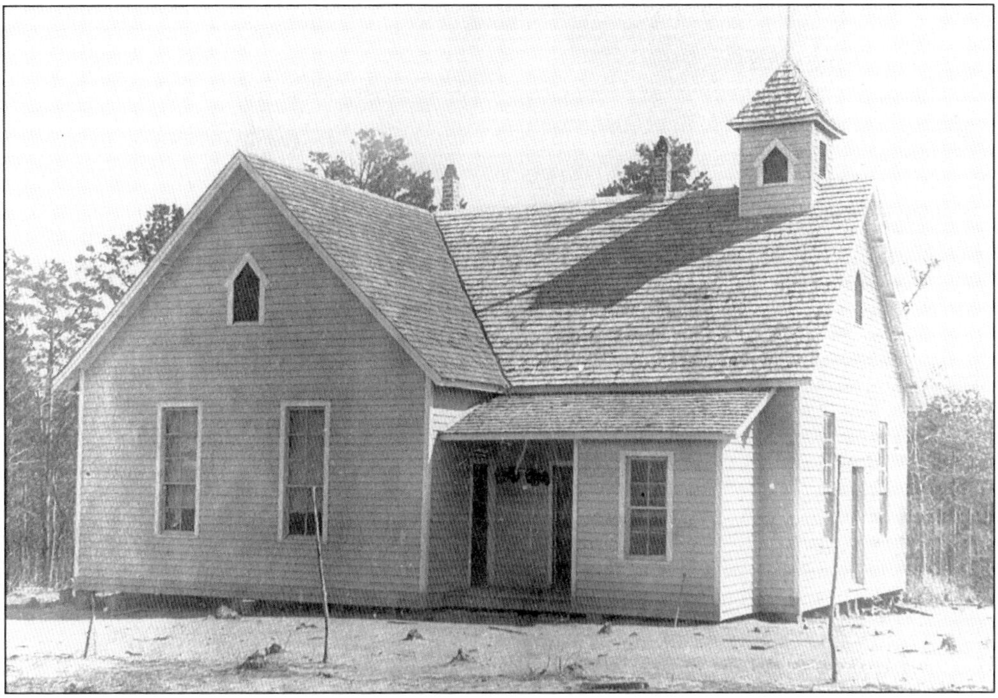

This photograph of the Beam School dates from 1901. The Beam School was northeast on the McKinney Mill Road and just past the intersection of the Red Barn Road and the McKinney Mill Road. The Beam School is no longer in existence. (Courtesy of Beth Beam King and Dan King.)

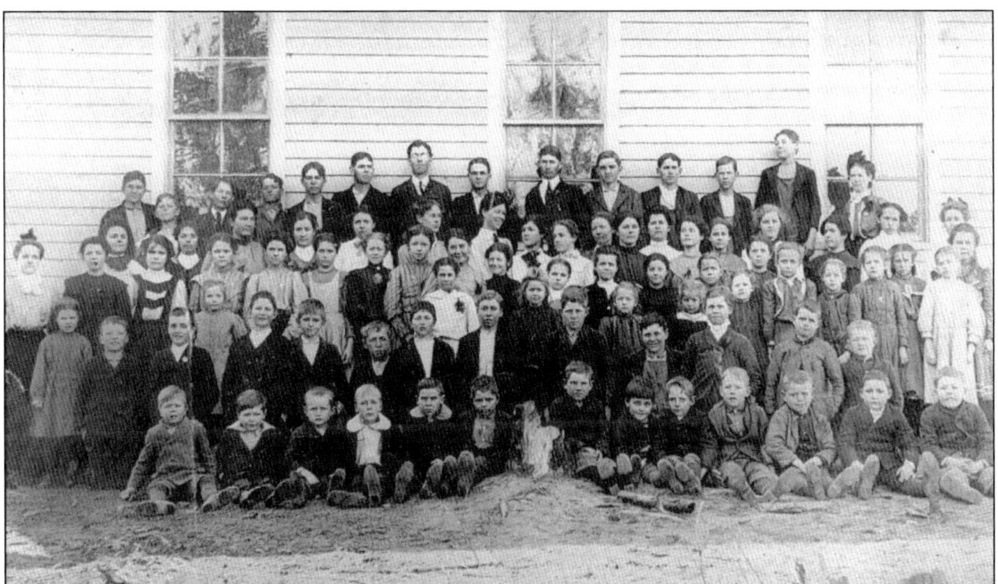

This photograph shows an unidentified class of students at the Beam School. (Courtesy of Beth Beam King and Dan King.)

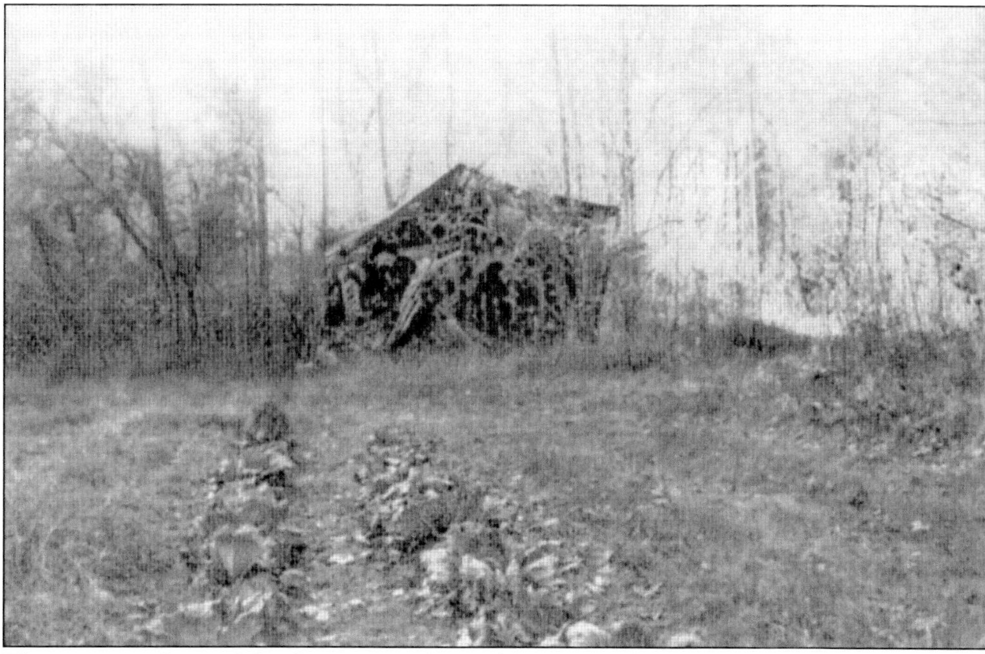

This one-room Bostic School was across the road from the old Withrow home near Hollis. It was in operation in the late 1800s. World War I veteran Zeno Gettys (1895–1987) attended school here. (Courtesy of Jefferson Gettys.)

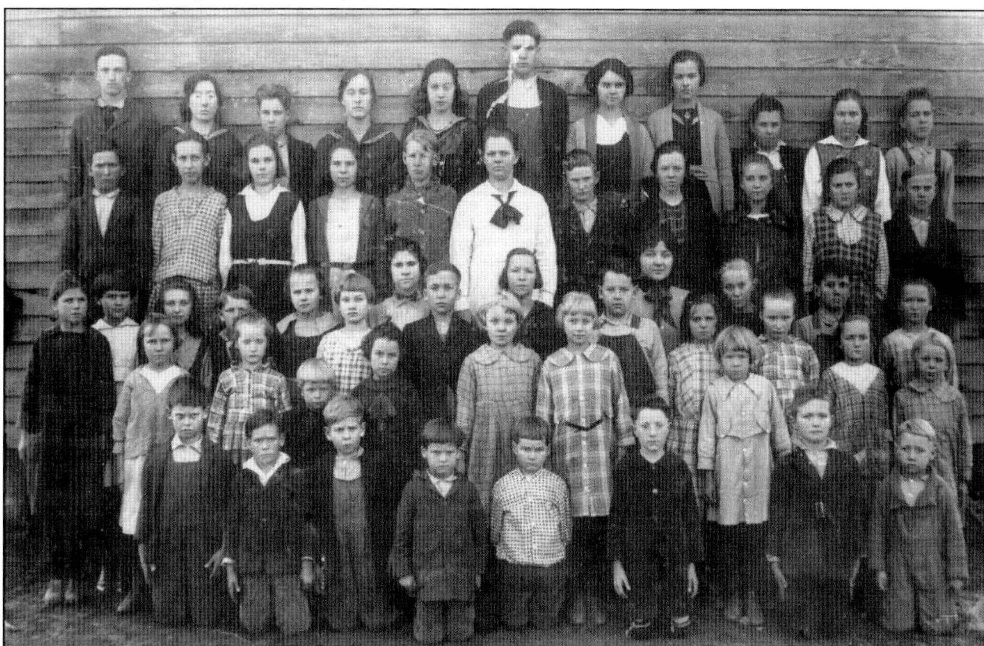

This photograph of the Race Path School dates from 1921. The school itself was in operation from the early 1900s. Race Path School was still in operation until 1924 when the new Ellenboro School opened. The teacher in this photograph was Vera Whisnant (Gettys). (Courtesy of Frances Gettys Bailey.)

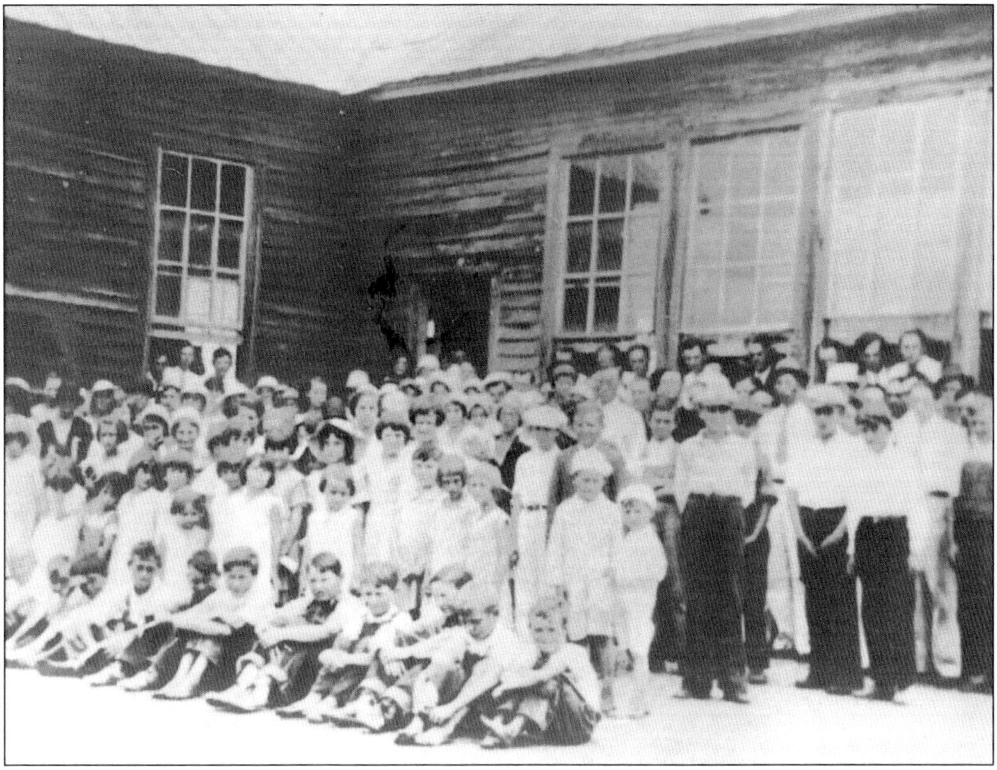

Hurricane Hill School took its name from its location on Hurricane Hill, behind Campfield Church. When staffing became a problem, the school was placed on skids and mules pulled the building beside where Campfield Church is now located; its name became Fairview Elementary School. Ed Campfield bought the Fairview school building and property. The school closed about 1927, and the students matriculated elsewhere. (Courtesy of Martina Toney.)

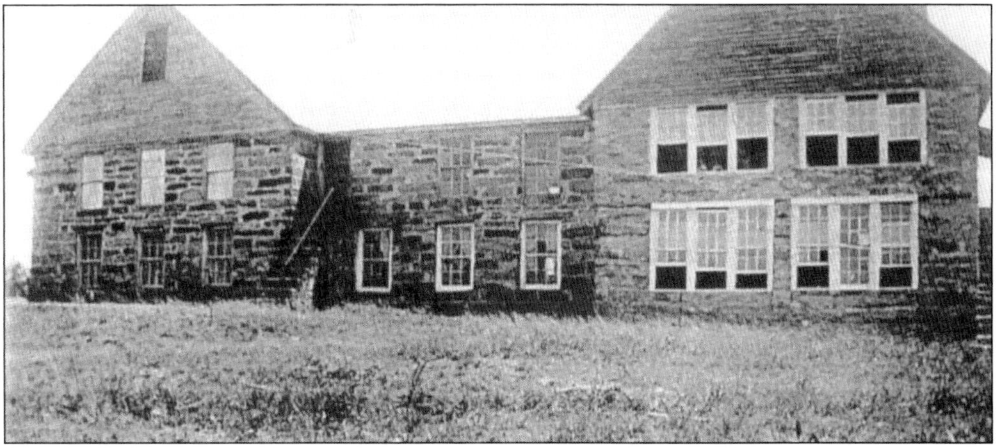

In 1890, Hollis had 25 students in all grades. After the wooden facility burned, a newly constructed rock building (1905) became the school. The four rooms to the right were a 1923 addition. In 1927, Grady Withrow (son of Julius Plato Durham Withrow) connected wires to the school building to provide electricity from his carbide plant. In 1950–1951, high school students began to attend Ellenboro, Polkville, and Sunshine; the rock building was no longer in use. (Courtesy of Ronald Hester and Vida Hester.)

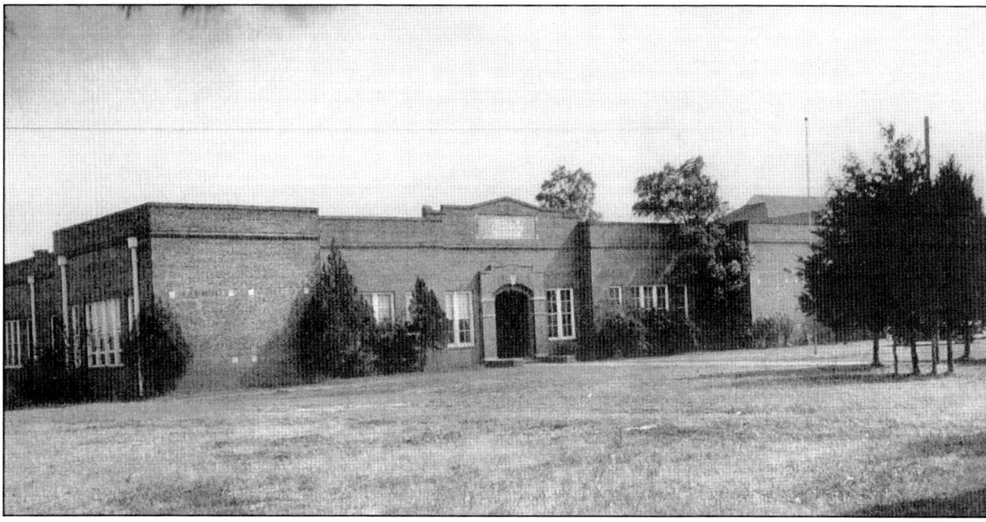

A brick building in Hollis had been constructed in 1925 as an elementary school. This brick structure burned in 1955, and the elementary school students moved to the rock building. In 1959, Hollis School closed, and the students were bused to other schools. (Courtesy of Ronald Hester and Vida Hester.)

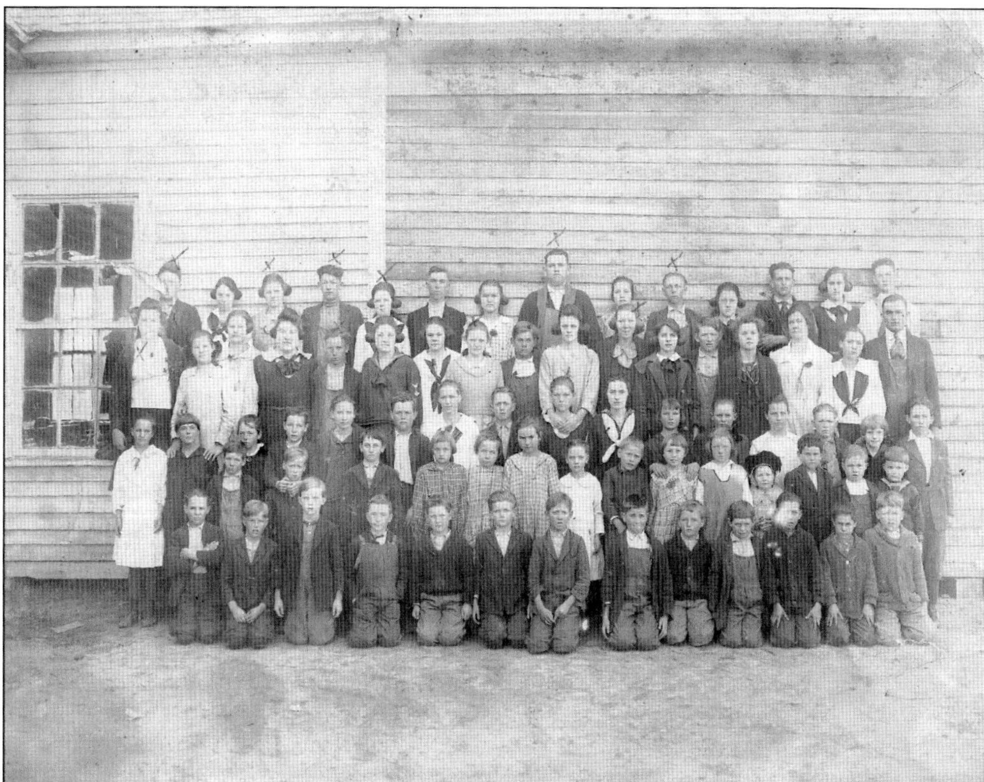

Colfax Township and the surrounding areas were rich in schools because the residents valued education. Another important school in the area was Oak Grove School near Oak Grove Methodist Church. This school was later used as a personal residence. (Courtesy of Jeanne Davis.)

Three

Work

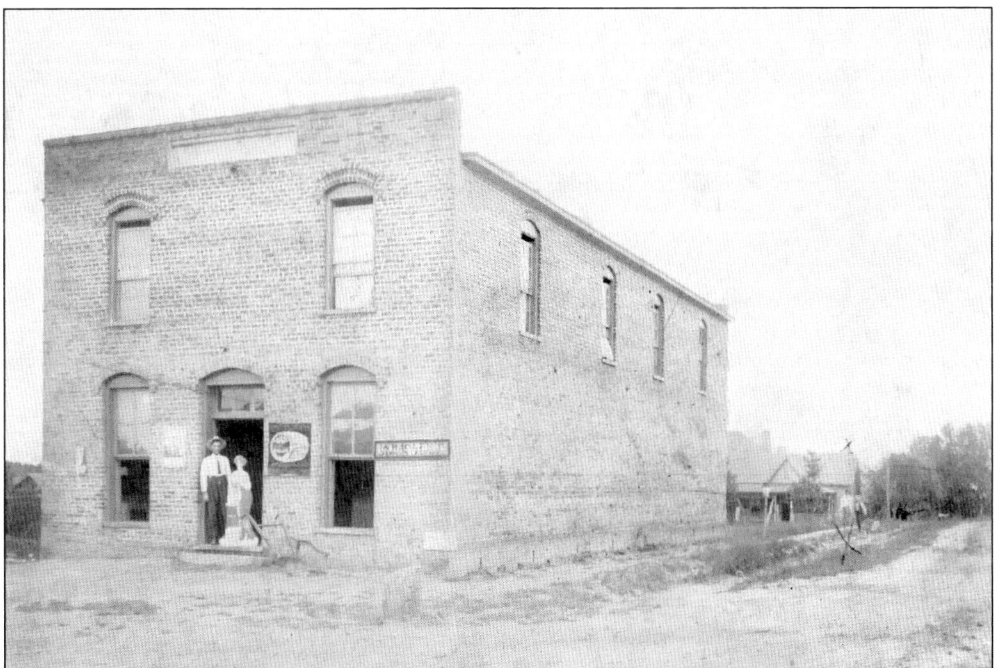

Audley McKinney wanted a brick store. Frank Byers had clay dug from Harrill Creek (near the Ice Box Swimming Hole) and down on the Jones property. Byers paid for bricks to be made and sun-dried for use in the 1903 structure. The upstairs was used as a meeting place for such groups as the Odd Fellows. (Courtesy of Jo Ann Martin.)

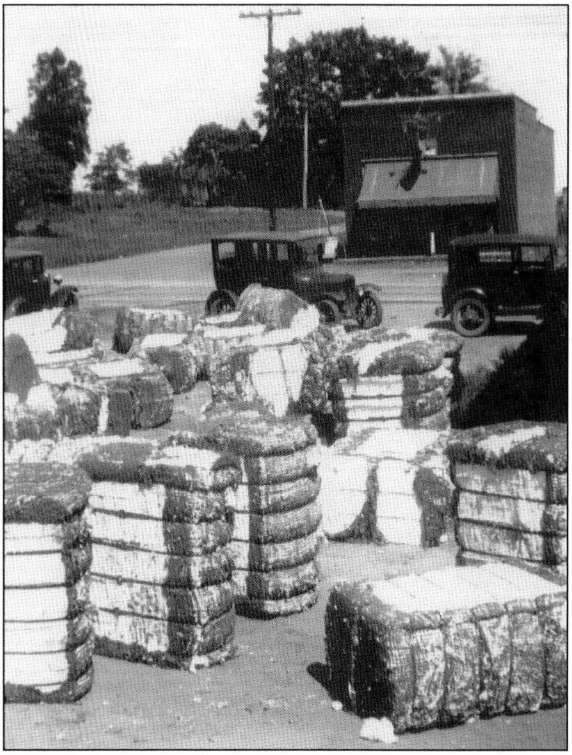

Van Harrill was a cotton speculator/broker and a local merchant. This photograph from the early 1920s shows his bales of cotton, which local people referred to as "Harrill's Cotton Patch." In the background is the old drugstore that became a bank in the 1960s. Several doctors located their offices in the back of the drugstore. (Courtesy of Paul Price.)

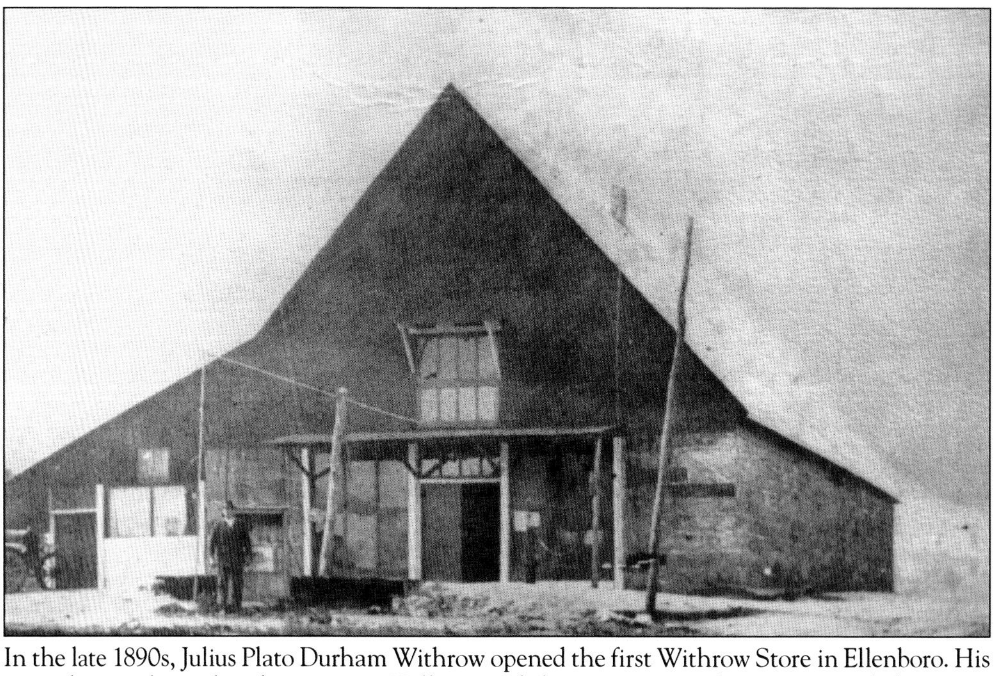

In the late 1890s, Julius Plato Durham Withrow opened the first Withrow Store in Ellenboro. His second general merchandise store in Hollis served that community from 1906 until the 1960s. Owners included J. P. D. Withrow, Grady Withrow, John Bell, and Horace Hunt. J. P. D. Withrow traveled by train to New York to purchase stock. The original building, constructed of stone from Cherry Mountain, stands today. (Courtesy of Ronald Hester and Vida Hester.)

John Bell was one of the last merchants in the former Withrow Store. He also had a store in Lattimore and one on Route 4. From the early 1930s until about 1943, he operated three "rolling stores," which employed bartering as a frequent means of exchange. This photograph shows Richard B. "Bud" McFarland in front of the Hollis establishment. (Courtesy of Norman McDaniel.)

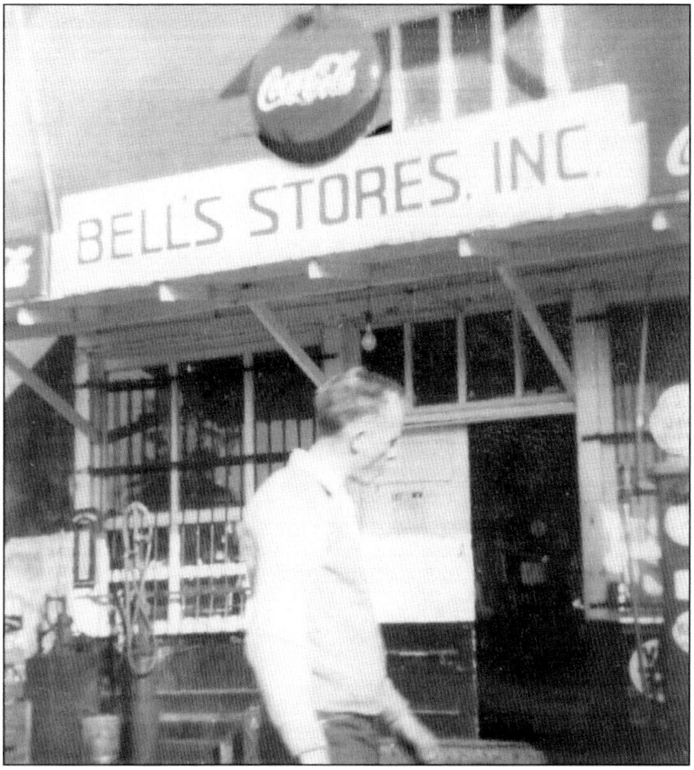

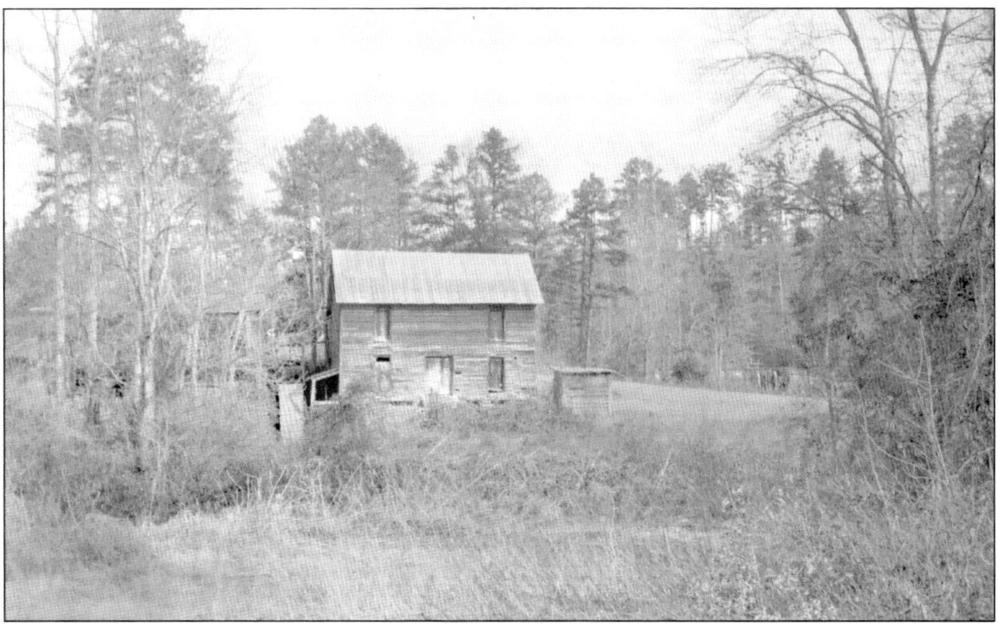

McKinney Mill dates from 1860. In 1910, the mill was moved 300 yards to its present location on McKinney Mill Road on Sandy Run Creek. Children enjoyed the millpond and the falls while parents had their corn and wheat ground. In 1965, Ivey Ray Mauney purchased the mill. Twenty-two years later, Junior Spratt rebuilt the dam and restored the plume, and Frank Waters rebuilt the wheel. Mauney continues to preserve the landmark. (Courtesy of Ivey Ray Mauney.)

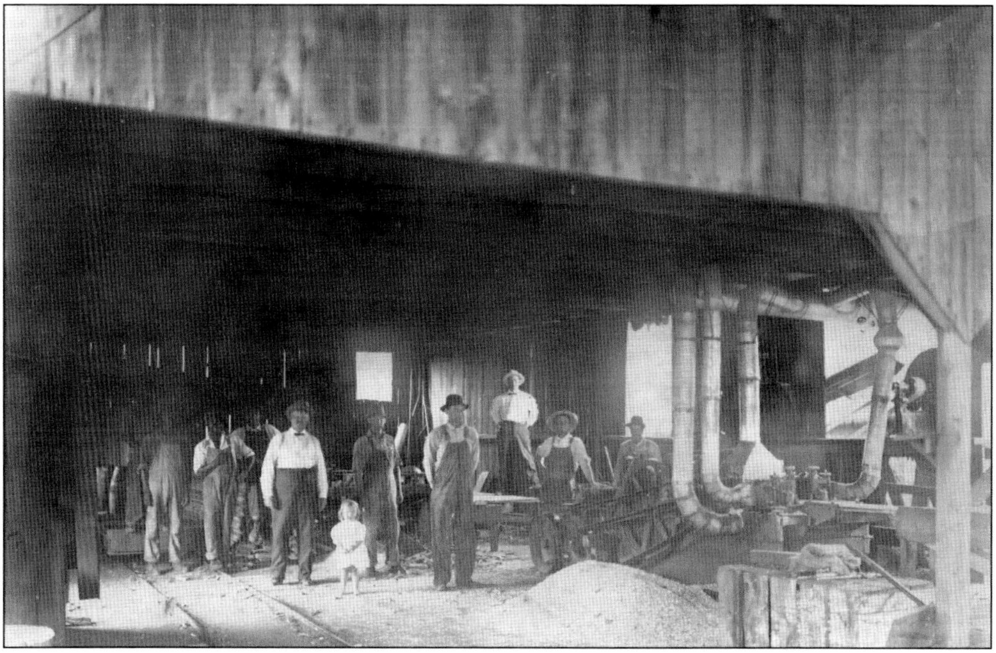

Hollis was the most distant northwestern point in Rutherford County for the cultivation of cotton. Areas to the north and west were generally too mountainous and had a shorter growing season. This photograph shows the interior of the Hollis Gin, which was a one-stand, hand-fed gin. J. P. D. Withrow—with a white shirt and bow tie—stands on the left. (Courtesy of Bill Withrow.)

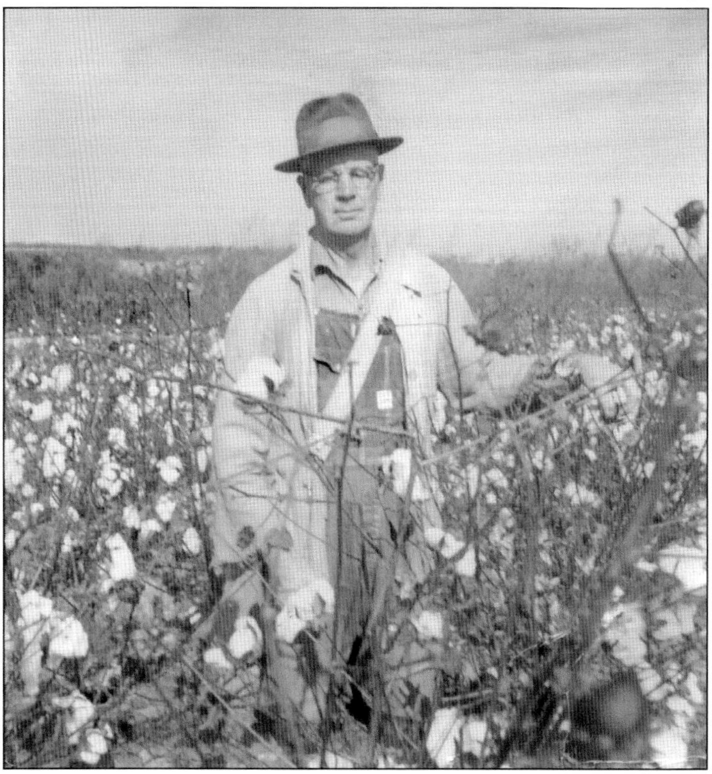

Cotton was the principal cash crop in Colfax Township, and activities centered around the crop. Schools began in mid-summer and adjourned for several weeks for students to pick cotton. The Colfax Free Fair coincided with the cotton harvest, and many students earned fair money by picking cotton. In the early 1950s, the going rate was a penny a pound. Local farmer Coran Toney, a World War II veteran, poses here with his bumper crop. (Courtesy of Rachel Toney Jones.)

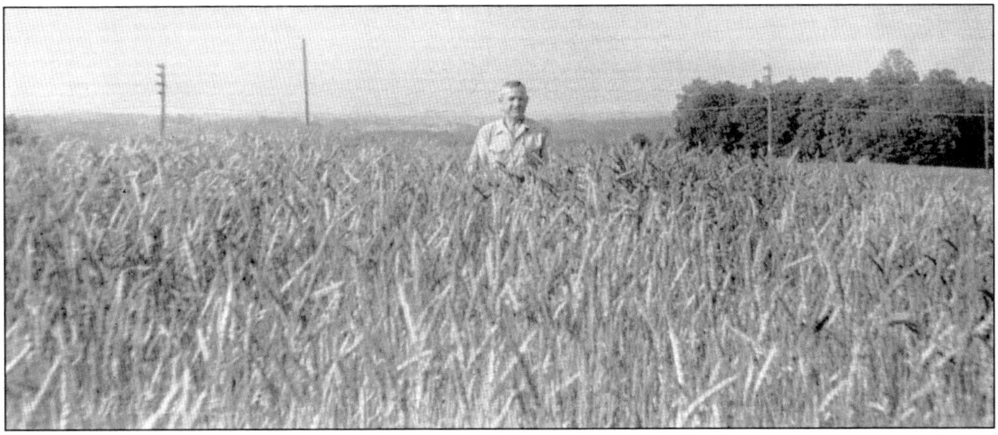

Ewart Burns (1904–1984) stands in his wheat field outside his Ellenboro home. His 1955 crop was mostly straw. A local electrician, Ewart worked also at the Cliffside Steam Station, wired every year for the Colfax Fair from the 1930s until his death, and in 1951, he hung Ellenboro's first traffic light. He married widow Nell Daves Price. Nell worked as deputy sheriff in the 1980s. (Courtesy of Anita Price Davis.)

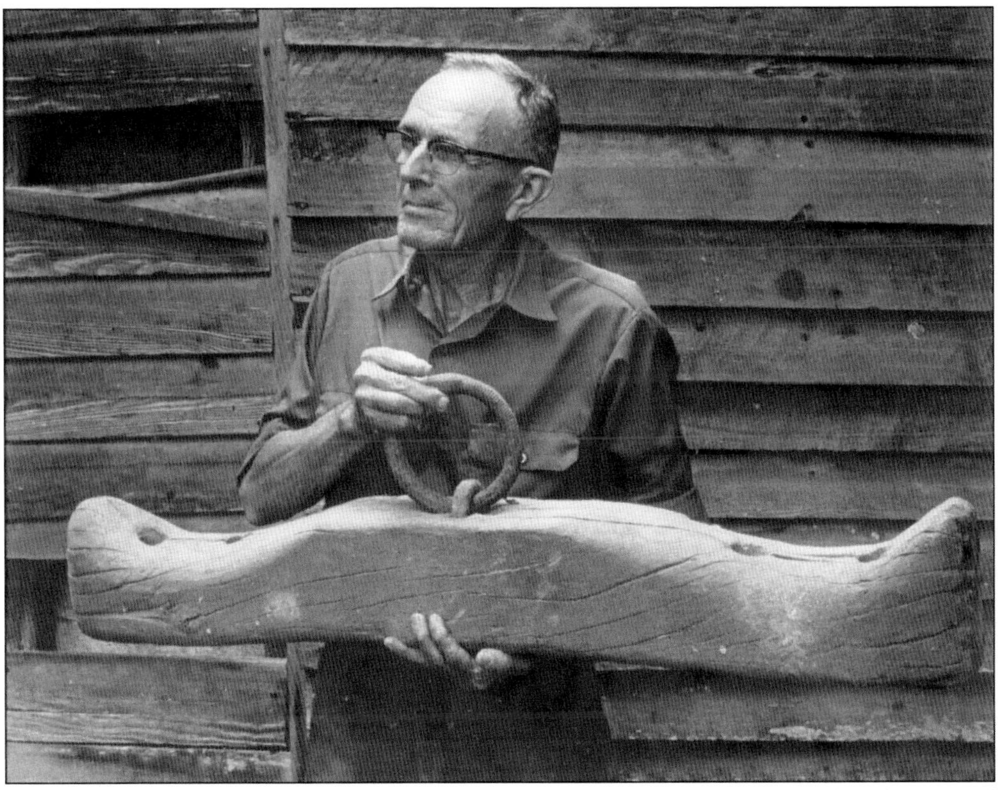

World War I veteran Zeno Gettys, the "Sage of Cherry Mountain," was a teacher, logger, and farmer. This oxen yoke belonged to his father, Thomas Jefferson Gettys. Zeno's wife, Vera Whisnant Gettys, was an Asheville Normal School graduate and taught at Race Path and Sunshine. Their children were Howard, Henry, Emmett, Kenneth, Jefferson, and Frances Gettys Bailey. Zeno's ancestors—Samuel Gettys and his son James—founded Gettysburg, Pennsylvania. (Courtesy of Frances Gettys Bailey and Jefferson Gettys.)

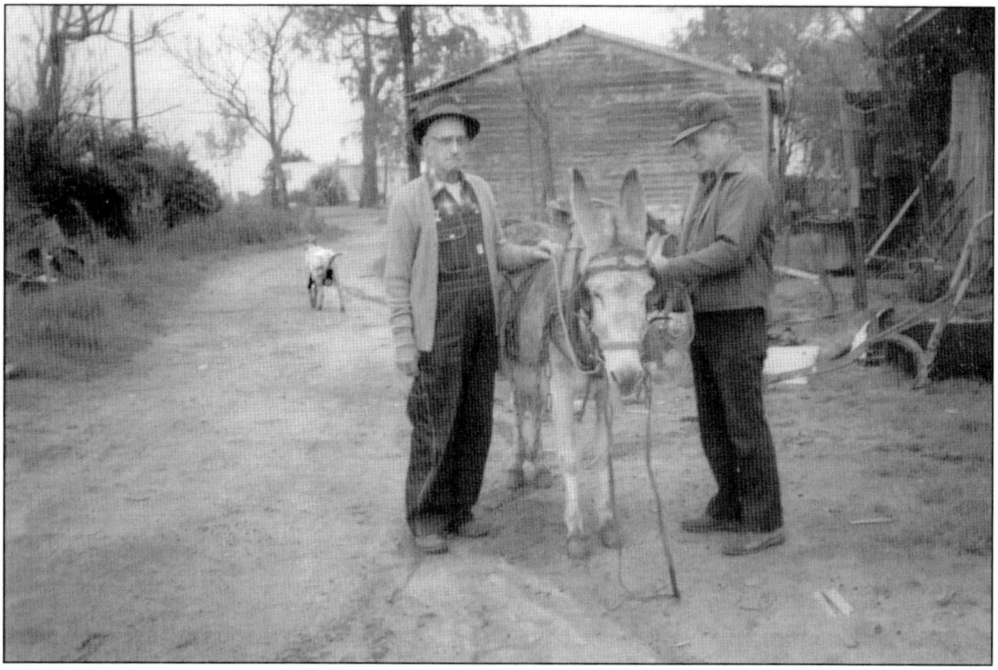

All the work was not done by the people alone. Odell Bridges (left) used a donkey to help him with his chores. Here he stands in his yard with his donkey Jenny and his son Obie. (Courtesy of Becky Bridges.)

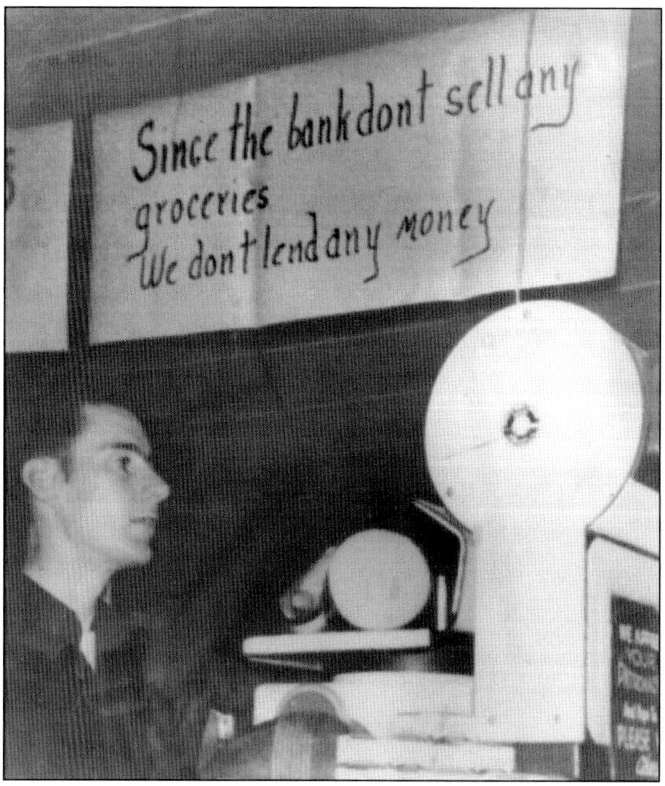

Grady Hamrick ran the store at Highway 74 Business and Piney Mountain Road for 22 years. In the 1950s, Grady bought Fred Hamrick's store in Ellenboro, which he operated until just before his death in 1968. In this photograph, Grady's son Lowell, who worked at the store, stands near a sign that reads, "Since the bank don't sell any groceries, we don't lend any money." Lowell later sold the store to Guy and Annie Greene. (Courtesy of Lowell Hamrick.)

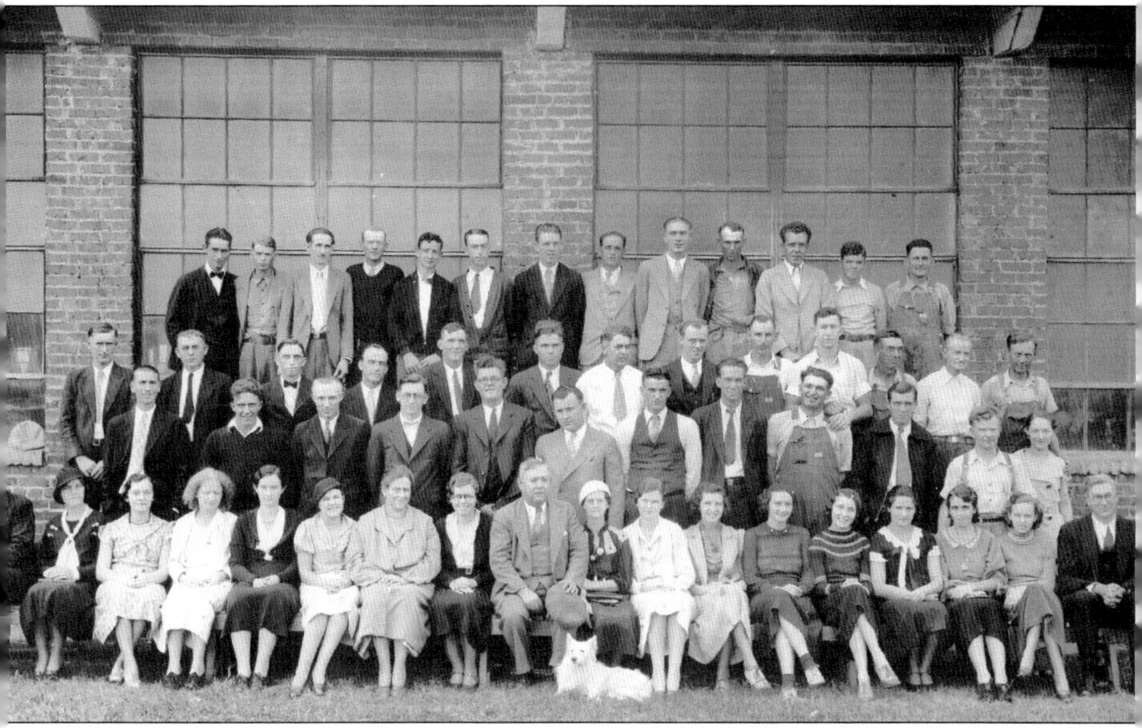

In July 1925, the Ellenboro Manufacturing Company opened under the name of Belk Manufacturing. A village sprang up around the plant. Later the company took the names of Queen Anne Mill, Neisler Mills, and Quaker Fabrics. Shown here from left to right are employees (first row) Reverend Taylor, Geneva Hill Bridges, Estelle Canton, Mutt Clary, Hester Greene, Net Martin, Annie Laura Limerick, Katherine Turner, Mr. and Mrs. Graham, Erie Martin, Lorene Harrill, Pauline Kendrick, Ruby Harrill, Beatrice Edwards, Irene Hill, Grace Horn, and Reverend Rooke; (second row) Fred Hamrick, Marine Martin, Harry Hope, Rush Greene, ? Martin, ? Canton, ? Hawkins, Leonard Hope, J. B. Padgett, ? Greene, Pete McGraw, and Inez Graham; (third row) unidentified, John Horn, Claude Bland, Ray Goldsmith, Carl Duncan, Welle Padgett, Oscar Harrill, Johnny McGraw, and five unidentified; (fourth row) Horace Bridges, ? Blanton, Dever Cleary, Bryon Bridges, Howard Duncan, Norris Callahan, Louie Duncan, two unidentified people, Gill Greene, ? Blackwell, Joe Allen, and Cliff Bridges. (Courtesy of Ellenboro Museum.)

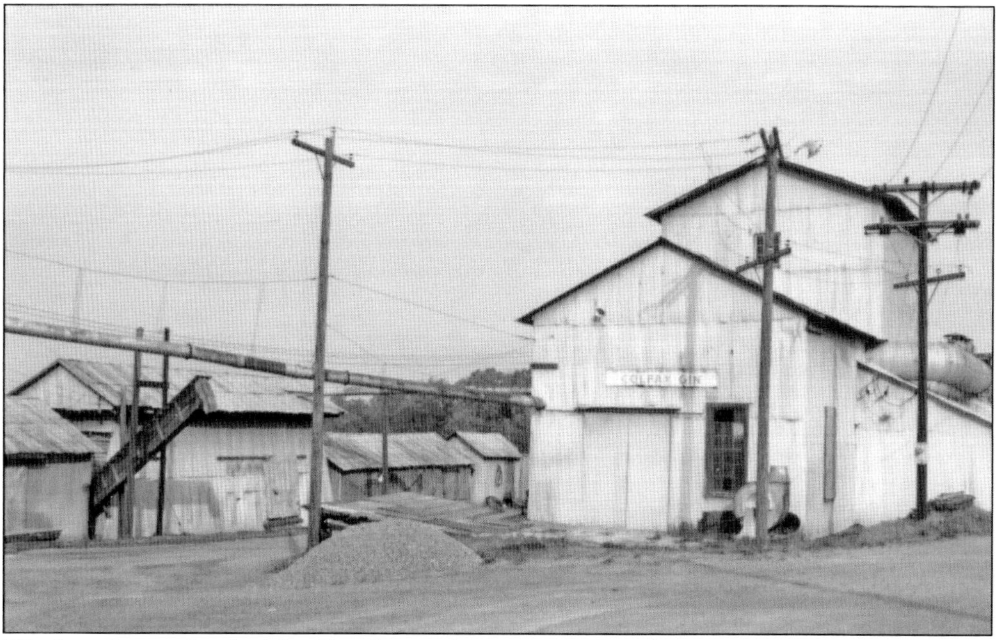

Ellenboro Cotton Gin, built by Chambers and Turner, Inc., dates from 1928. William Van McDaniel helped install the original equipment. When Chambers and Turner declared bankruptcy, the Lancaster Cotton Oil Company purchased it. In 1959, McDaniel began operating the gin. Farmers tried to earn the distinction of having the year's first bale of cotton. The average bale weighed 480–500 pounds. (Courtesy of William Joe McDaniel.)

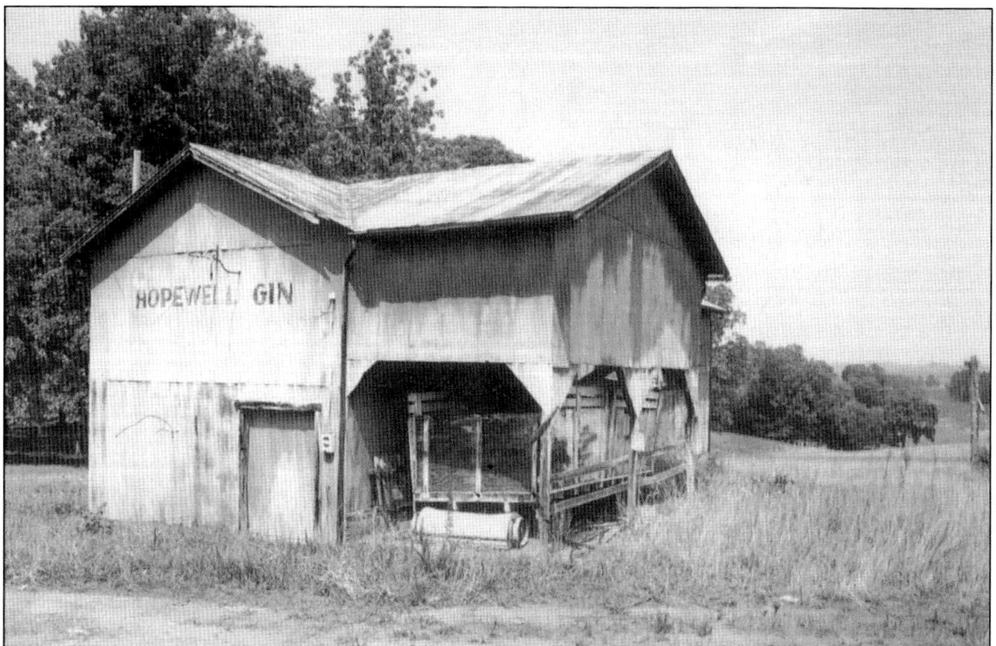

Hopewell Gin was built by the Lee Robbins family after 1928. Victor Cotton Oil Company of Gaffney later purchased the gin. In 1947, William Van McDaniel purchased the Hopewell Gin; he closed it in 1959. (Courtesy of James M. Walker and Anita Price Davis.)

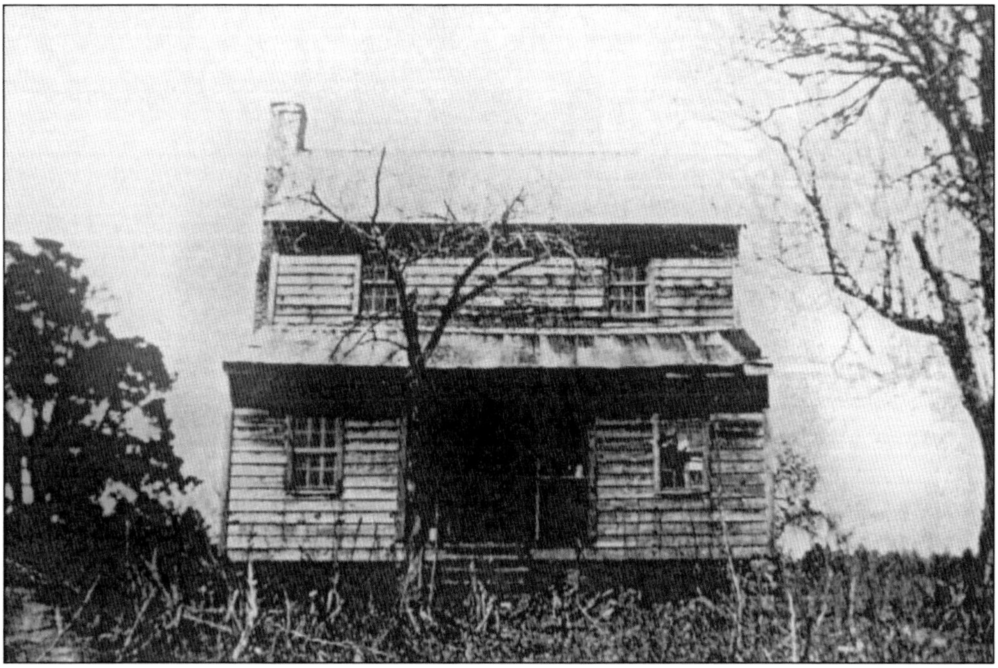

The Memory Post Office dates from March 5, 1883. David B. Harrill was the postmaster; the post office was on his land in what is now the Dobbins Church community. Though discontinued on April 9, 1884, the post office was reestablished on June 27, 1884, and it continued to operate until July 30, 1904. The building, which was later used as a residence, still stands. (Courtesy of Dan and Beth Beam King.)

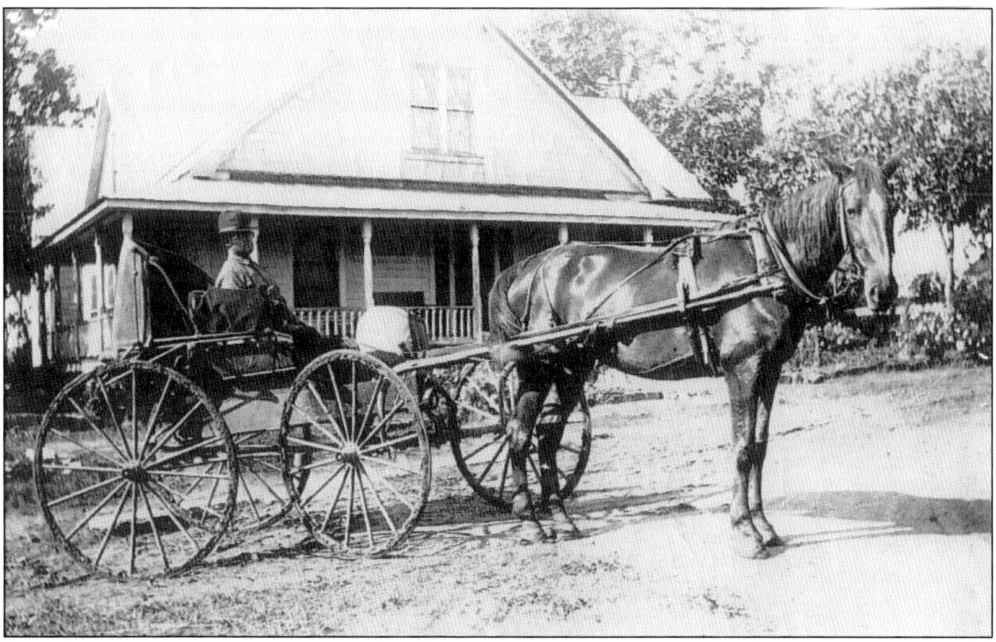

Elizabeth "Beth" Beam King's uncle, Joseph Beam, delivered mail from Ellenboro in 1911. Joseph was the son of Samuel Monroe Beam. The home in the background belonged to Samuel and Sara Elizabeth Beam on Red Barn Road. (Courtesy of Dan and Beth Beam King.)

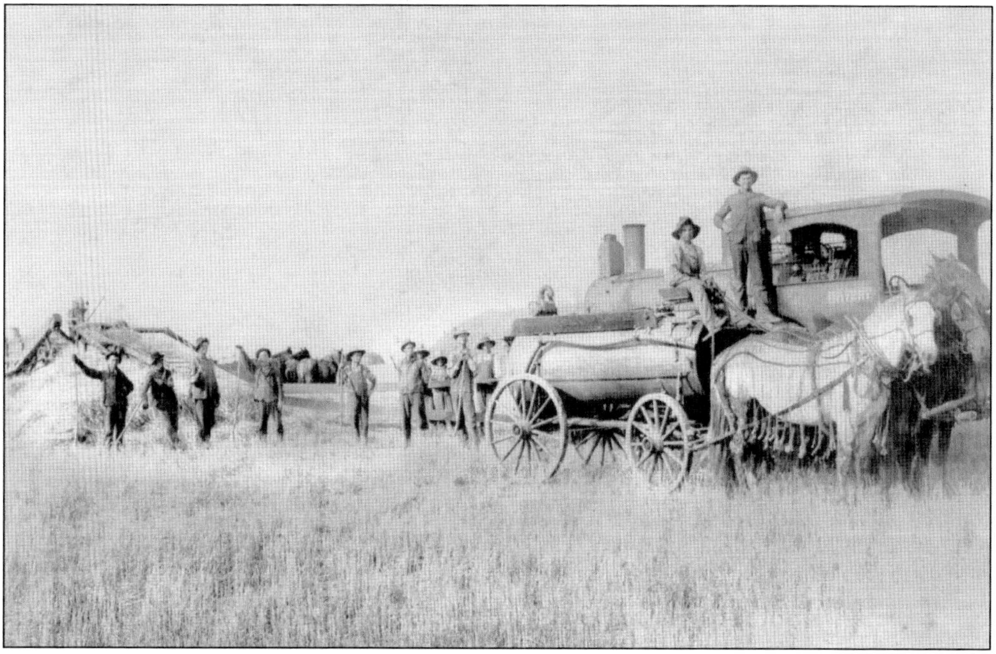

Harvesting wheat required expensive equipment that most Colfax farmers could ill afford. Those who did own sophisticated threshing machines were in great demand for hire at other farms. To entice the threshers to come to one's farm, families served a large midday meal. "Thrashers" appreciated this perk and often gave that family preference on their work schedule. The term "threshers' meal" meant any large meal. (Courtesy of Mary Pruette.)

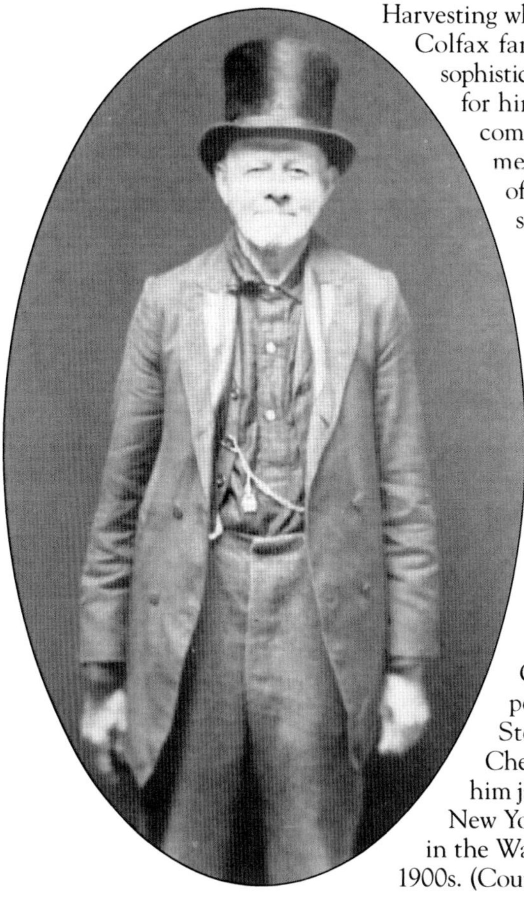

Some local residents made illegal liquor to sell to others for profit and for home use as "medicine." Born in 1821 on Sandy Run Creek, famed local moonshiner Amos Owens perfected Cherry Bounce—a blend of 44 Blue Steel whiskey, honey, and cherry juice from Cherry Mountain cherries. His profession brought him jail time and even a stay in Sing Sing Prison in New York. A Confederate veteran, Amos has rested in the Walls Baptist Church Cemetery since the early 1900s. (Courtesy of Joe Stockton.)

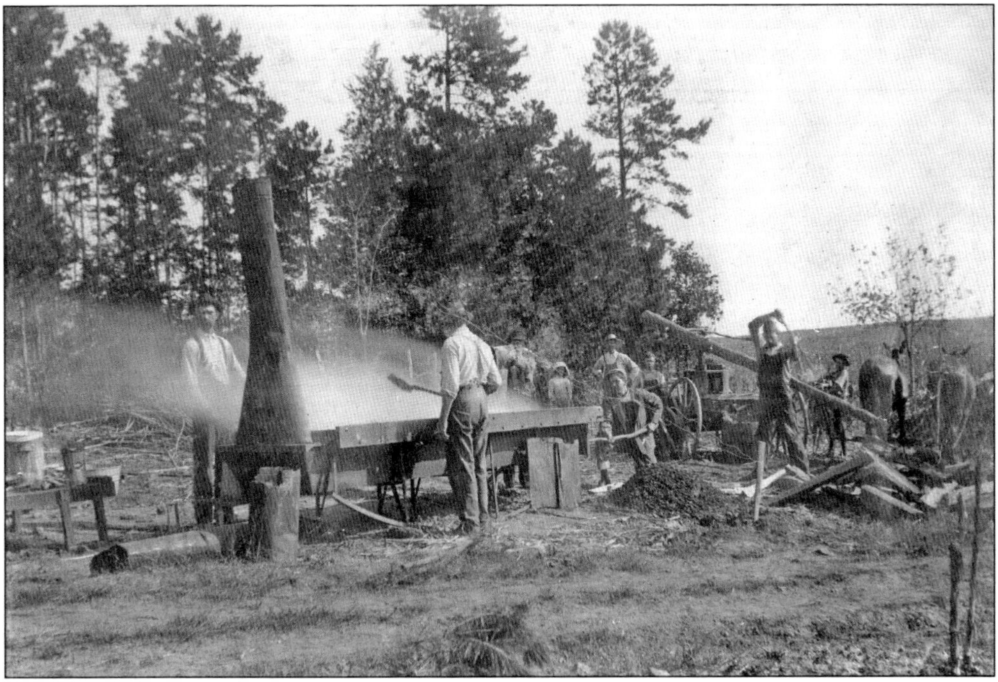

Sorghum cane, originally from Africa, was a common crop in the Colfax area. Farmers extracted the liquid from their harvested sorghum with a cane mill; numerous "lassy" (molasses) mills dotted the countryside. After cooking the sugary juice in an evaporator, the result was molasses. Some cane farmers invited neighbors in to cook the molasses further and to celebrate with a taffy pull. (Courtesy of Jo Ann Martin.)

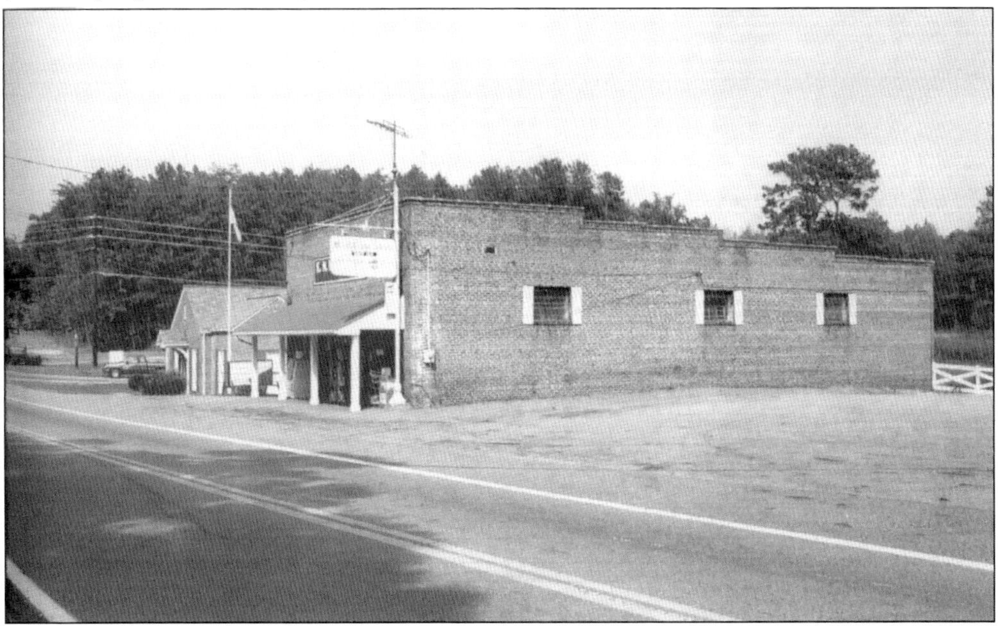

The Washburn family and their Washburn's Store, established in the early 1830s, gave their name to the surrounding community. Still in operation, the store is part of a historic district listed in the National Register of Historic Places. (Courtesy of James M. Walker and Anita Price Davis.)

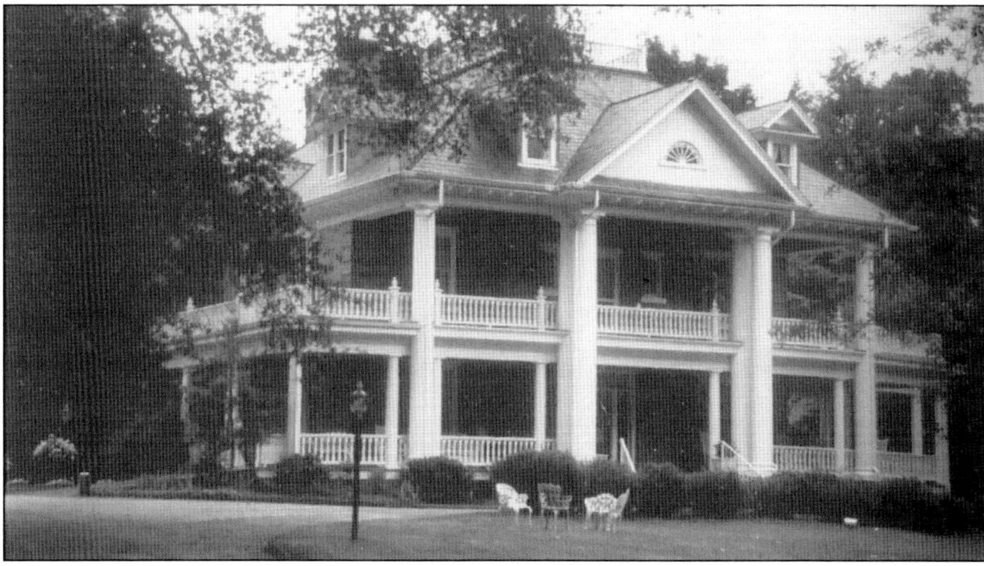

The Washburn historic district includes the Washburn House, across the road from Washburn's Store. The house was listed on the National Register of Historic Places on February 20, 2002. (Courtesy of James M. Walker and Anita Price Davis.)

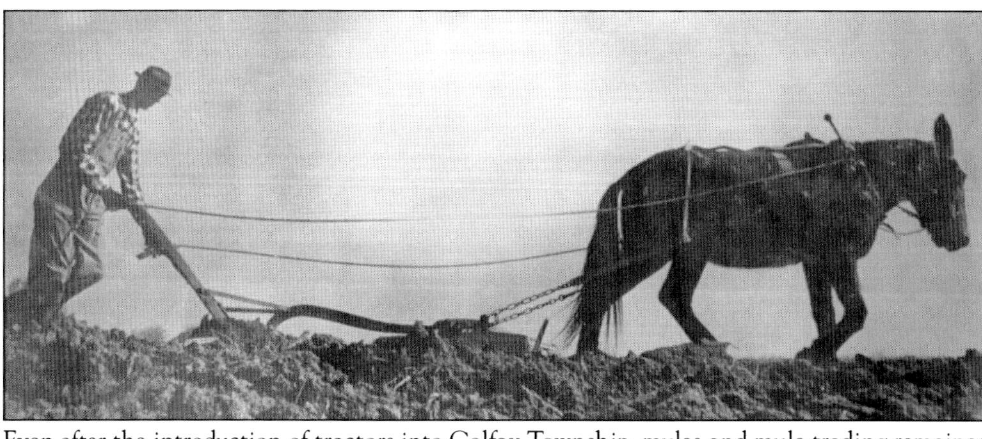

Even after the introduction of tractors into Colfax Township, mules and mule trading remained an important part of the agricultural economy. Many farmers preferred mules to horses. Valued for their strength and endurance, each mule often had its own name and personality. Here Fay Toney plows with a mule in the Campfield Memorial Baptist Church community. (Courtesy of Betty Toney Davis.)

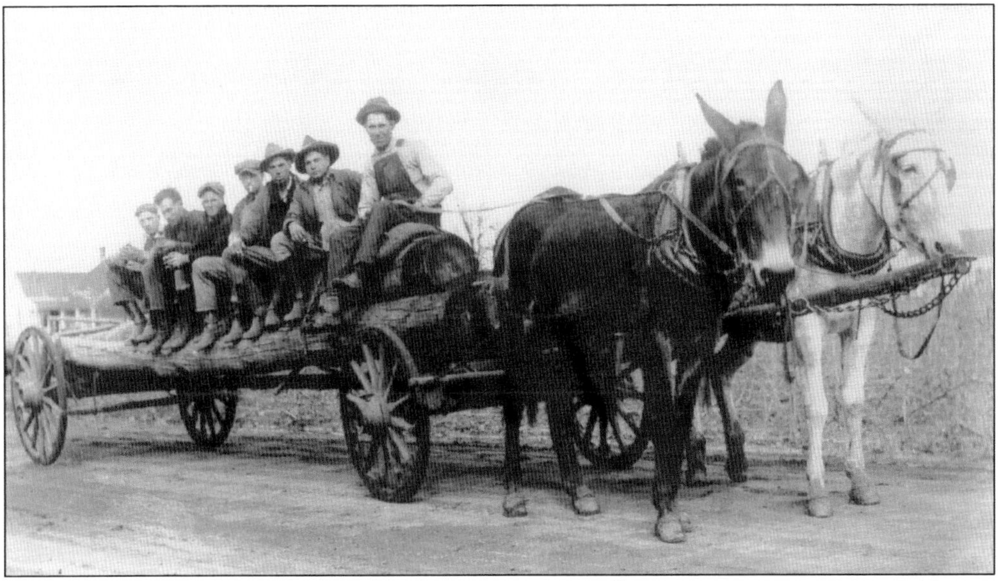

With its forest resources, Colfax Township saw many small logging operations. Here Ed Pruett holds the reins to the mules. (Courtesy of Mary Pruette.)

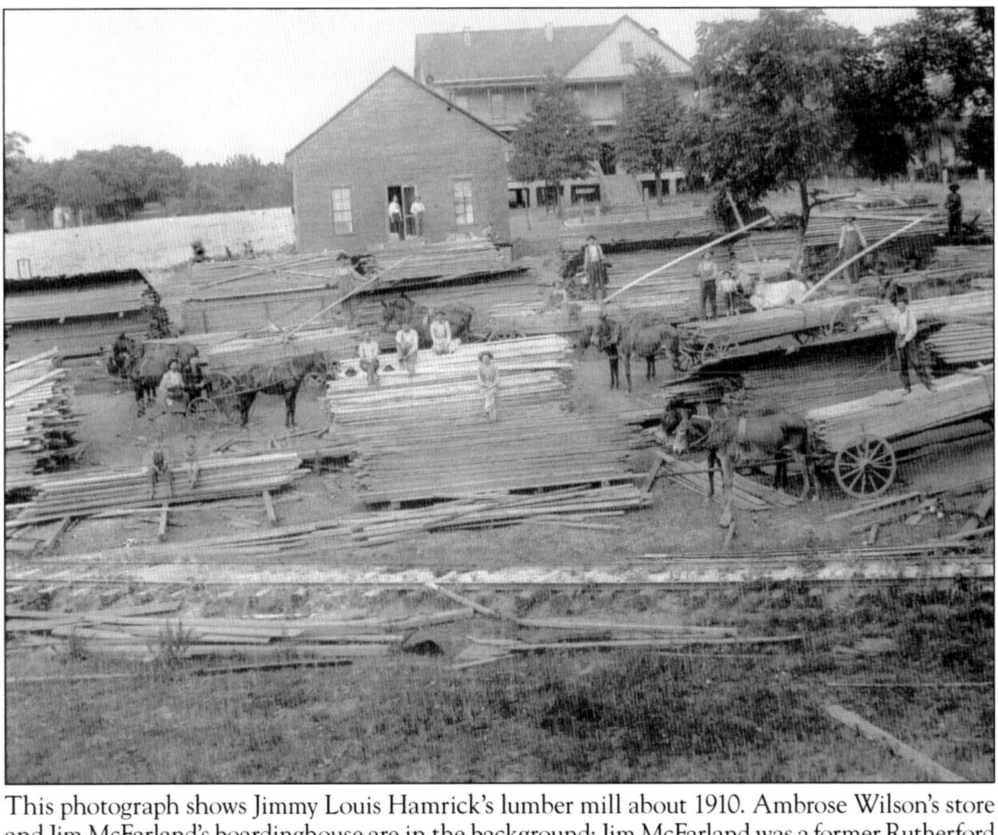

This photograph shows Jimmy Louis Hamrick's lumber mill about 1910. Ambrose Wilson's store and Jim McFarland's boardinghouse are in the background; Jim McFarland was a former Rutherford County sheriff. In the foreground of the picture are railroad tracks leading to a planer mill. The lumber mill burned in the early 1950s. (Courtesy of Mary Pruette.)

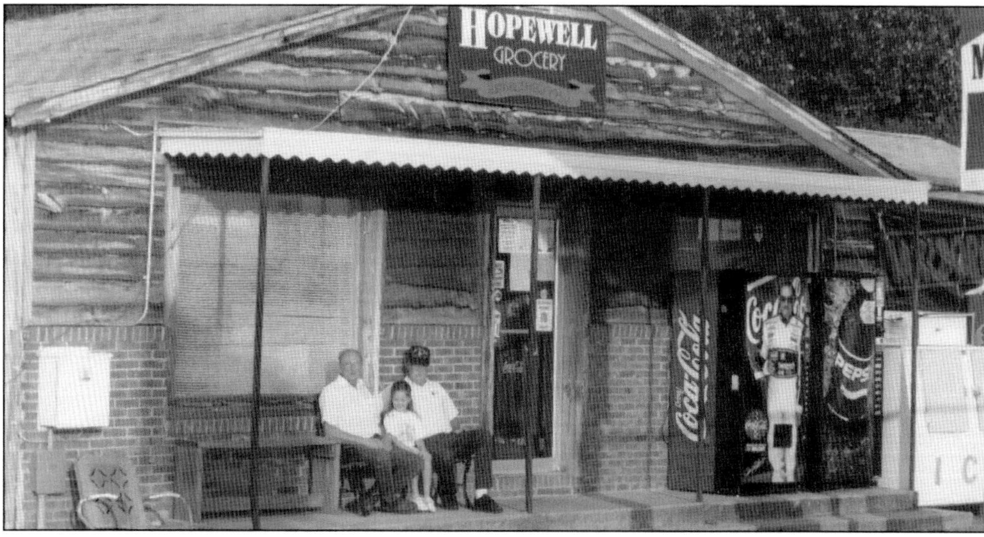

Hopewell Grocery, seen here, still operates as a community store. Many residents remember bartering with owner O. C. Waters in this same building in the 1920s. The people gathered around the store attests to its friendly atmosphere. (Courtesy of Joyce Waters McFarland and Brenda McFarland Toney.)

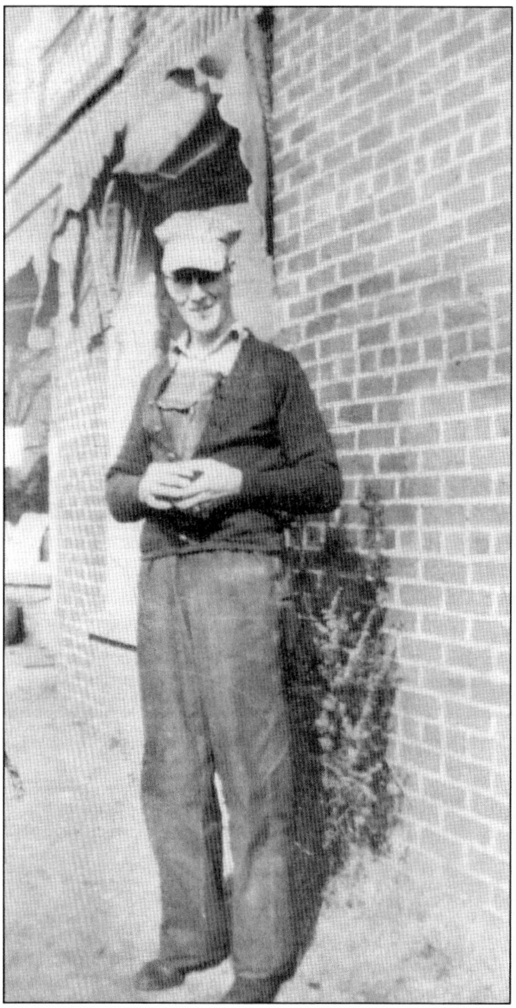

The main Seaboard Air Line Railroad and the Southern Railroad traversed Colfax Township. Engineer Edward Rollins Price, Colfax resident and founder of Capri Park (1956), stands in front of Ervin M. Grindstaff's general store, which he operated from 1940 to 1945 at the corner of Hollis Road and Highway 74 Business. Grindstaff sold to Ernest Self; the store burned in 1947. Ervin later opened Grindstaff's Interiors in Forest City. (Courtesy of Anita Price Davis.)

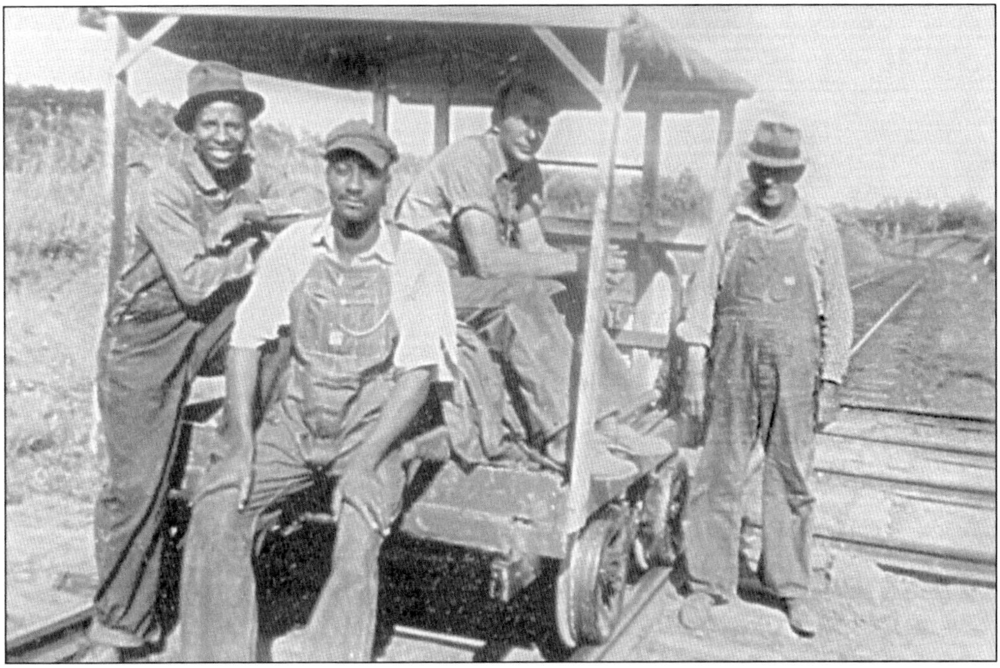

Section foreman Corbett Mauney (right) poses with a Southern Railroad train track crew. Corbett was the father of Ivey Ray Mauney, who also became a railroad engineer and the owner of McKinney Mill, mentioned earlier in this chapter. (Courtesy of Ivey Ray Mauney.)

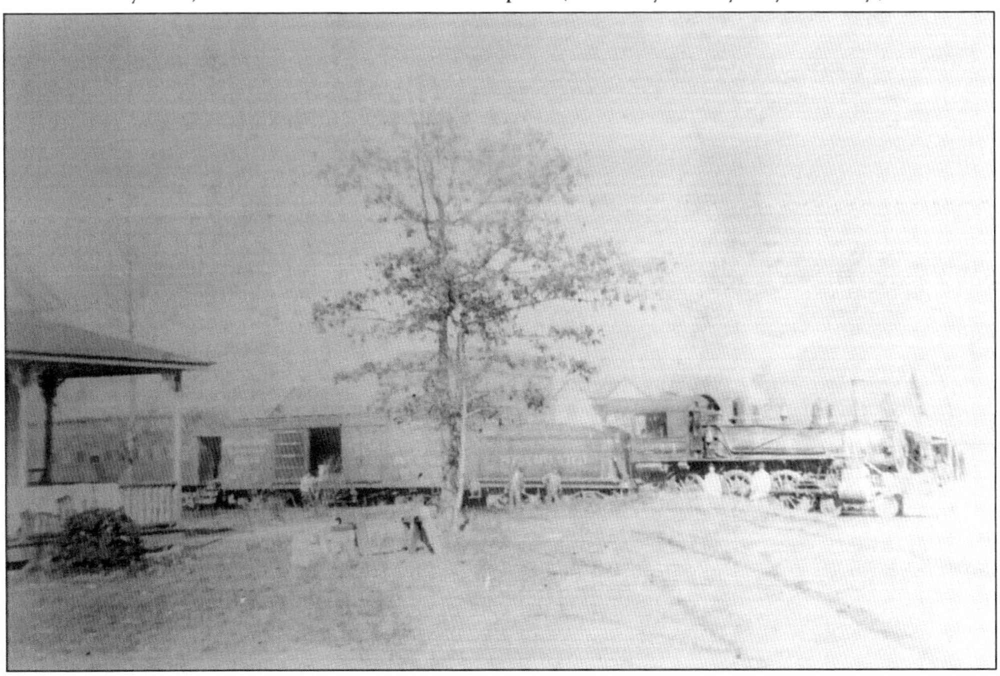

This train dates from the late 1800s and is on the tracks crossing Glenn Street in Ellenboro. The house in the foreground is that of Walter Lee "Captain" Black and later belonged to son Orland Hugh "Babe" Black and his wife, Sarah Summey Black. Both men were section foremen. (Courtesy of Ellenboro Depot/Colfax Museum.)

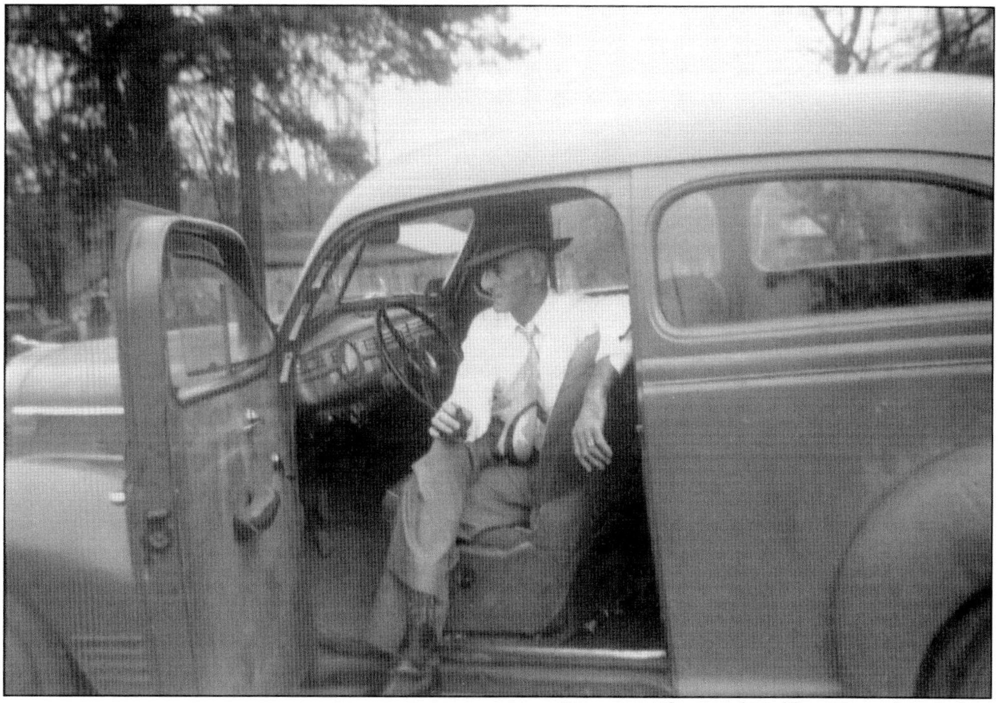

Some residents of Colfax Township left temporarily to aid in the war effort. Here Sherwood Glenn Withrow rests in his Dodge at the Dismal Swamp. During the Korean War, Withrow worked at the U.S. naval base in Newport News, Virginia. The family returned to Colfax Township near the end of the war. (Courtesy of Scott Withrow.)

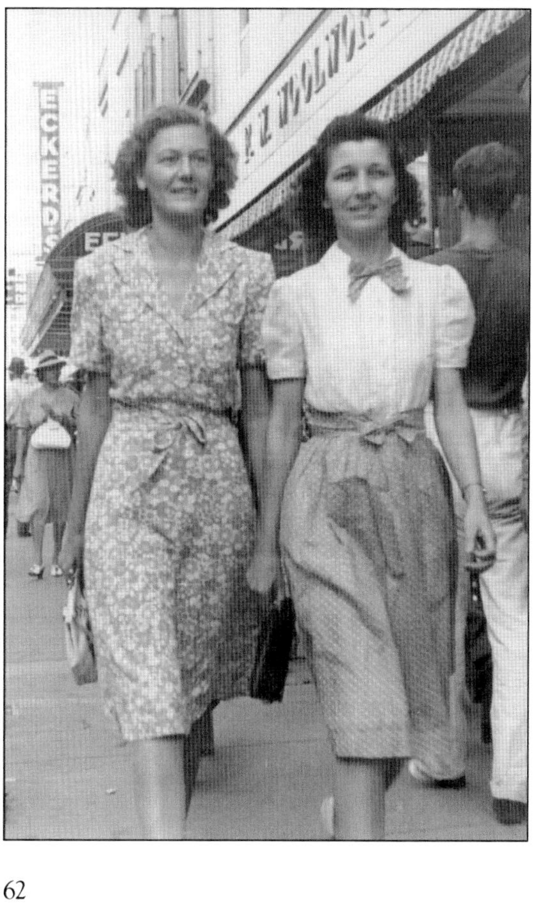

Like many women, Mae Virginia Hamrick (Withrow) and Sarah Harrill (Martin) found employment in nearby urban areas. Both Mae (left) and Sarah worked in Charlotte in 1941 before returning to Colfax Township. (Courtesy of Scott Withrow.)

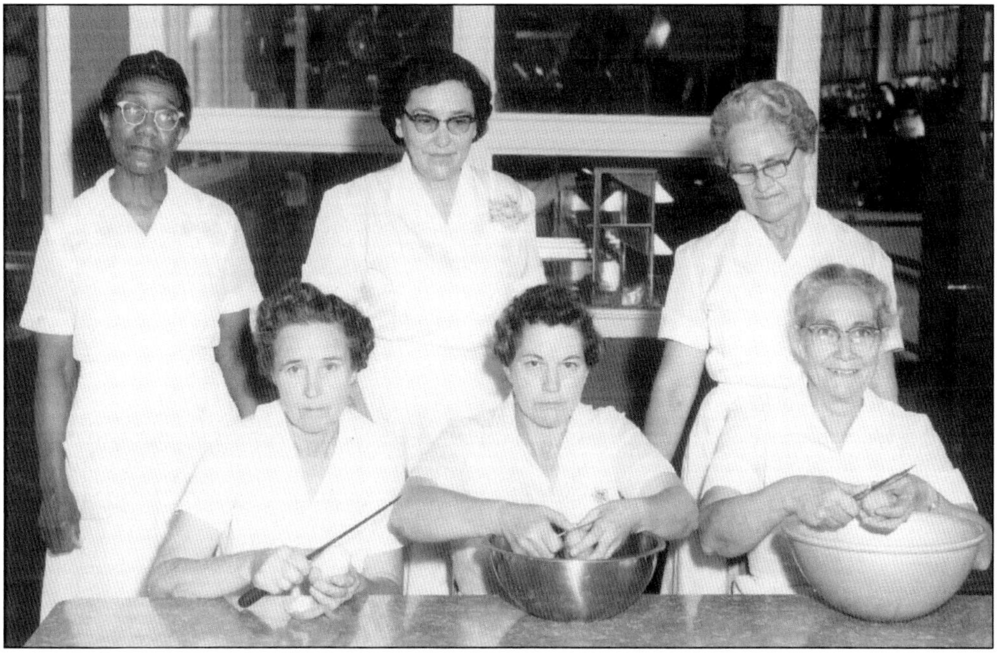

Women also contributed to the family income. These cafeteria workers and their Southern cooking were welcome sights to the hungry students at Ellenboro School. Seen here from left to right are (sitting) Lucille Edwards, Mrs. Zeno Davis, and Mrs. John Spurlin; (standing) Elsie Lomax, Ollie Rea Randall, and Cora Lee McDaniel. (Courtesy of Jelma Hamrick Daves.)

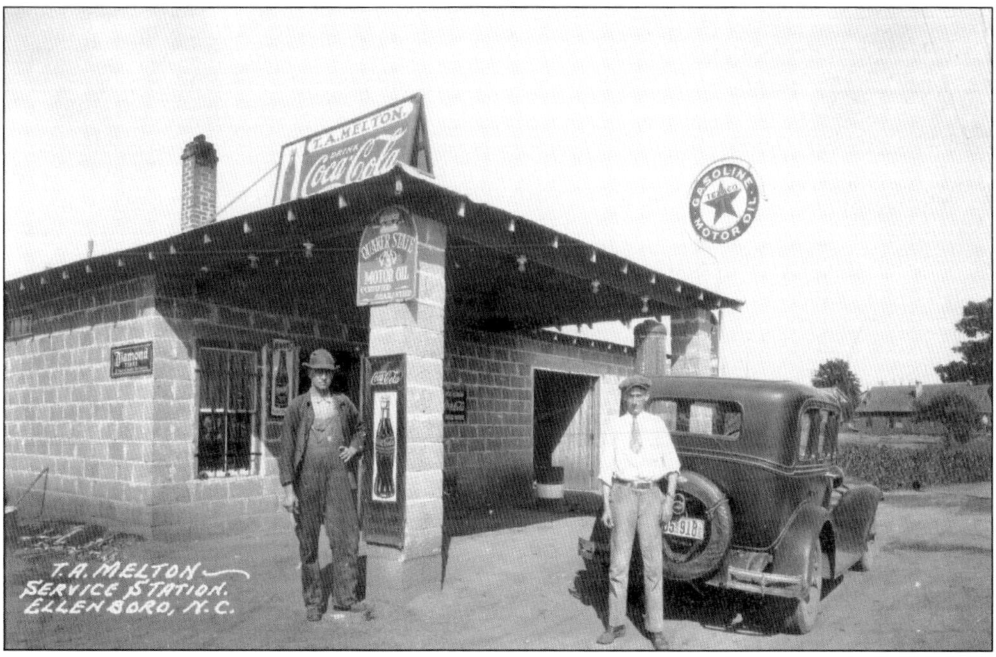

This photograph of T. A. Melton's Service Station in Colfax Township dates from the early 1930s. Shown here are T. A. Melton (left) and Grady Hamrick. A Model A idles at the pump, and signs advertising Coca-Cola, Quaker State Motor Oil, and Texaco products appeal to the customers. (Courtesy of Scott Withrow.)

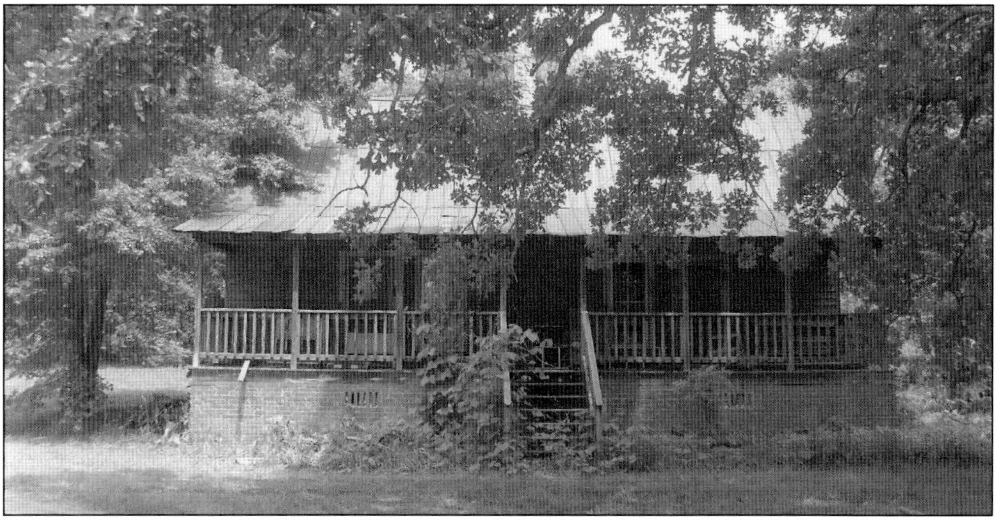

The Smart Store was a true country store. Located off Tiney Road near Corinth Church, the store's owners and operators were Ulyess (1897–1984) and Lona (1904–2000) Smart. The store was in operation for about 30 years (late 1940s to mid-1970s). (Courtesy of Pat Rhyne.)

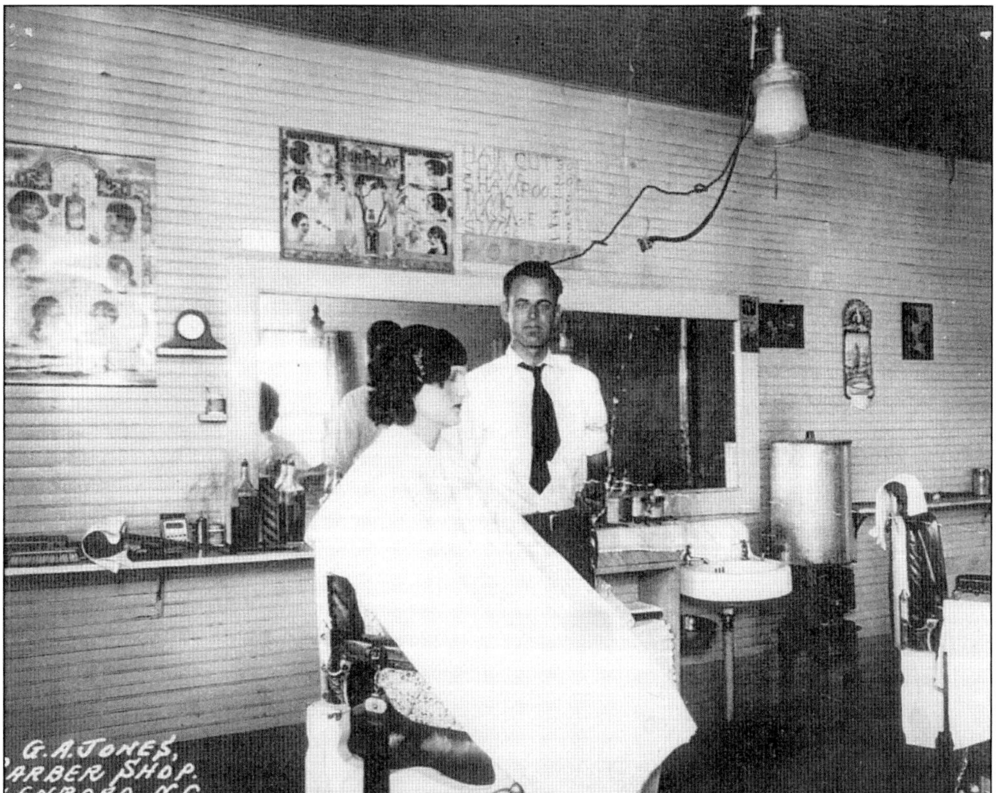

Born in 1897, Gordon Jones in seen here in his barbershop in 1923. Seated in the chair is Pansy Jones, Gordon's wife. Gordon cut hair from 1923 until shortly before his death in 1978. In addition to haircuts, the shop offered shaves and showers. Gordon's son Clyde Jones continues to cut hair there today. (Courtesy of Colfax Museum.)

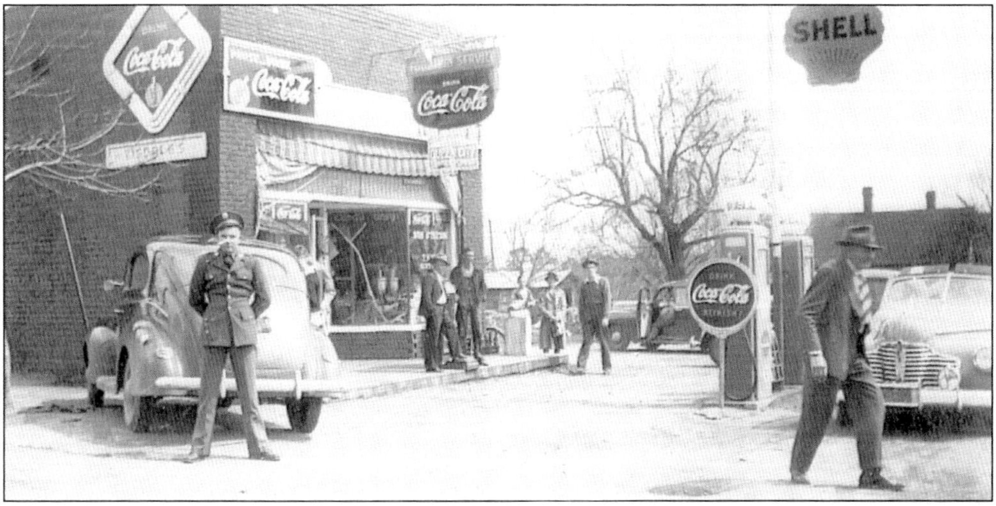

In the 1940s, a uniformed Charles Thomas "T" Lawson stands before the building that served concurrently as Tisdale's Store and Service Station, Queen City Bus Station, and Dr. King's office. The pre-1925 building (owned by Howard Greene) served as drugstore, bank, and jewelry store. Orus Woodrow "Woody" Hamrick sold Masury paint there; his wife, Hattie Mae Jones Hamrick, operated the front soda fountain. Jimmy Louis Hamrick is on the right. (Courtesy of Jeff, Frank, Tom, and Charles Lawson.)

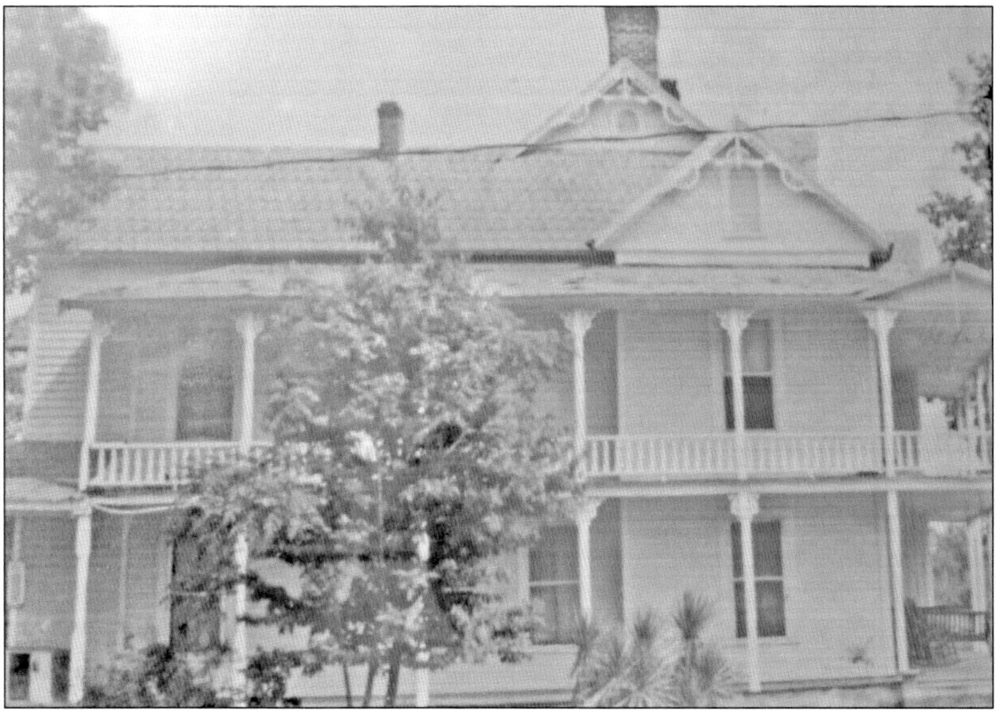
In 1906, John Audley and Mary Louise Harrill Martin built the 14-room Piedmont House, which included two indoor bathrooms. The 1930 census lists four boarders, all of whom were teachers employed at the newly built Ellenboro School. "Ma Lou" and "Pa John" ran the boardinghouse until 1941 when son Yates (1900–1965) married Sarah Harrill (1911–1992). Sarah ran the house, and Yates worked in the mill in Ellenboro. (Courtesy of Jo Ann Martin.)

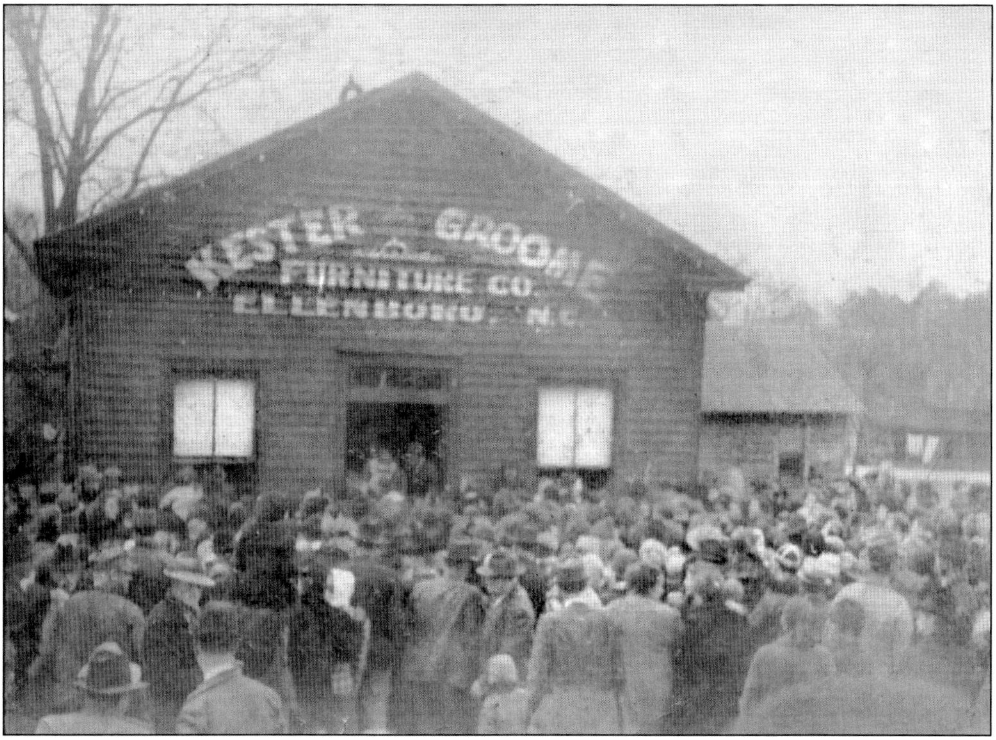

Kester Groome Furniture Store in Colfax Township was originally beside what is now the U.S. Post Office in Ellenboro before relocating to the east end of Depot Street. The Kester and Groome families started their furniture enterprise in Shelby, North Carolina. This photograph shows the opening of the Ellenboro store in the late 1930s or early 1940s. (Courtesy of Geneva Groome.)

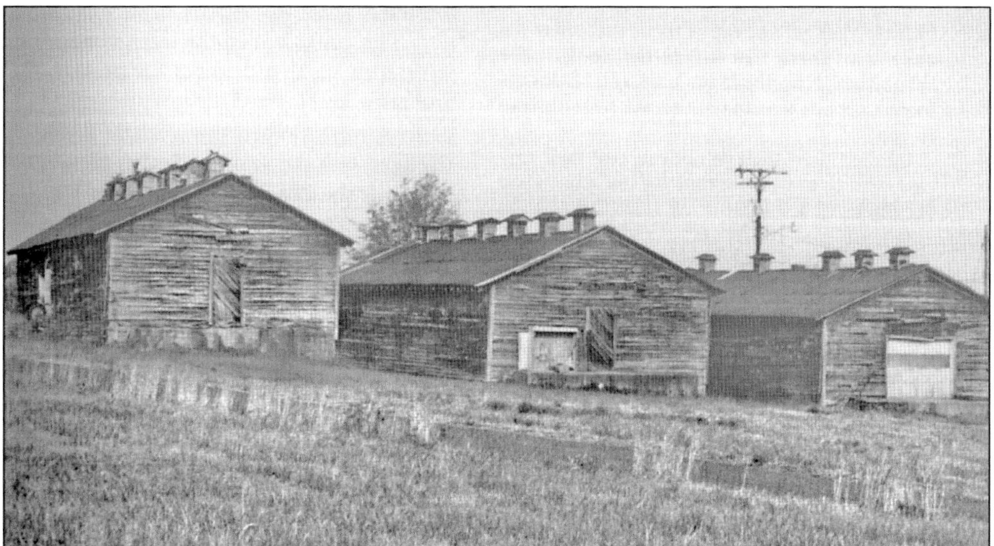

A. B. Bushong, agriculture teacher at Ellenboro High School, was instrumental in introducing the sweet potato as a cash crop in Colfax Township in 1927. With the help of financing from the Farmers Federation, sweet potato houses such as these in Ellenboro provided a place for curing and storing the crop. (Courtesy of James M. Walker and Anita Price Davis.)

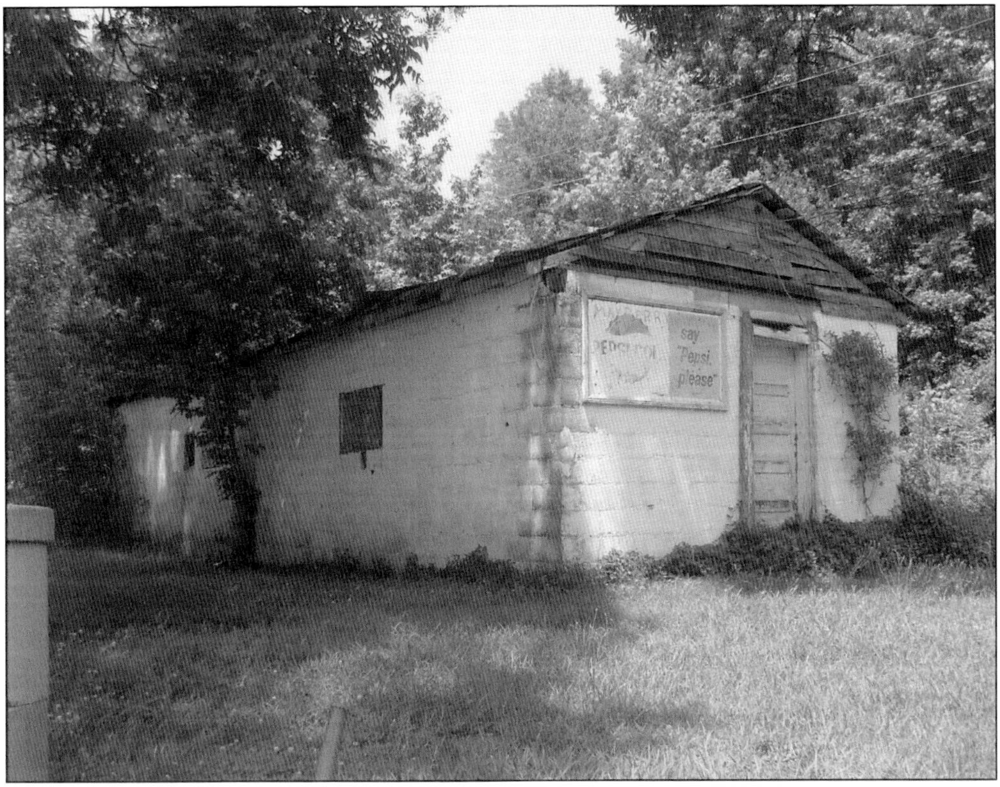

Smug's Place stood on Hamrick Drive in Ellenboro. Leo "Smug" Greene and J. L. McSwain built the establishment in the late 1940s, and it remained in operation until the mid-1990s. Smug's was a gathering spot with a grill and pool tables in the back. The store also served the community as a site for group dinners, dances, music, fellowship, and reunions. (Courtesy of Pat Rhyne.)

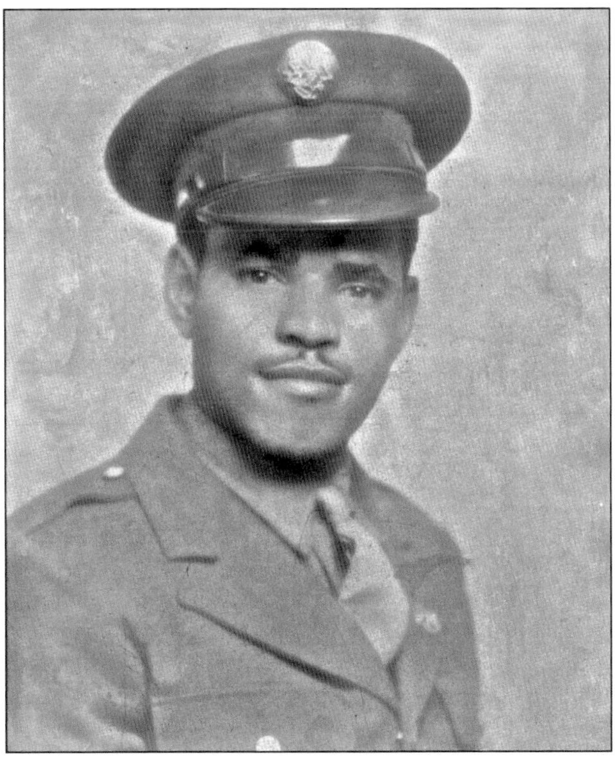

Leo Greene (1920–1981) was a trustee of Webb First Baptist Church. Affectionately called "Smug" by those who knew him best, Leo and wife Lois had a daughter, Celia Greene Davenport, and two sons, Alvin and Stanley, both of whom eventually moved to Maryland. Leo served in the U.S. Army during World War II. (Courtesy of Alvin and Stanley Greene.)

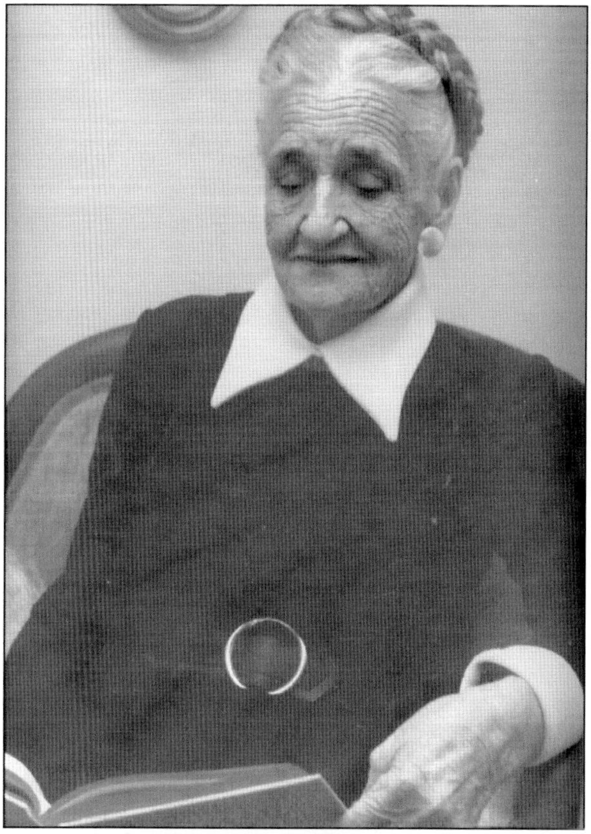

Doctors were few in rural areas. As a child, Ella Turner Daves (1887–1980) accompanied her grandmother Rachel Sims Black as she served her neighbors as a midwife, tended the sick, and helped with "laying out" the dead. They often rode horses in the mountainous areas. Ella later used onion poultices and other mountain remedies on her own 13 children, her grandchildren, and other Colfax residents. (Courtesy of Anita Price Davis.)

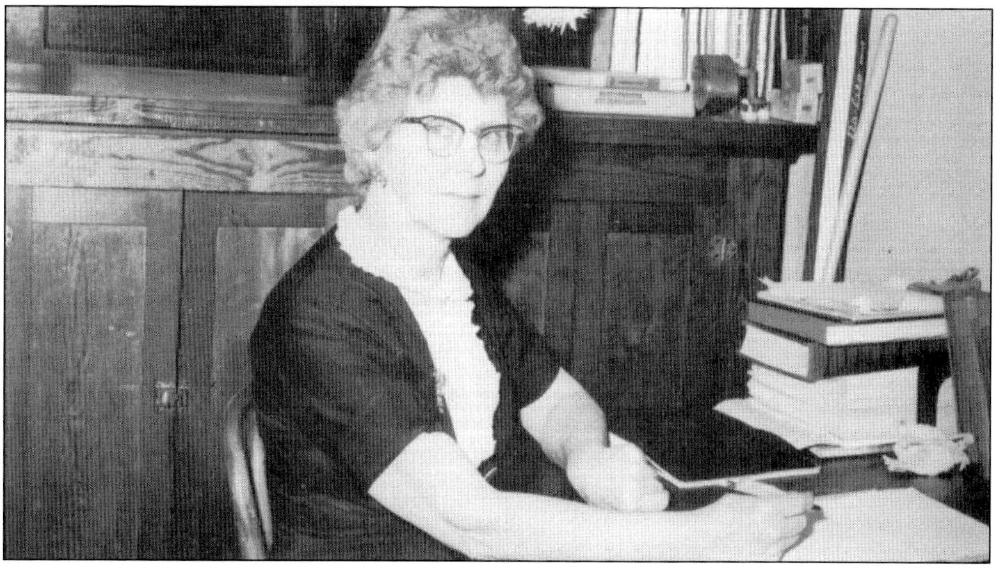

Born in Caroleen to Will and Mary Byers Griffin, Elizabeth Byers Griffin Rhyne (1908–1992) worked as a teacher and secretary at Ellenboro School from 1961 until 1974. The mother of six boys—Joe, Bill, Bob, John, Jim, and Mike—and daughter Betty, Elizabeth moved permanently back to Ellenboro from Spindale in 1948. Known to everyone in the community, Elizabeth was a renowned local historian. (Courtesy of Mike Rhyne.)

Four

Fun Times

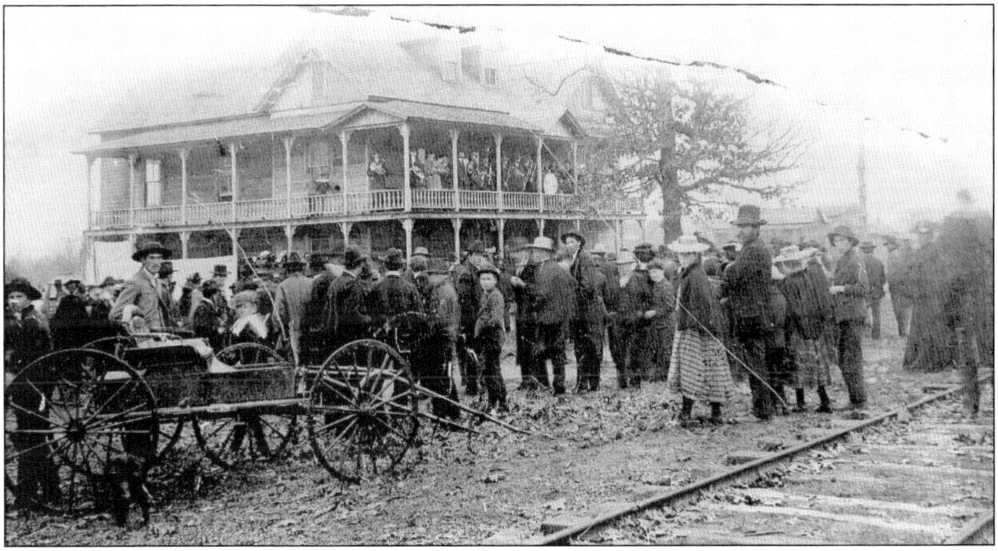

Residents of Colfax Township worked hard, but they found time for varied recreational activities. Big Day celebrations were an annual event typically held on the Fourth of July. Dating back to the early 1900s—and possibly the late 1800s—these well-attended get-togethers featured patriotic themes. Residents celebrated with picnic lunches, picking, singing, speeches, group games, and popular contests such as the greased-pole climb. Such summer foods as watermelon and ice cream were always a treat. The Big Day celebrations continued through the years, but by the 1960s, they were sporadic events. The town fathers formally revived Big Day in Ellenboro in 1979 to celebrate the 200th anniversary of Rutherford County. The Big Day celebration of 1989 recognized Ellenboro's 100-year anniversary. Mayor Wilbur Wright headed the planning for this event. Since 2007, Big Day has become an annual event once more. This Big Day photograph in Ellenboro dates from the early 1900s. Pictured in the background is the Piedmont House, noted in the previous chapter. Notice the band on the second-floor balcony. (Courtesy of Jo Ann Martin.)

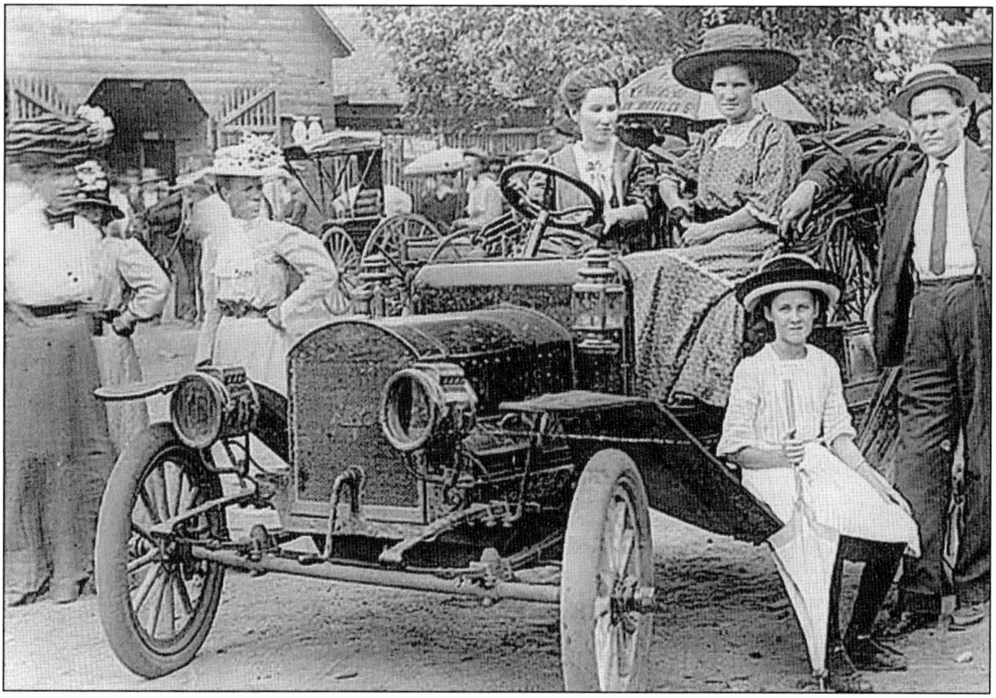

In this Ellenboro Big Day photograph from the early 1900s, Ola Humphries Whisnant, wife of dentist J. F. Whisnant (standing), sits behind the Maxwell's wheel. The woman on the running board is Mattie L. Whisnant, who married Dr. T. C. "Claude" Lovelace, the legendary Henrietta-area doctor who made house calls in the lower part of Rutherford County. (Courtesy of Ben Humphries.)

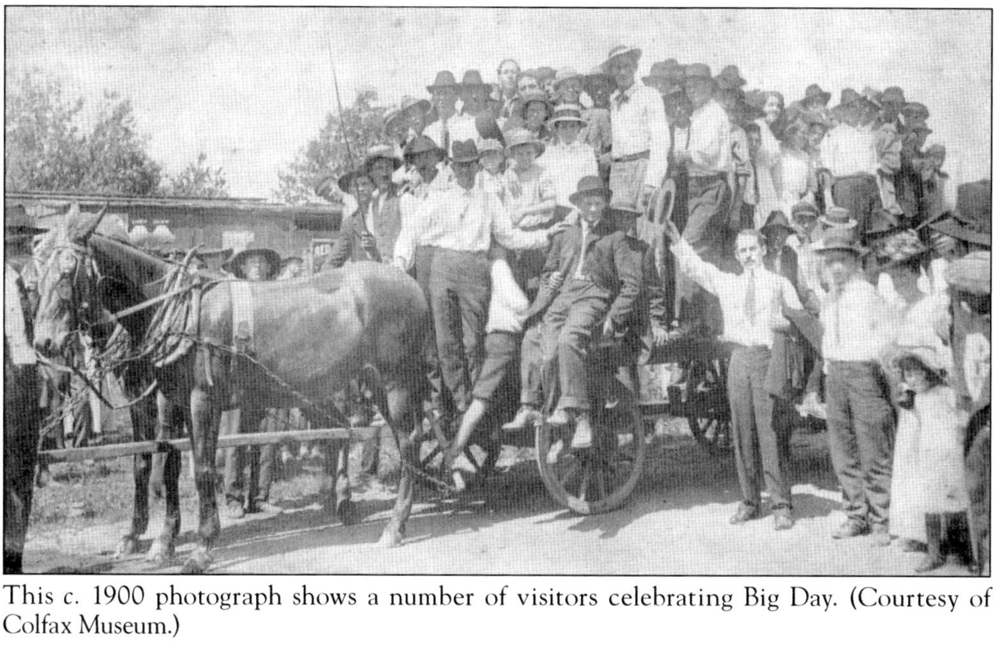

This c. 1900 photograph shows a number of visitors celebrating Big Day. (Courtesy of Colfax Museum.)

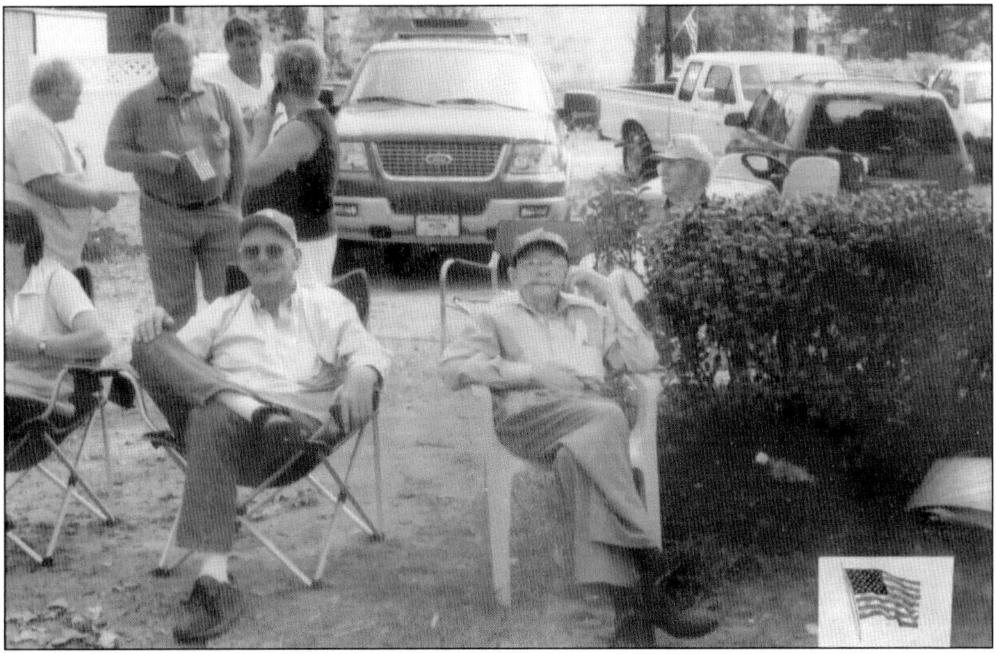

This photograph from the July 4, 2007, Big Day celebration shows, from left to right, (first row) Joan Hutchins, Fred Hutchins, and Charles "Bass" Wright; (second row) Darlene and Jeff Lawson, Herman Wright, and an unidentified student. Seated behind the bushes is Joe Stockton. (Courtesy of Herman Wright.)

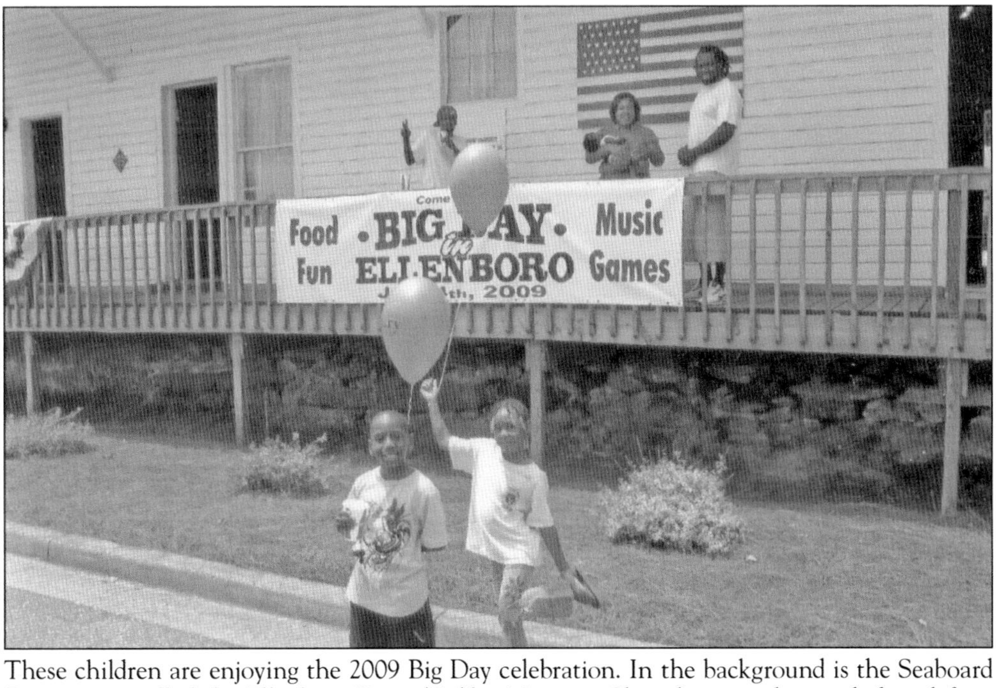

These children are enjoying the 2009 Big Day celebration. In the background is the Seaboard Depot, now called the Ellenboro Depot/Colfax Museum. Show here on the porch from left to right are Bryan Ross, Tammy Rogers, and Justin Rogers. On the ground are Matt and Rogier Ross. (Courtesy of Colfax Museum.)

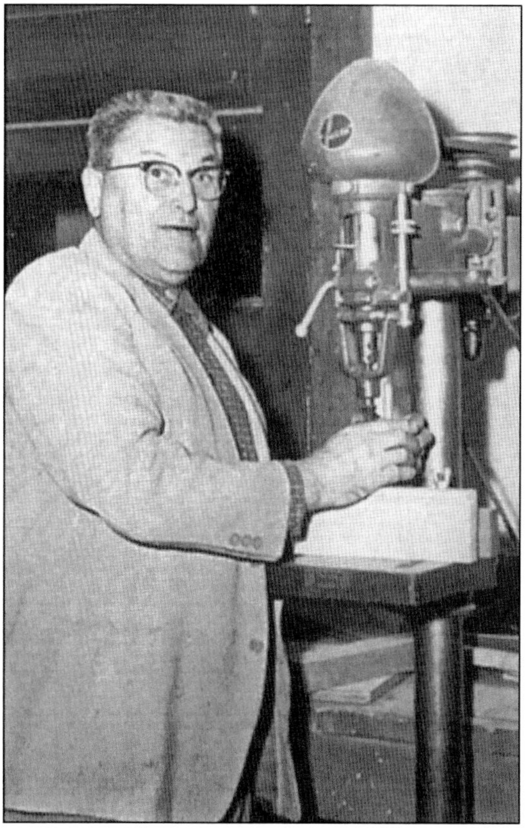

A. B. Bushong was Master Teacher of Vocational Agriculture of the South, a title earned from competition among agriculture teachers of Southern vocational agriculture. Bushong instituted sweet potatoes as a local cash crop, started a 7,000-egg chicken hatchery, organized a local cannery, served as chief observer of the World War II Aircraft Warning Post, trained returning veterans and area adults, organized tours of Washington, D.C., and started the Colfax Free Fair in 1929. (Courtesy of James M. Walker.)

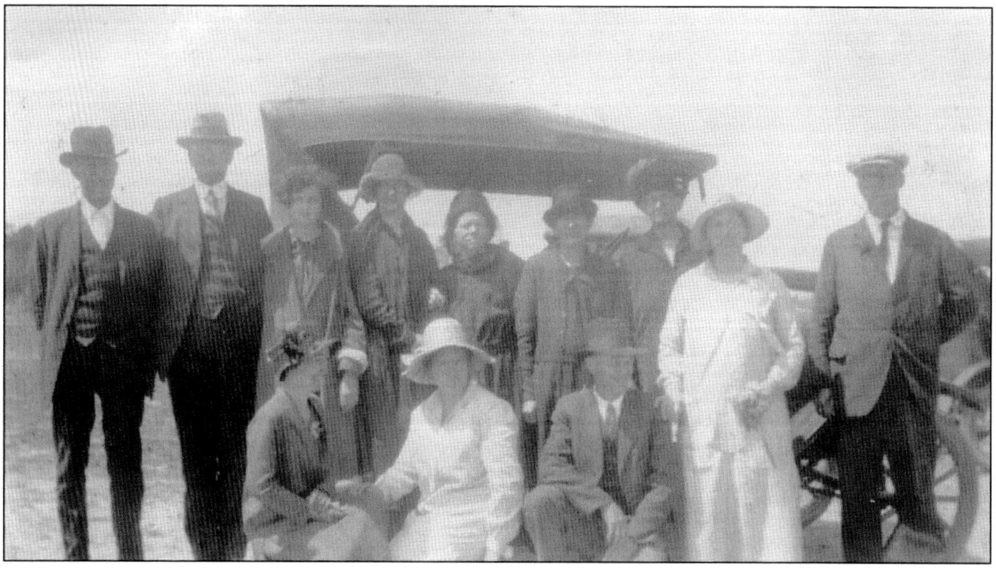

This 1930 photograph shows visitors to the Colfax Free Fair, first envisioned by A. B. Bushong. Seen here from left to right are (first row) Lela P. McKinney, Cova Wilson Beam, Plato Wilson, Lola Wilson, and an unidentified visitor; (second row) Bob McDaniel ?, Elmer McKinney, two unidentified people, Vici Bridges, Hessa Edwards Wilson, and Octivia P. Bridges McKinney. (Courtesy of Colfax Museum.)

This photograph of the Ferris wheel at the Colfax Free Fair dates from the late 1930s. The R. C. Lee Company provided the rides from 1929 until the 1970s. Other popular activities were bingo, games, contests, entertainment, plays from The Sauline Players, exhibits, concessions, entertainment, fellowship, and the Miss Colfax Fair Contest. (Courtesy of Colfax Museum.)

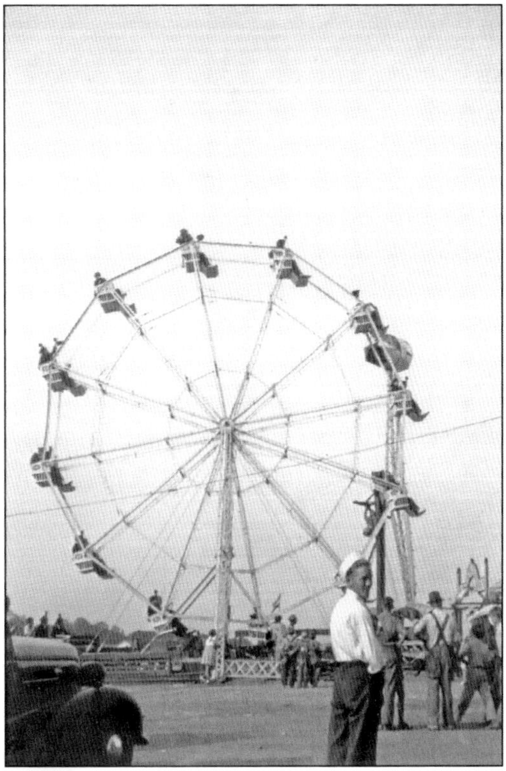

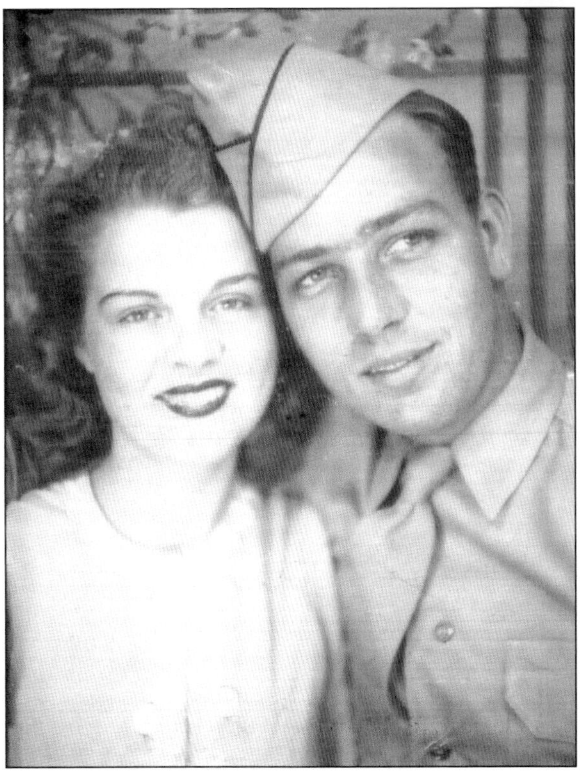

In 1943, Arthur F. Price received a furlough after completing basic training. Even with limited time to spend together, he and wife Nell Daves Price (later Burns) considered attending the Colfax Fair a "must." They had their picture taken at a photograph machine there. This was Arthur's last trip home before his death on December 28, 1944, from a land mine. (Courtesy of Anita Price Davis.)

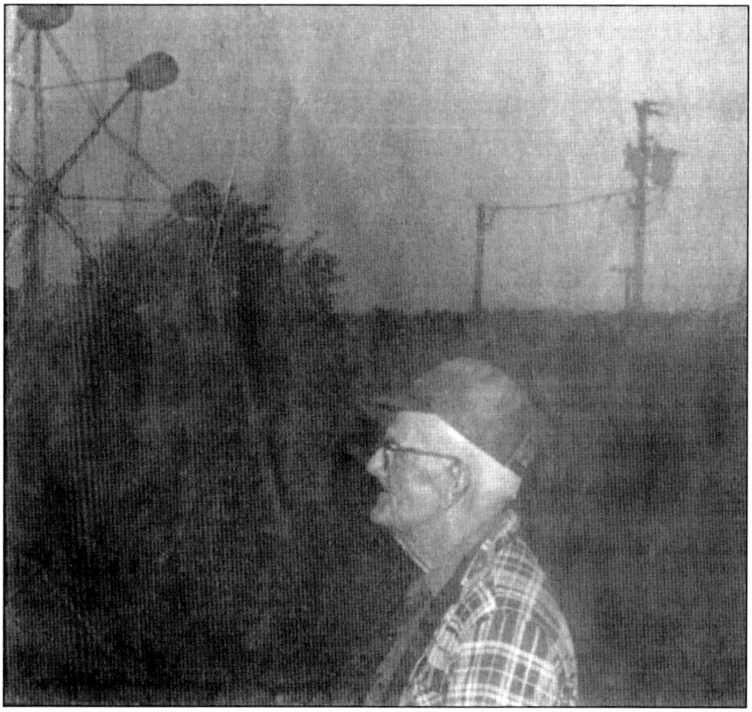

R. P. Freeman, who lived near the fairground, was vitally interested in education, students, and the fair. Each year he gave freely of his time to help in the set up and dismantling of the rides. In the background of the photograph is the popular Rollo-Plane. (Courtesy of Stacey Dodson.)

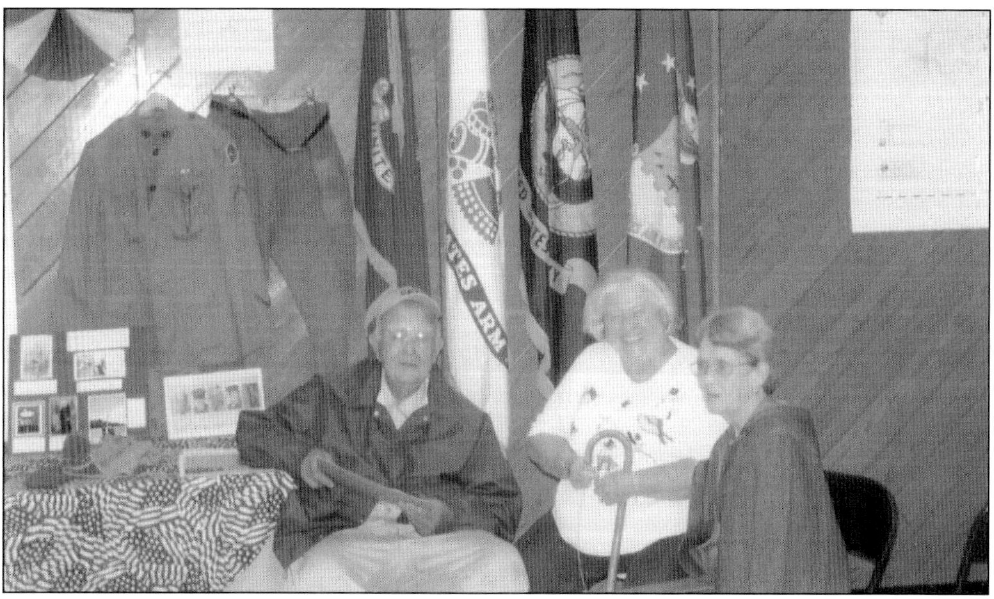

John Tedder (left), Peggy Edwards Hines (center), and Jelma Hamrick Daves discuss the display of veteran memorabilia at the Colfax Free Fair. (Courtesy of Pat Rhyne.)

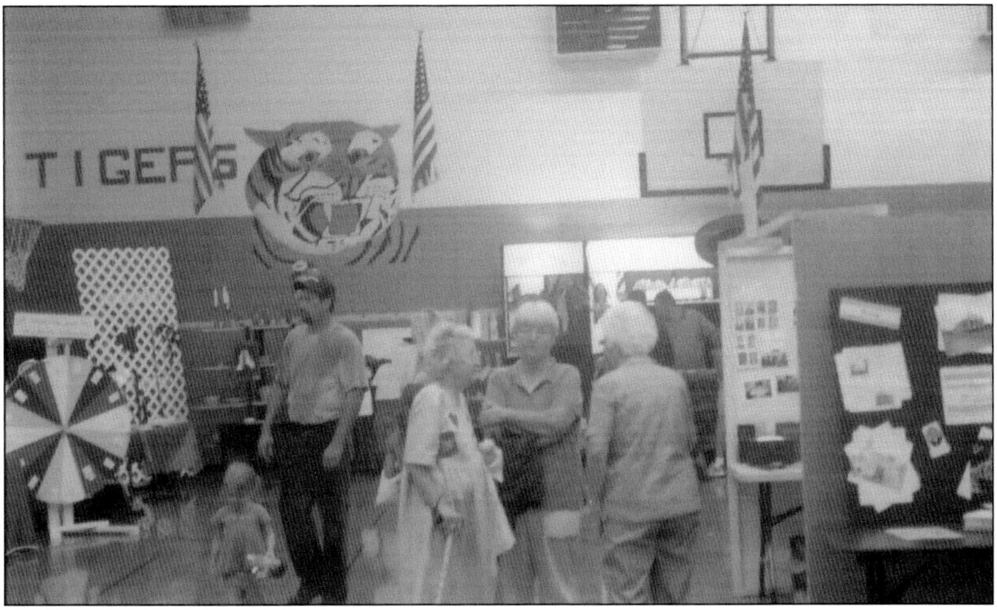

Sunshine (Mrs. John) Tedder (left) and daughter Mary (center) enjoy fellowship with Nellene Whitaker at the exhibit hall in the Mike Davis Gymnasium. (Courtesy of Pat Rhyne.)

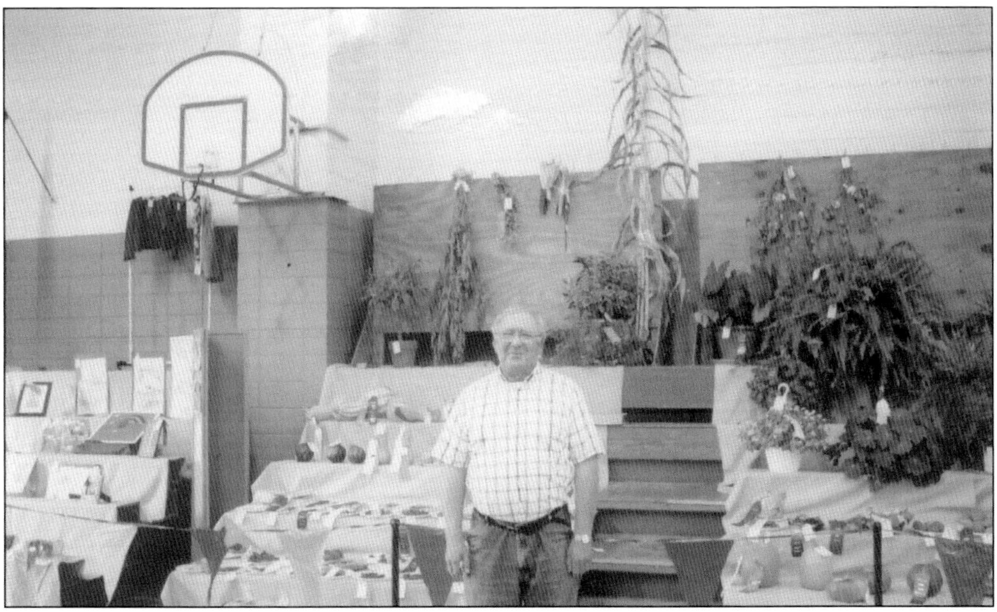

Here William Joe McDaniel of the Colfax Gin stands in front of a farm exhibit. This type of display has always been a standard of the Colfax Free Fair. (Courtesy of Pat Rhyne.)

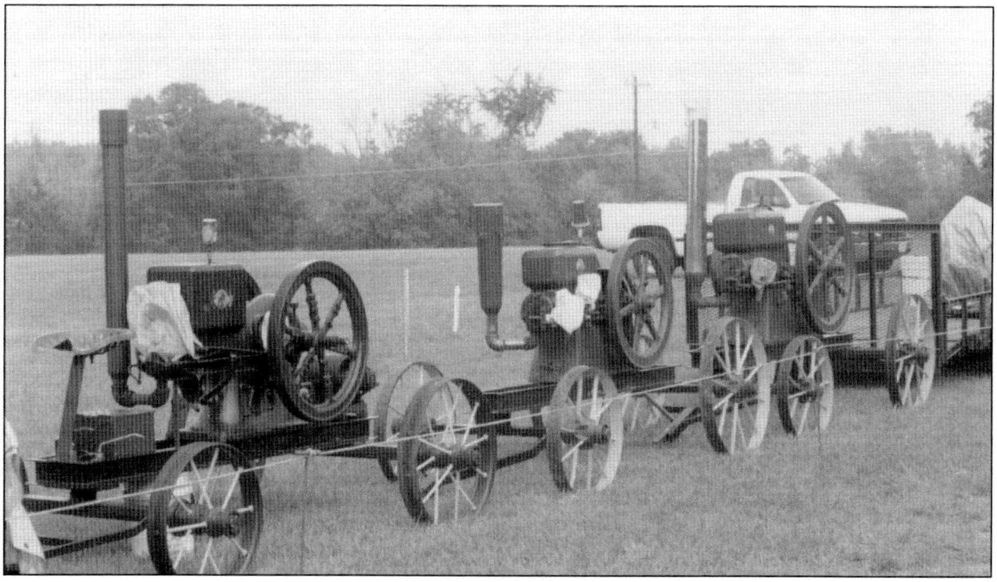

Hit-and-miss engines have become a regular part of the Colfax Free Fair's tractor show. (Courtesy of Pat Rhyne.)

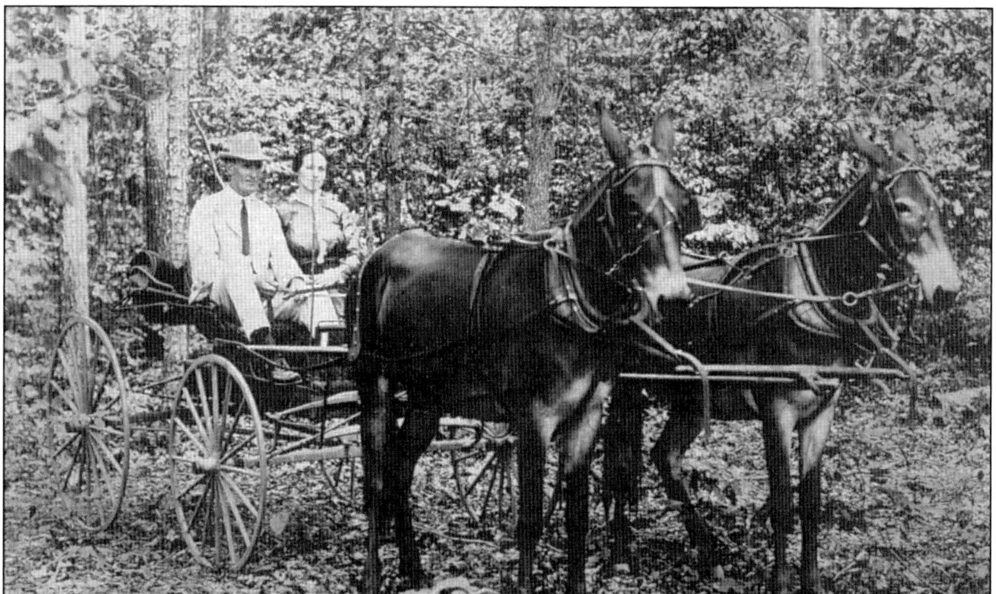

Entertainment in Colfax Township could also be very simple. In this early-1920s photograph, David G. Carpenter (1894–1955) and his wife, Ellen Short Carpenter (1887–1947), take a buggy ride along Hopewell Road. Today the two are buried in the Hopewell United Methodist Church Cemetery. (Courtesy of Roger Carpenter.)

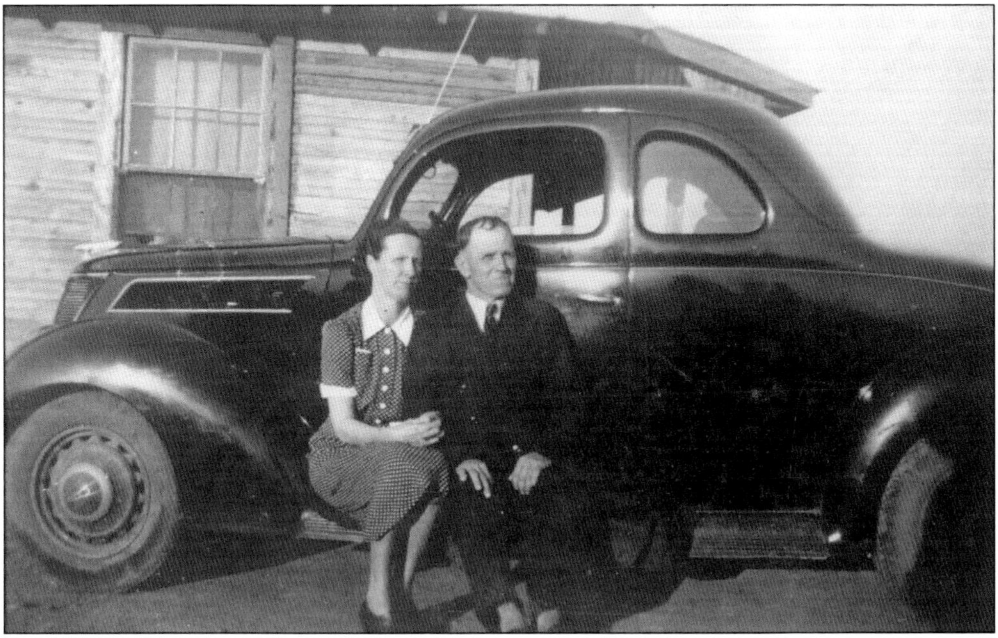

Jim Callahan was a familiar figure in Colfax Township during the 1920s and 1930s. He sold home products to families throughout the area. Here he and his longtime girlfriend Mag Allen pose beside a 1939 Ford coupe. (Courtesy of Bobby Callahan.)

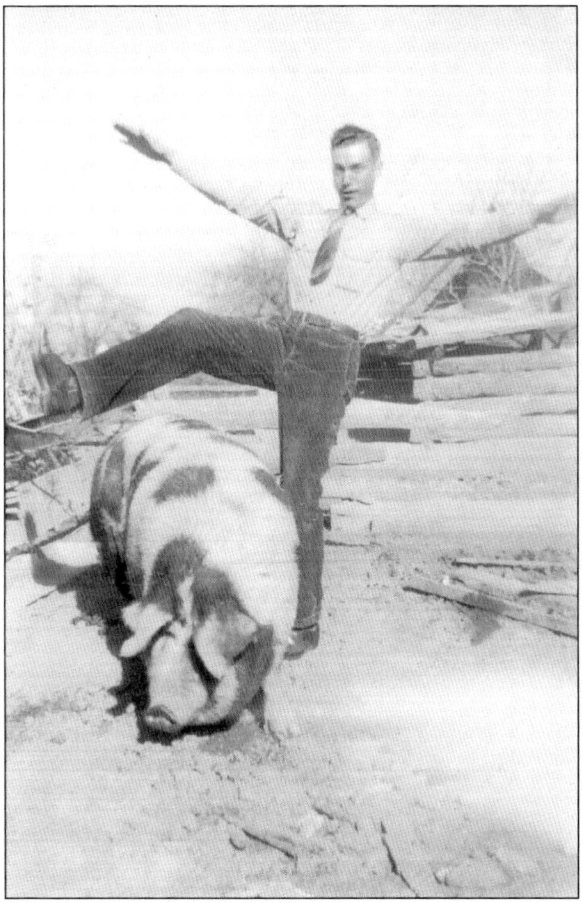

Edmund Blanton had a reputation in the area for working hard and helping others. Despite the effort involved in successful farming, Edmund sometimes found some time to "cut up." Here he is, having fun—even though he is in a pigpen. (Courtesy of Mae Blanton.)

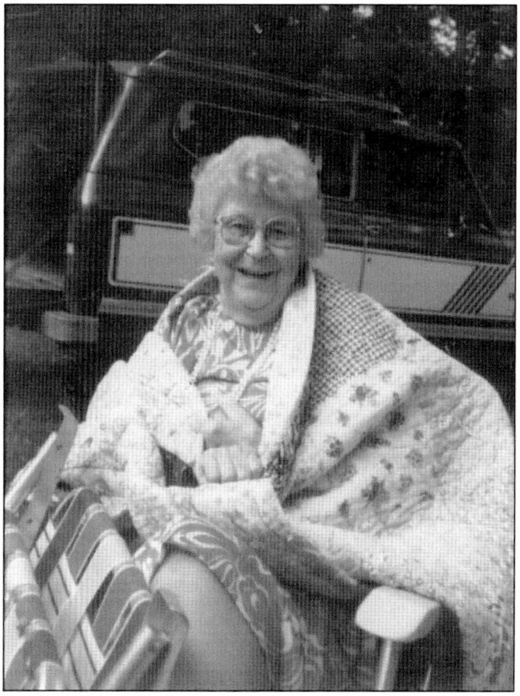

Quilting was a popular pastime; the resulting coverlets were essential to most households. Many women quilted in traditional quilting patterns. Quilts have become a respected art form in recent years. Here Elizabeth Griffin Rhyne (1908–1992) cloaks herself with a quilt made by her mother, Mary Byers Griffin. (Courtesy of Mike Rhyne.)

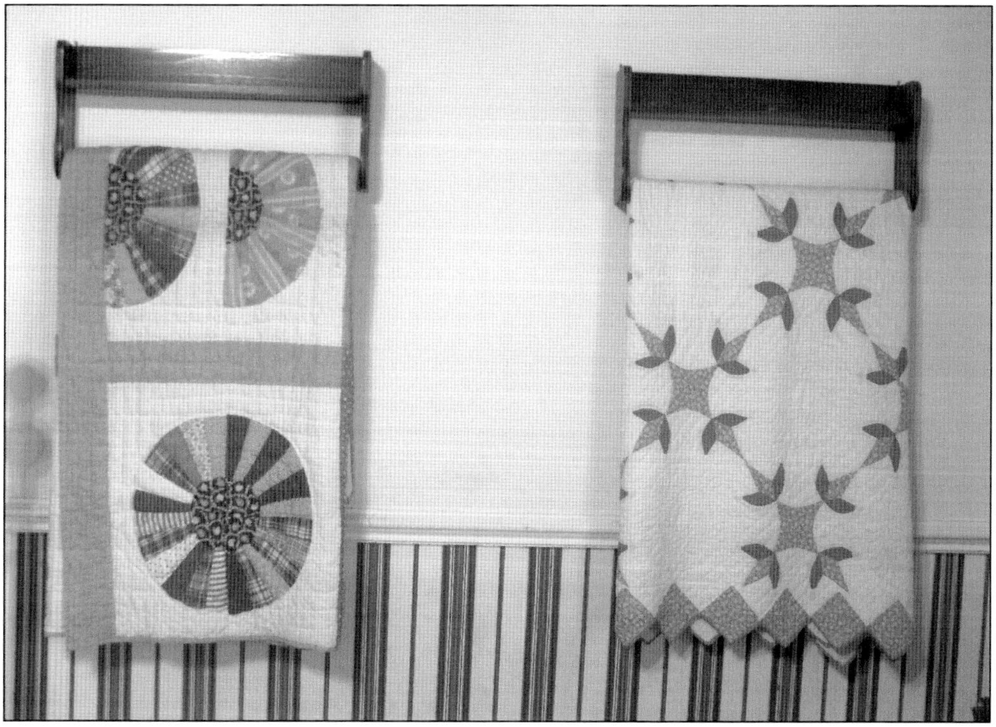

These quilts—over half a century old—are the products of Mary Byers Griffin and her quilting friends, who included Beulah Pruette, Zuda Harrill, Cleo Burns, Betty Greene, and Ethel Culbreth, among others. The quilt on the left features a Dresden plate pattern. Quilting bees were a way of socializing and sharing in the work at hand. (Courtesy of Pat Rhyne.)

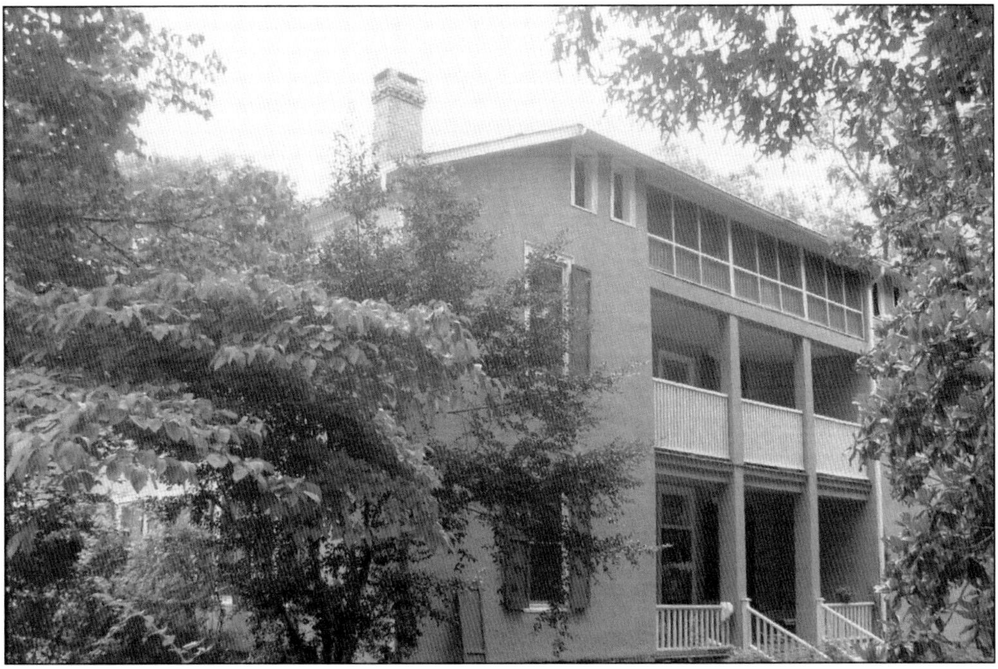

Built in 1909, the Byers/Rhyne House just off Highway 74/20 in the Ellenboro city limits was a teacherage and a popular place to hold quilting bees. The practice of being able to drop in without invitation and find a welcome has continued through the years in the house. A frequent sight in the yard are the spreading feathers of peacocks who migrated to the place and found a welcome. (Courtesy of Pat Rhyne.)

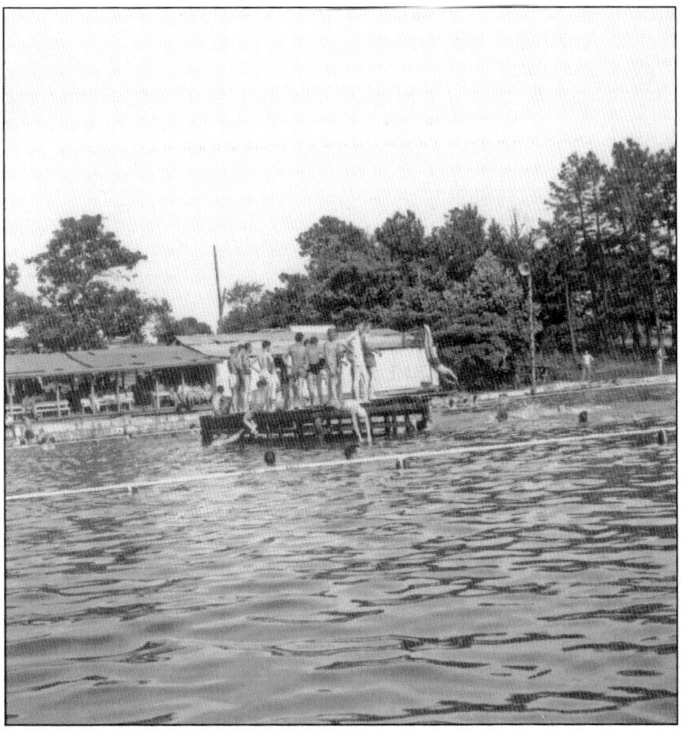

Located off Highway 74/20 Business in Ellenboro on Sunshine Lake Road is the man-made Sunshine Lake. Grover Hamrick built the lake in 1926–1928 for people from Colfax Township and surrounding areas. A favorite activity for swimmers to Sunshine Lake was using the diving board and tower. (Courtesy of Paul Price.)

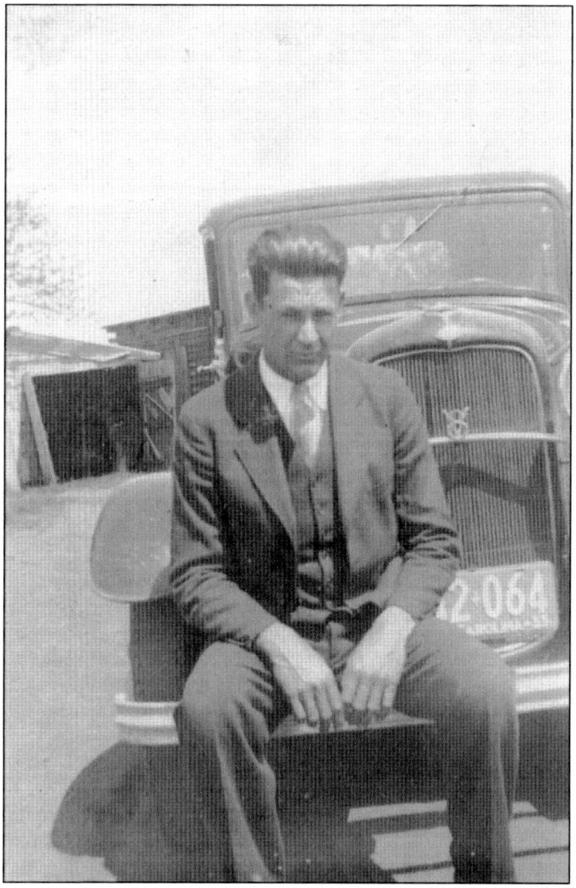

Ewart Burns and Grover Hamrick traveled in Ewart's V-8 Ford (shown here) to the 1933 Chicago World's Fair. Grover brought statuettes and lily pads for Sunshine Lake back in the car. Grover told an attendant at a Chicago park about Sunshine Lake, and the attendant advised the men to cross the major highway beside the park if they wanted to see a "real" lake. When they did, they were staring at Lake Michigan. (Courtesy of Anita Price Davis.)

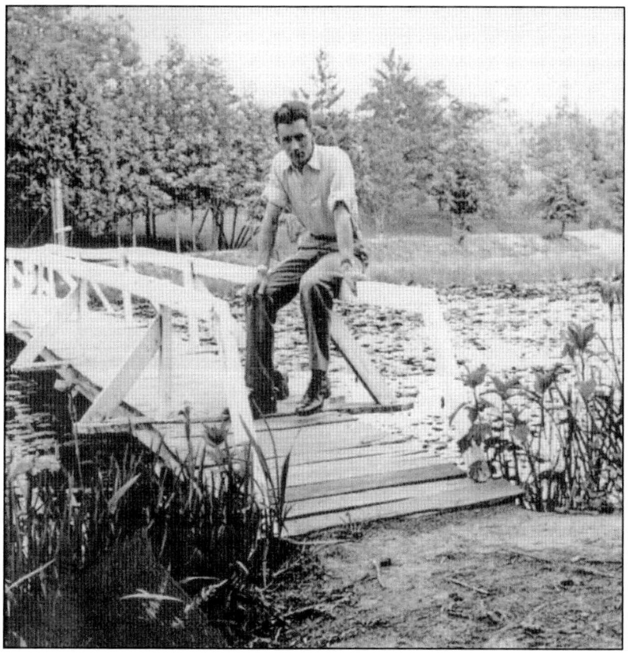

This view of Sunshine Lake shows Grover Hamrick seated on a scenic wooden bridge over the lake. Notice the luxuriant lily pads that Grover was able to cultivate on the lake. (Courtesy of Paul Price.)

Grover Hamrick erected a building to the side of Sunshine Lake. The pavilion had hardwood floors and a jukebox. Hamrick rented the pavilion for dances and family reunions. The lake closed as a swimming lake in 1952 because of the polio scare, but it continued for several years as a fishing spot. (Courtesy of Paul Price.)

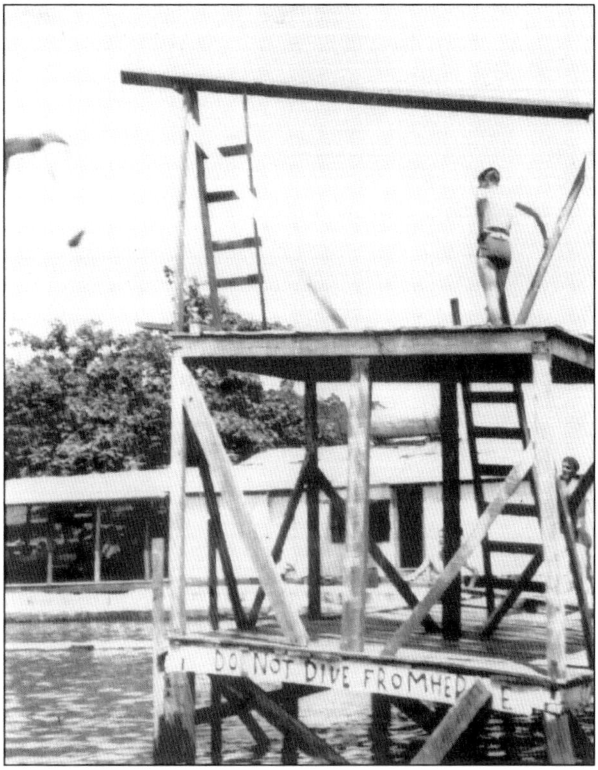

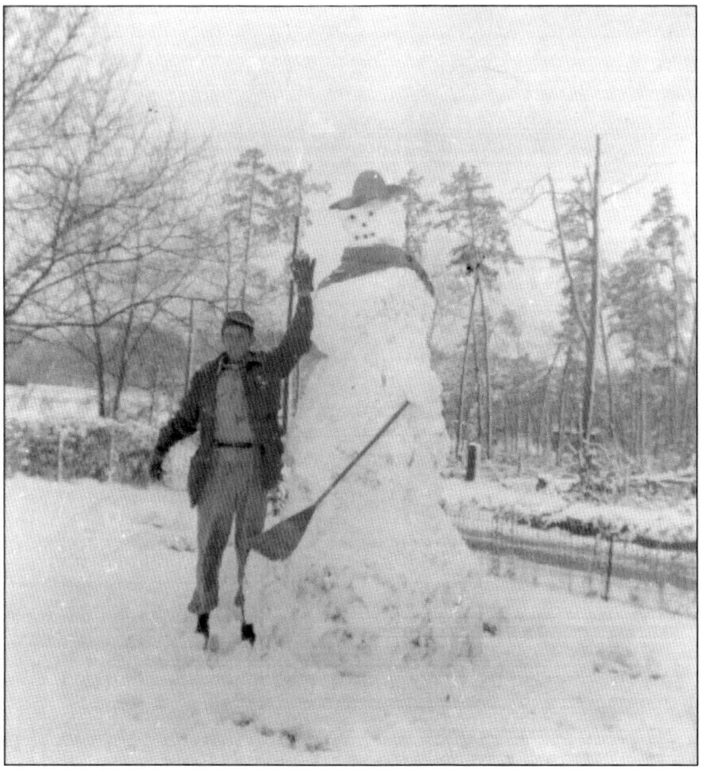

A veteran, farmer, and merchant, Zeb Daves (1919–1964) is seen here enjoying a snowstorm. Zeb and Selma Philbeck Daves had one child, Ted, who was born in 1947. Undaunted by severe burns in a early-1960s service station accident, Ted finished East High with the Key Award for excellence and graduated from Western Carolina University with an engineering degree. Ted was cofounder and 30-year president of Hi-Test Labs, a successful Virginia engine manufacturing company. He also cofounded Performance Counts Automotive. (Courtesy of Anita Price Davis.)

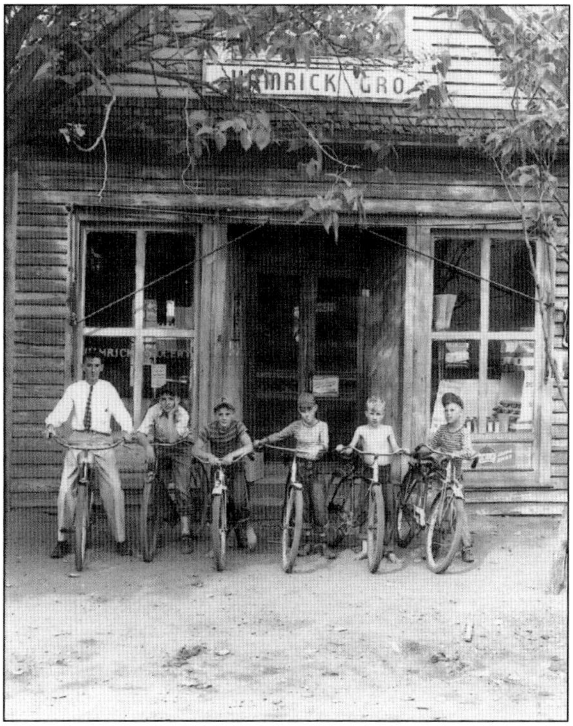

A familiar sight around Depot Street in Ellenboro in the mid-1940s was that of the "town boys" who often rode their bicycles around town. From left to right are Merchant Gray Hamrick, Zeno Daves, Don "Buckshot" Edwards, Wallace Billingsley, Dean Jolley, and Horace Billingsley. (Courtesy of Paul Price.)

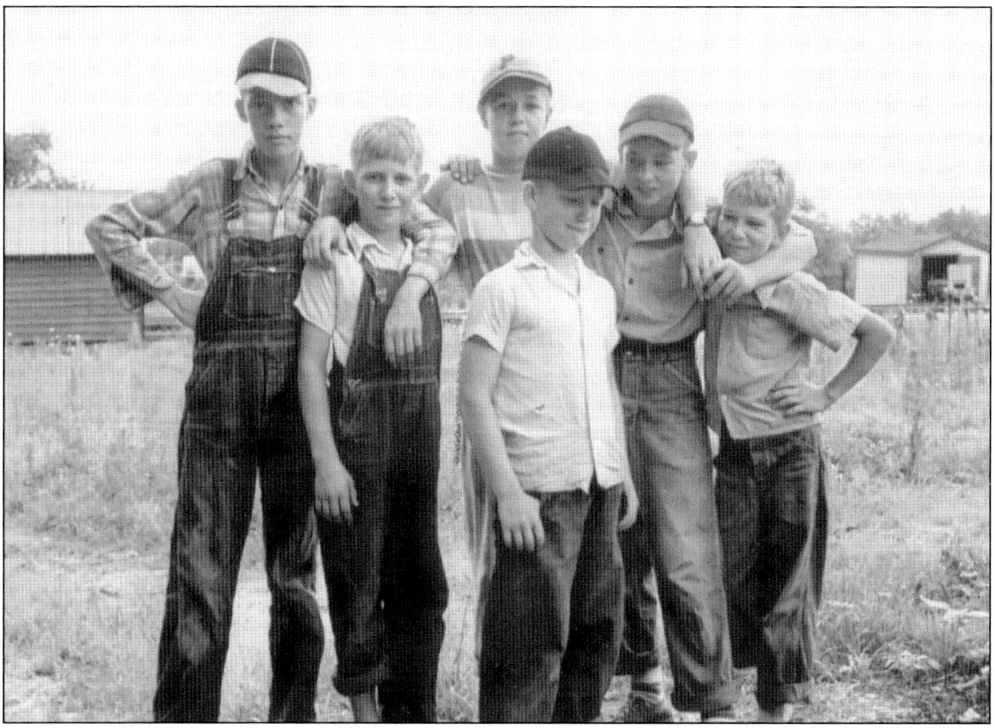

The camaraderie among the local boys in the area is evident in this early 1940s photograph. From left to right are Donald Black, Kenneth Daves, Lowell Bushong, Donald "Buckshot" Edwards, Zeno Daves, and Jerry "Cooter" Daves. (Courtesy of Paul Price.)

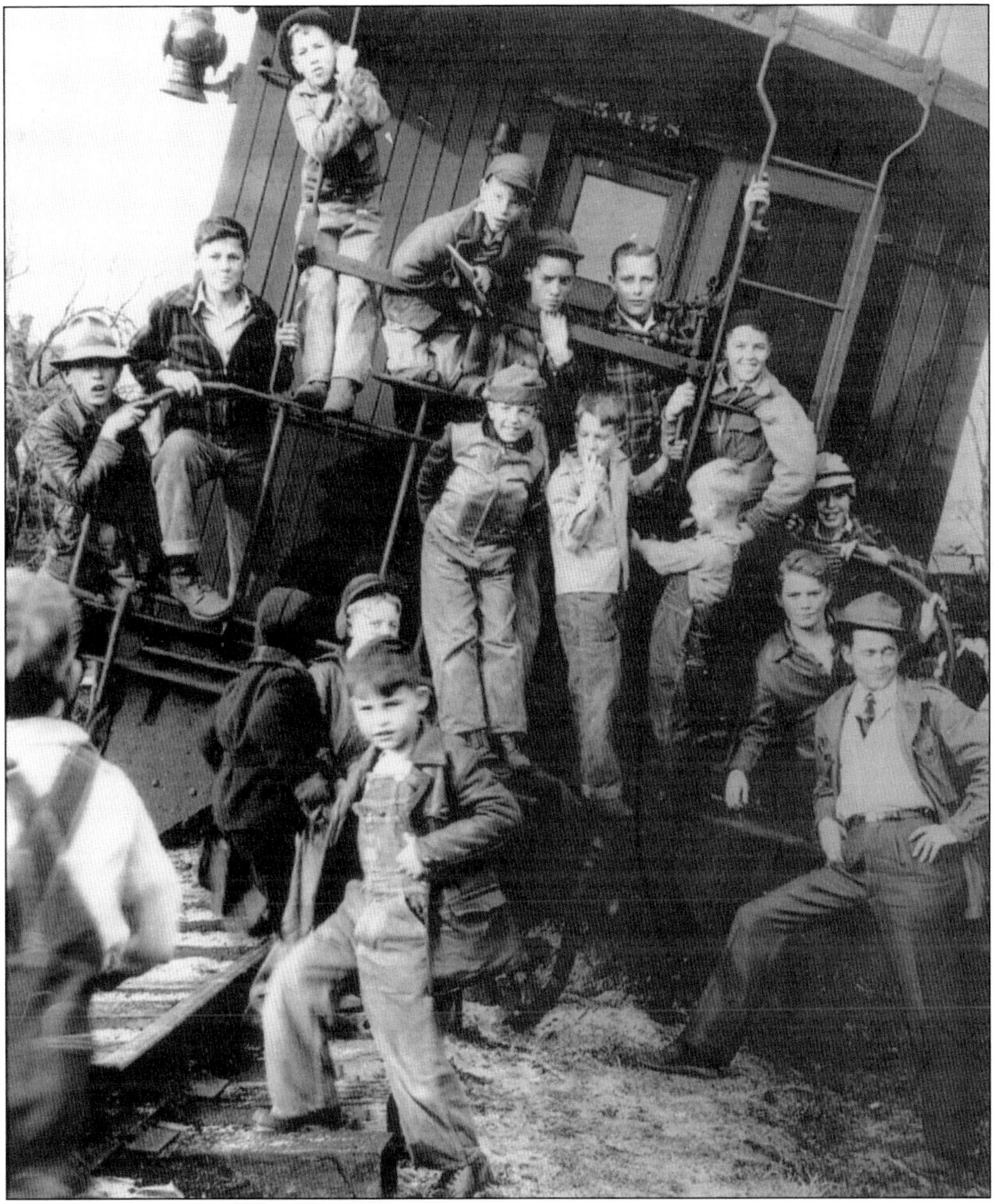

When a caboose from the Seaboard Air Line Railroad jumped the track near Ellenboro around 1945, many people suspected local boys of throwing the switch. Jerry "Coot" Daves remembers that they were in school, were not responsible, and speculates that the conductor failed to correct the switch. Seen in this picture standing on the ground are Joel Walker (center, wearing overalls), Durward Hamrick (man at far right), and three unidentified boy companions. Standing on the caboose from left to right are (first row) Tommy Walker, Jerry Daves, Jimmy Daves, and Vito Hamrick; (second row) an unidentified boy (with hat over eyes, mouth open) Everett Wilson, Wallace Billingsley, Horace Billingsley, Donald Black, Bobby Culbreth, Lowell Bushong,and Don Hamrick. (Courtesy of Paul Price.)

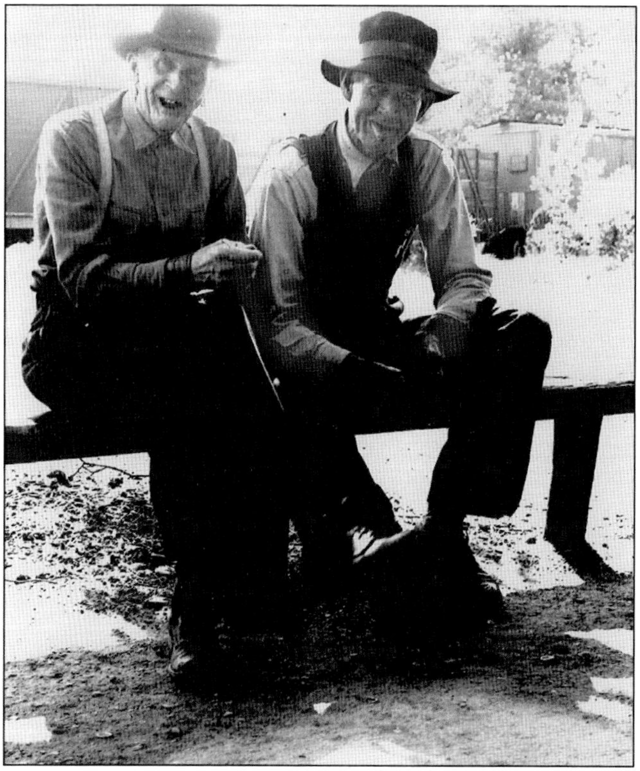

Some of the local men in the Ellenboro area found enjoyment in meeting and talking with each other on a regular basis. Here Walter Lee "Captain" Black and Joe Pink Wright enjoy a laugh on the Liar's Bench in front of Van Harrill's Store. (Courtesy of Robert Watkins.)

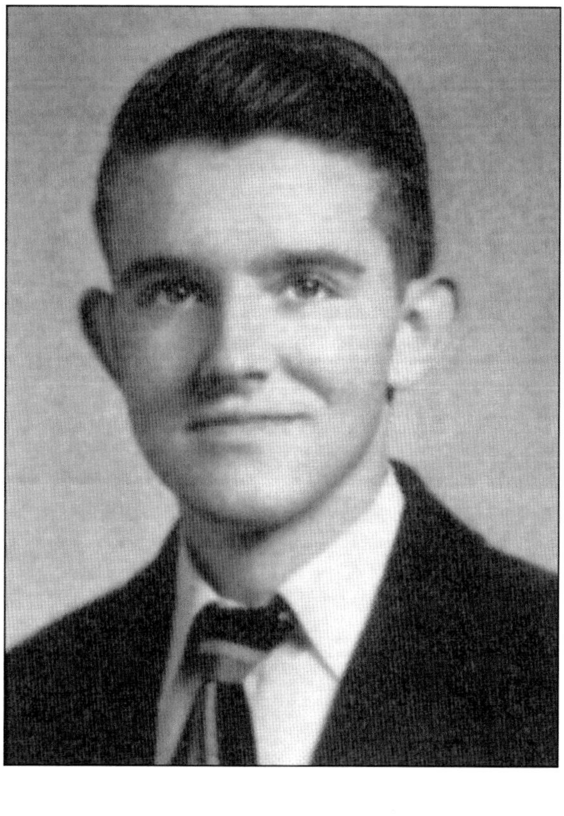

Many Colfax residents were NASCAR fans. Herman Beam (1929–1980) was the son of W. Vaughn Beam, stationmaster at the Bostic Railroad Yard. A graduate of the University of North Carolina and a chemist, Herman was also a NASCAR driver, chief mechanic, and team owner from 1957 to 1963. He earned the nickname "The Turtle" for finishing 84 races without a win. As of 2010, the record still holds. (Courtesy of North Carolina Collection, University of North Carolina at Chapel Hill Library.)

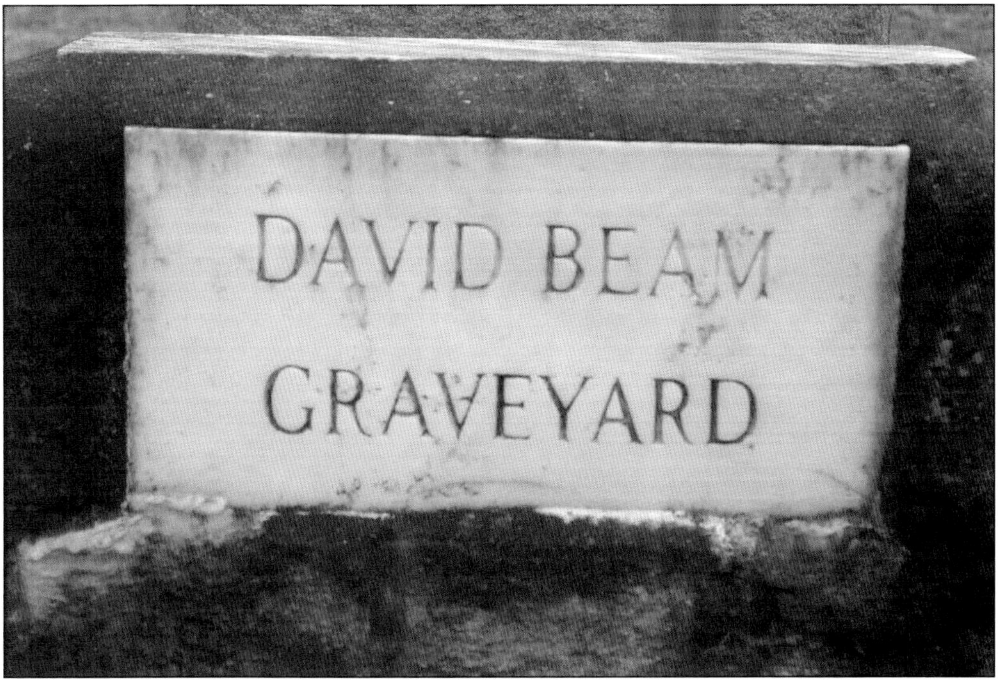

Herman Beam died at the young age of 50. His burial was in the David Beam Cemetery in Colfax Township near the Memory Post Office, pictured earlier in chapter three. (Courtesy of Scott Withrow.)

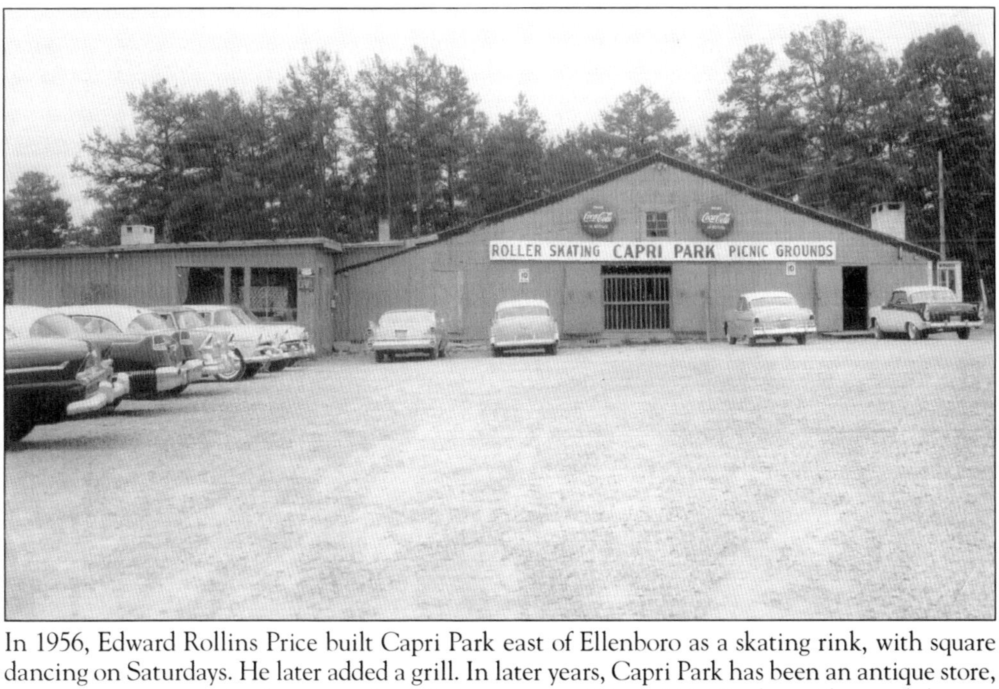

In 1956, Edward Rollins Price built Capri Park east of Ellenboro as a skating rink, with square dancing on Saturdays. He later added a grill. In later years, Capri Park has been an antique store, a restaurant, an auction house, and a religious retreat. Price's 1956 Dodge with a push-button transmission (far right) later became the "wheels" for his older daughter Jeanne Price. Edward Price also built the Park House at 217 Capri Park Drive. (Courtesy of Mike Rhyne.)

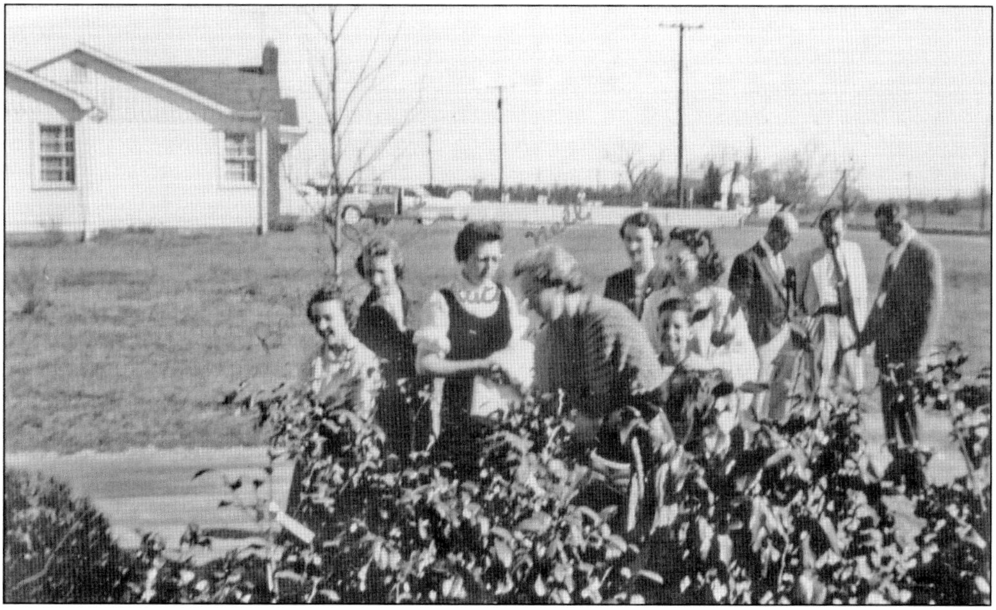

The families of Claude Casey, Edward Price, and Ervin Grindstaff socialize in the Prices' yard at 1499 Highway 74 East in March 1956. They were enjoying time together and discussing plans for Capri Park, of which Casey and Price became partners. Seen here from left to right are recording artist Barbara Grindstaff, Jeanne Price, Ruth Price Grindstaff, Nell Braswell Price, Carolyn Grindstaff Barbee, Ruth Casey, young Mike Casey, Ervin Grindstaff, Claude Casey, and Edward Price. (Courtesy of Carolyn Grindstaff Barbee.)

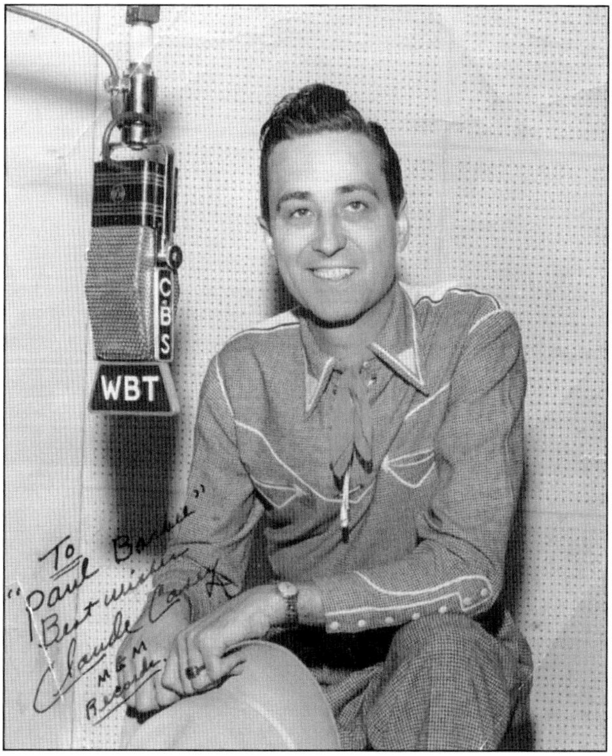

Claude Casey, lead singer and emcee for the country-and-western group the Briarhoppers, recorded for RCA and MGM and founded both WJES-AM and WKSX-FM. His first of 10 movies was *Swing Your Partner* with first-time actress Dale Evans. Casey (1912–1999) lived three years in the Park House adjacent to Capri Park, where he played, sang, and called dances. Ed Price (1913–2004) enjoyed his last years in the Park House. (Courtesy of Carolyn Barbee Grindstaff.)

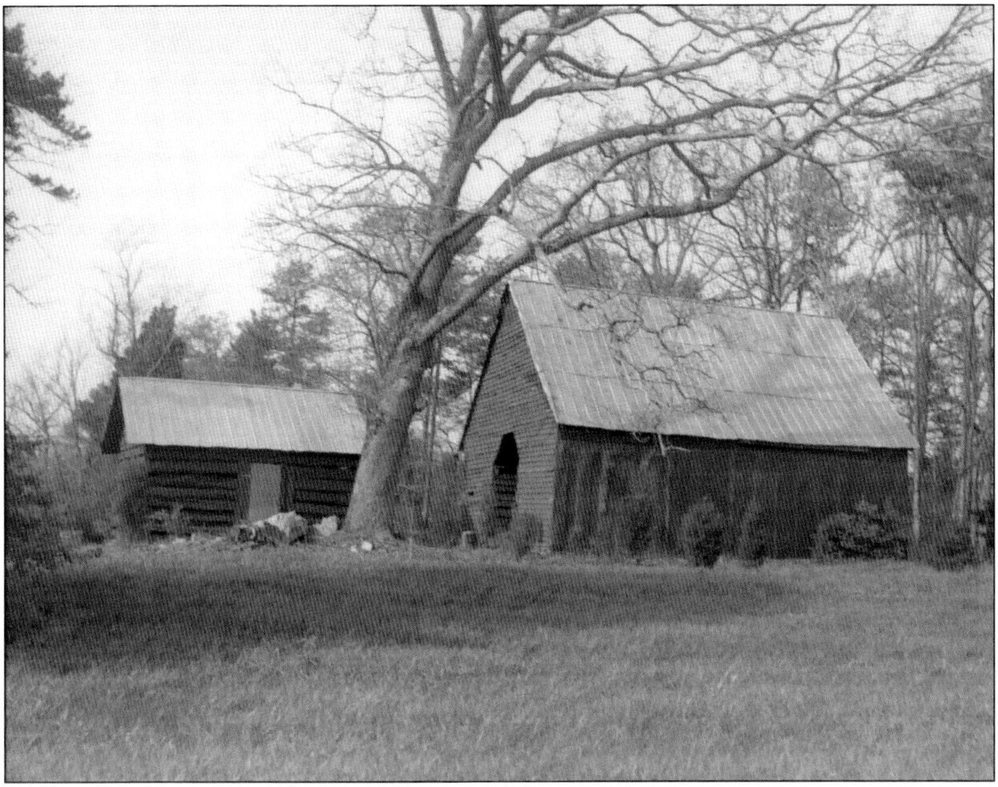

In the early 1800s and most of the 1900s, children in Colfax Township devised their own entertainment, without expensive toys and games, when they were not busy with chores and school. The barn on the farm became a haven for children to read, climb, look for newborn kittens and hen's nests, and escape the rest of the family. One rule, however, always applied: no smoking in the barn. (Courtesy of Robert Watkins.)

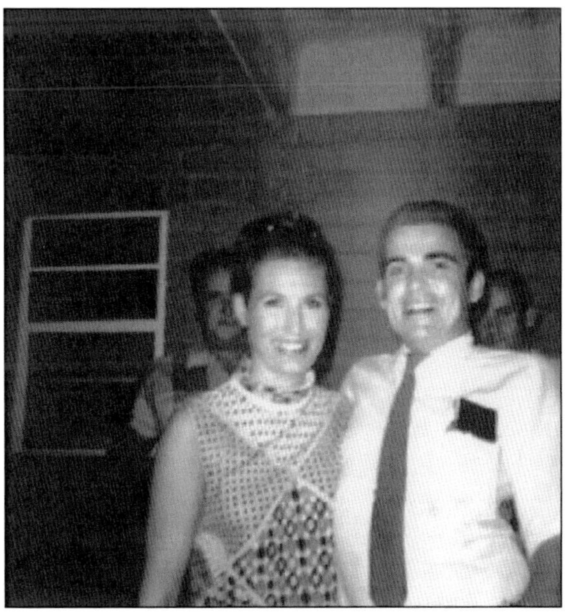

Radio voices and music filled most homes in the township. Jerrell S. Bedford from Colfax Township went into radio broadcasting as a young man in 1962. He worked on and off at WSPA-TV for 20 years, worked full-time at WAGY for 15 years, and worked for WGMA. In total, he was involved in the broadcast industry for 38 years. In this photograph, "Pappy" stands with renowned country singer Loretta Lynn. (Courtesy of Jerrell S. Bedford.)

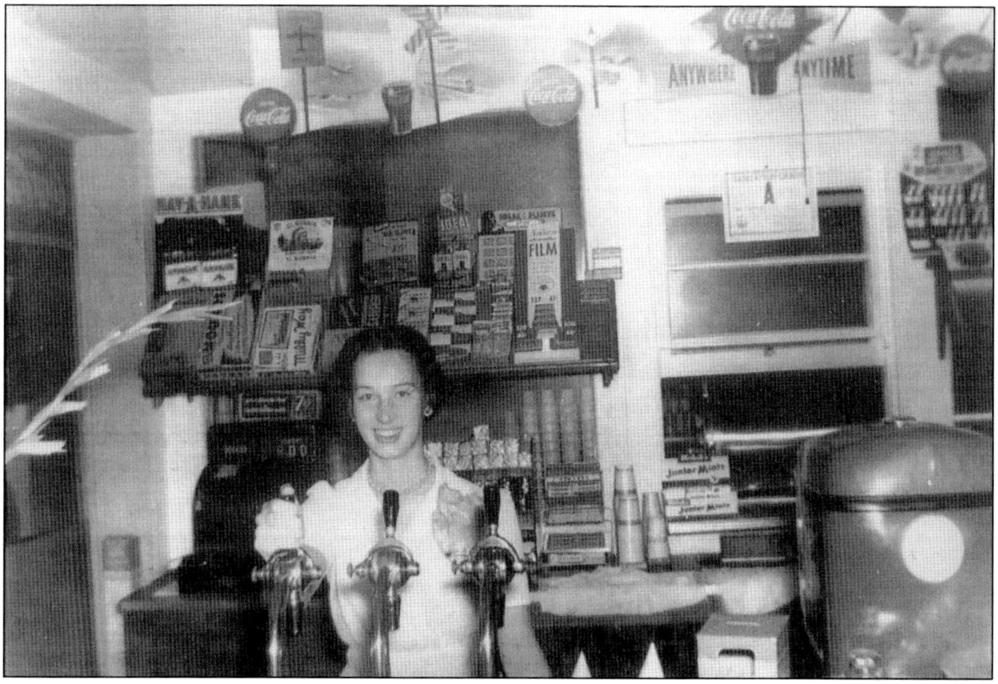

Teenagers in the 1950s loved to cruise the Dairi-O and Grill at the Rutherford and Cleveland county line before stopping in to order from the standard fare—sandwiches, fries, fountain drinks, and shakes. Shown here is Carolyn Grindstaff Barbee, who owned and managed the popular drive-in during the mid-1950s. Later Carolyn sold the establishment to Lonnie Owensby. The building no longer exists. (Courtesy of Carolyn Grindstaff Barbee.)

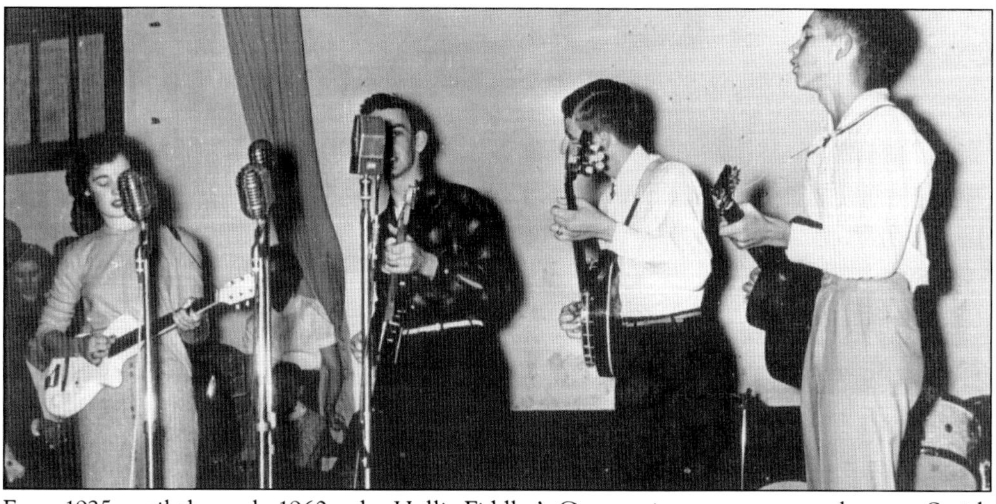

From 1925 until the early 1960s, the Hollis Fiddler's Convention was an annual event. Smith Hammett, Snuffy Jenkins, Earl Scruggs, Laura T. Jenkins, and Uncle Dave Macon performed there. In this photograph are the Teen Timers—Irene Crawley, Mike Lattimore, Dan X. Padgett, and Jack Crawley—performing in 1951 just before Dan won first place for banjo. Now called the Annual Ellenboro Fiddler's and Bluegrass Convention, the event remains a one-evening event on the Saturday before Thanksgiving. (Courtesy of Dan X. Padgett.)

Nell Daves (later Price Burns) remembered traveling to Lake Junaluska as a Hopewell 16-year-old to receive training on how to establish Methodist Youth Fellowship groups in local churches. Nell (1923–1998) talked often of traveling more than an hour from Hopewell for the first time, learning more about Methodism, and going swimming in a suit borrowed from her sister Ellie. (Courtesy of Anita Price Davis.)

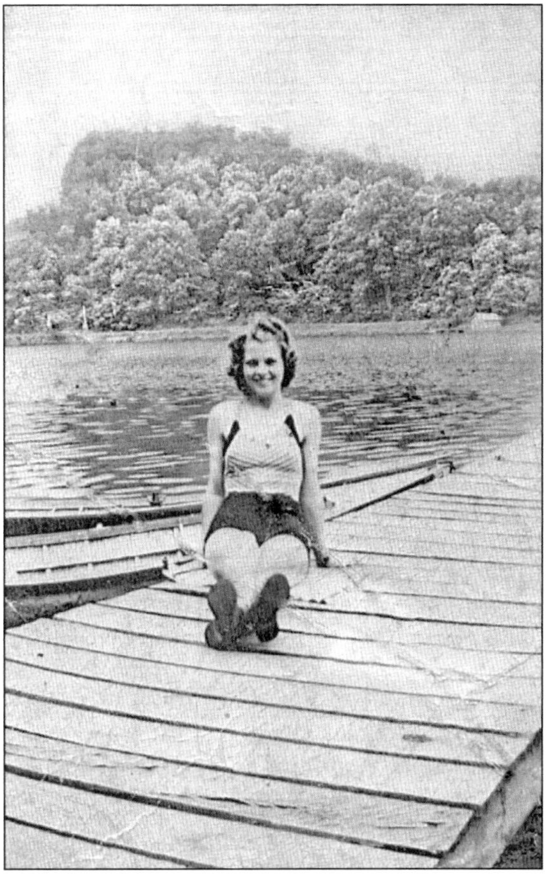

After World War II, more Colfax Township families were able to afford vacations. Here Scott Withrow, age 9, stands atop a sand dune during a family trip to North Carolina's Outer Banks. (Courtesy of Scott Withrow.)

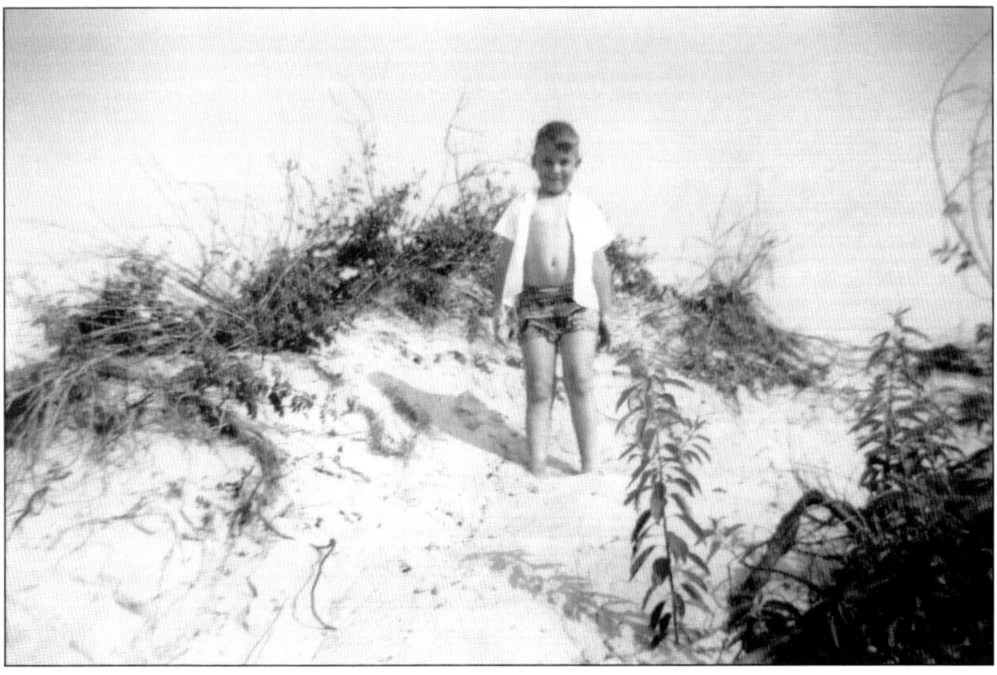

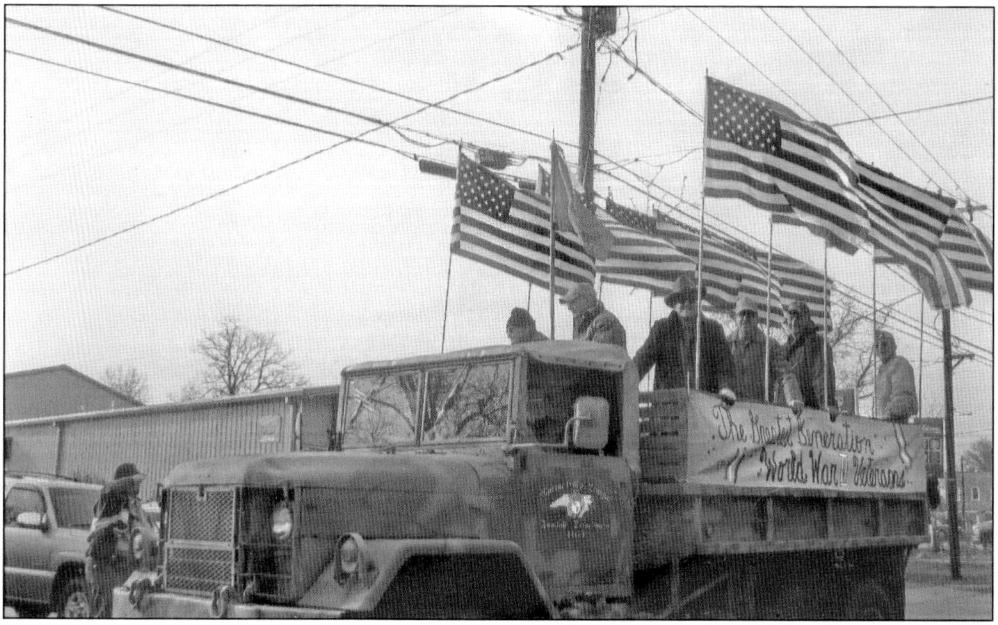

The Christmas parade of Colfax Township is an annual event in early December. In 2009, the grand marshals of the parade were some of the area's few surviving World War II veterans. The deuce-and-a-half in which they rode featured American flags and a banner reading, "The Greatest Generation." Shown here from left to right are John Tedder, Robert Watkins, Ray Mauney, J. T. Doty, and two U.S. Marine escorts. (Courtesy of Mike Rhyne.)

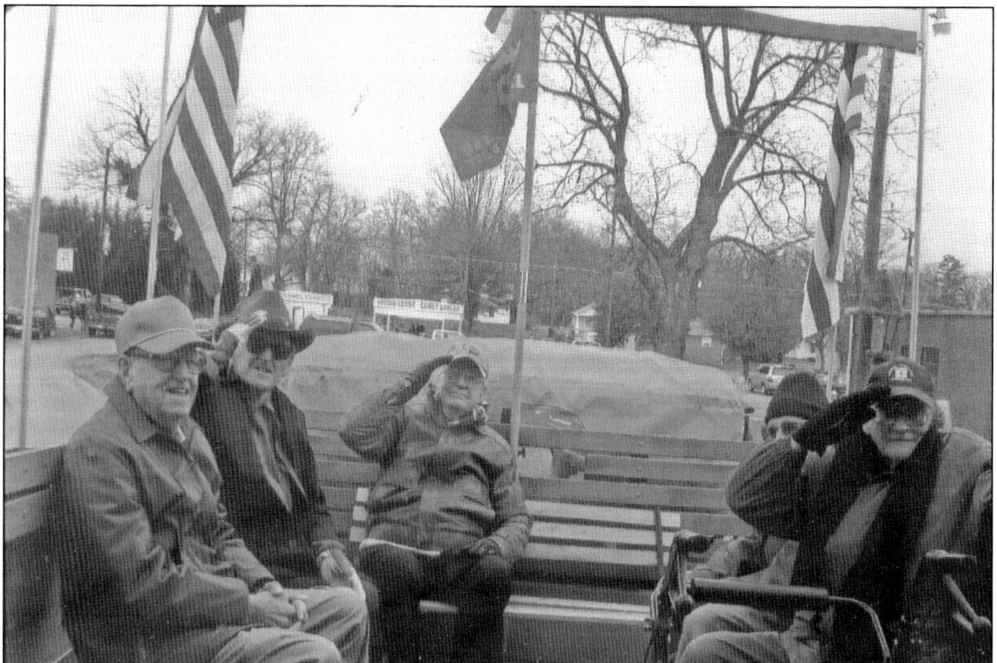

From left to right, the 2009 Christmas parade grand marshals shown here are Colfax World War II veterans J. T. Doty, Ray Mauney, Robert Watkins, John Tedder, and Gerald R. Medd. (Courtesy of Mike Rhyne.)

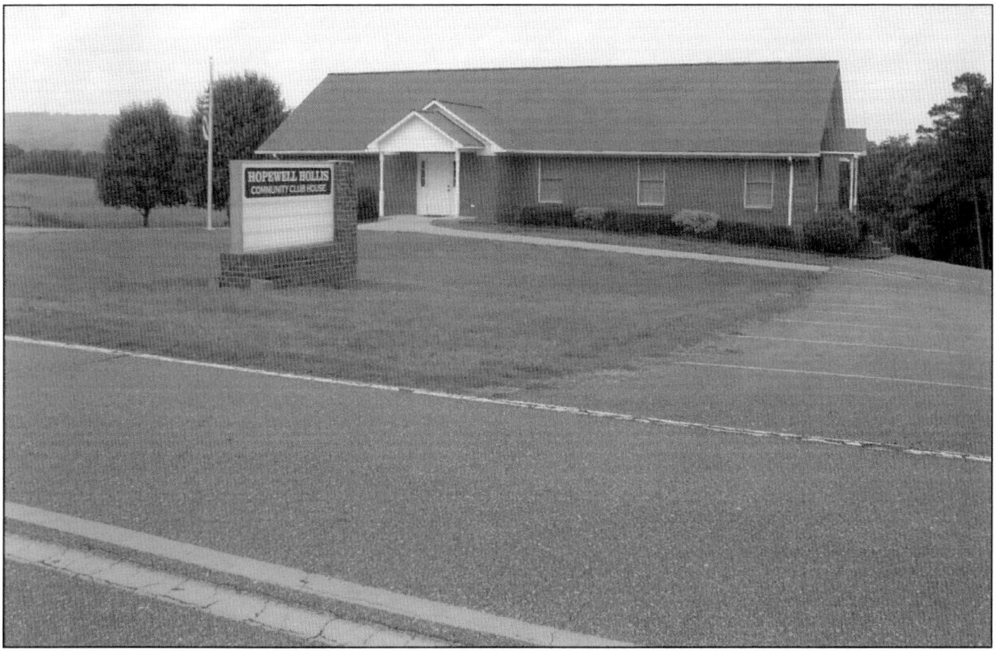

The Hopewell Hollis Community Center on Hollis Road in Hopewell is a popular meeting place for local residents. The center is also a meeting place for the Ruritan Club. (Courtesy of Mike Rhyne.)

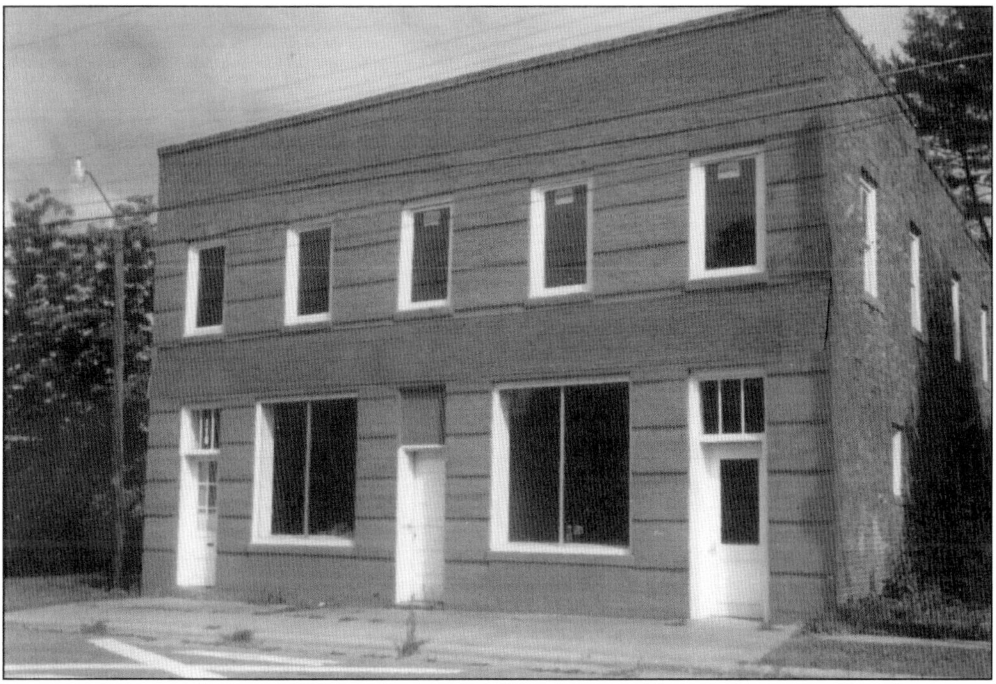

The first Ellenboro bank building dates from about 1906. The two-story structure (still standing in 2010) has changed little in structure through the years and is used a meeting place for various groups. Over the years, it has also housed a bank, a post office, and an antique shop. (Courtesy of Anita Price Davis.)

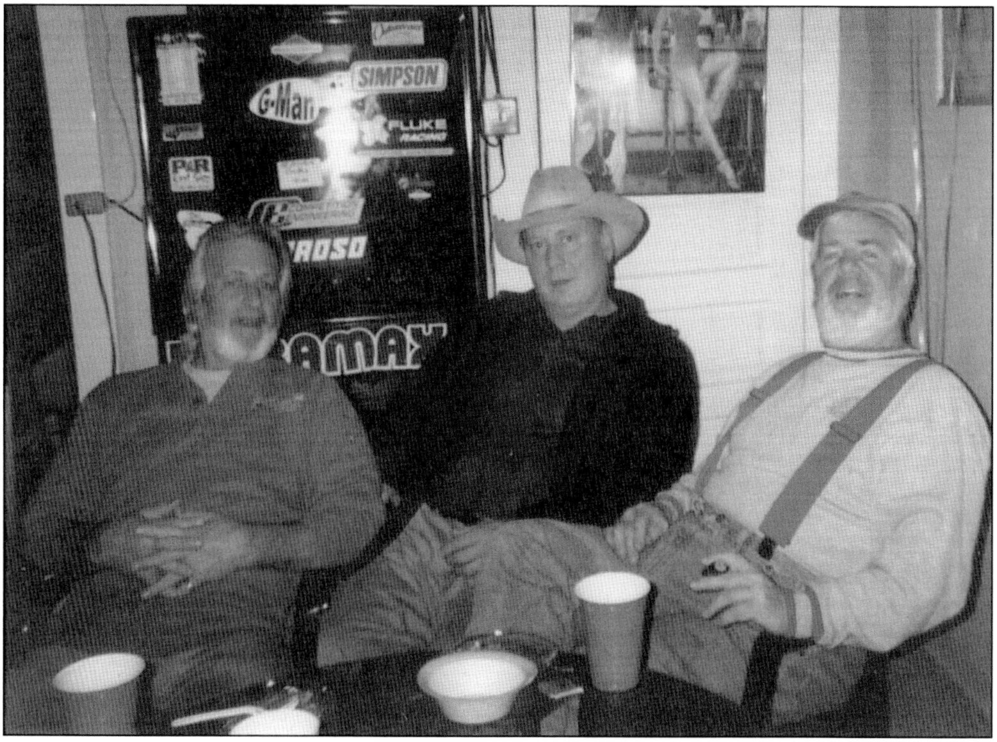

Jim Rhyne, John Logan, and Mike Rhyne relax after deep-frying wild turkey for a social hour at the old Ellenboro bank building. (Courtesy of Mike Rhyne.)

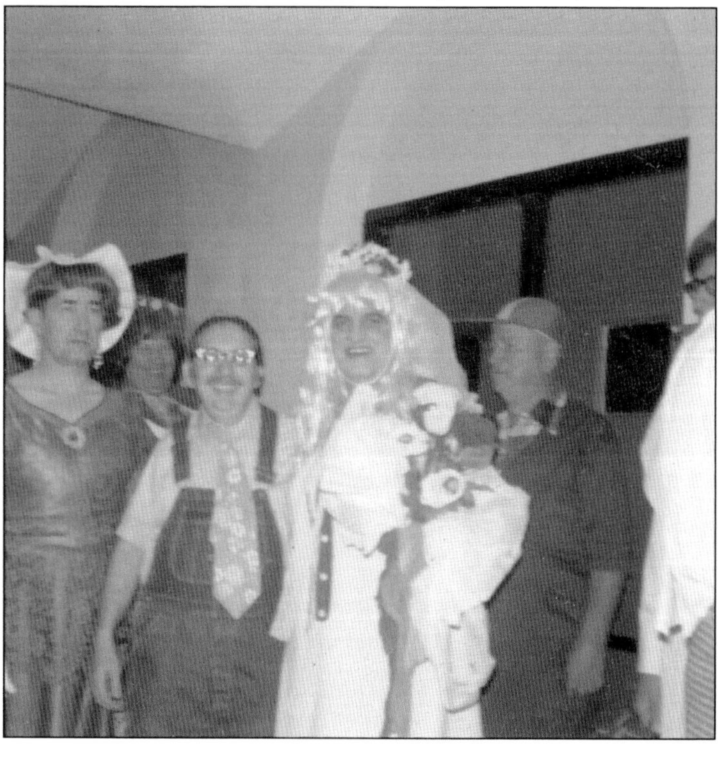
Area residents enjoyed an occasional program and get-together for relaxing and socializing. From left to right, Gene Brooks, J. V. Jones, Thomas Tisdale, and Emmett Hamrick present a womanless wedding for visitors. The well-attended event remains a topic of local conversation and amusement. (Courtesy of Frances Gettys Bailey.)

Five

Groups and Organizations

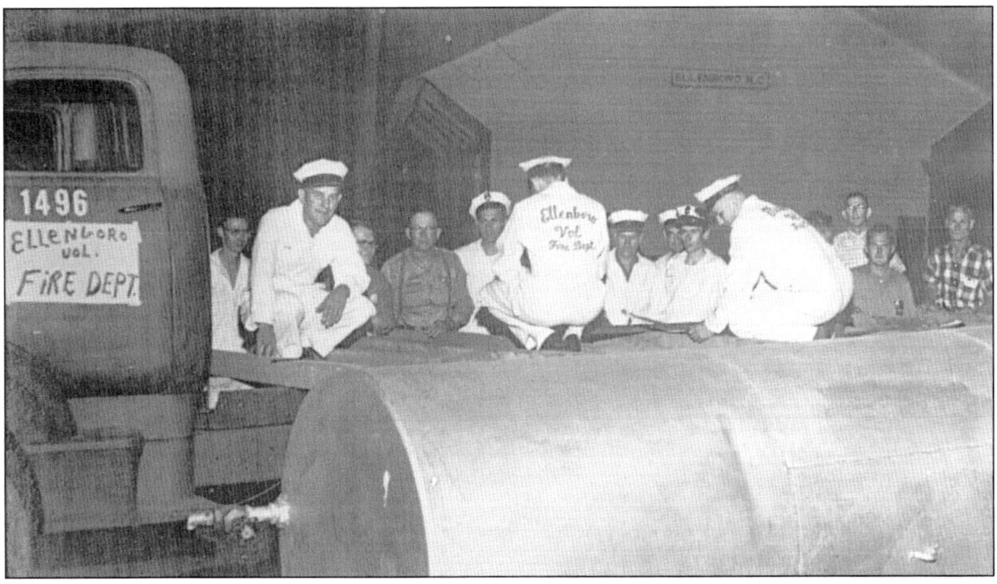

Essential to the safety of Colfax residents was the Ellenboro Fire Department, which serves the entire Colfax Township and other areas when necessary. Seen here is the first fire truck for the Ellenboro Fire Department. Shown from left to right in this photograph are Henry Jones, Joe Francis, Wilbur Allen, Howard Green, John Edwards, Drewey Jones, an unidentified man, James Brooks, Lowell Hamrick, Norman McDaniel, Bob Hamrick, Grady Hamrick, and Carl Bradley. (Courtesy of Colfax Museum.)

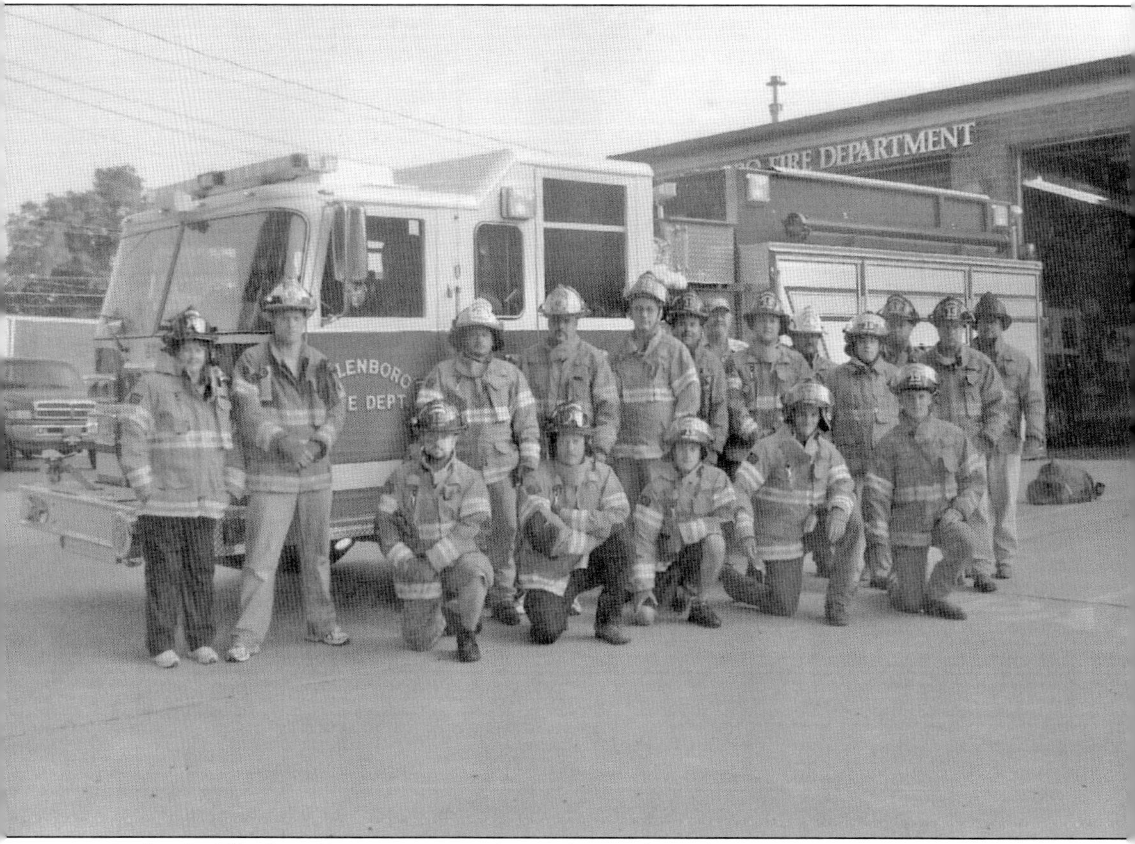

Today the Ellenboro Fire Department has 12 fire trucks and 30 members, of whom 13 are qualified as first responders. The firefighters hail from all parts of Colfax Township. From left to right, they include (kneeling) Tyler Lovelace, Bill Greene, Nick Downey, Tyler Hoyle, and Matt Rhodes; (standing) Sonya Moody, Daniel Edwards, Kenny Edwards Jr., Robbie Downey, Dixon Crow, Danny Holtzclaw, John Edwards Jr., Dustin Byers, Derek Bridges, Mike Jones, Ray Ponder, Brian Lowery, and Cliff Propes. (Courtesy of Pat Rhyne.)

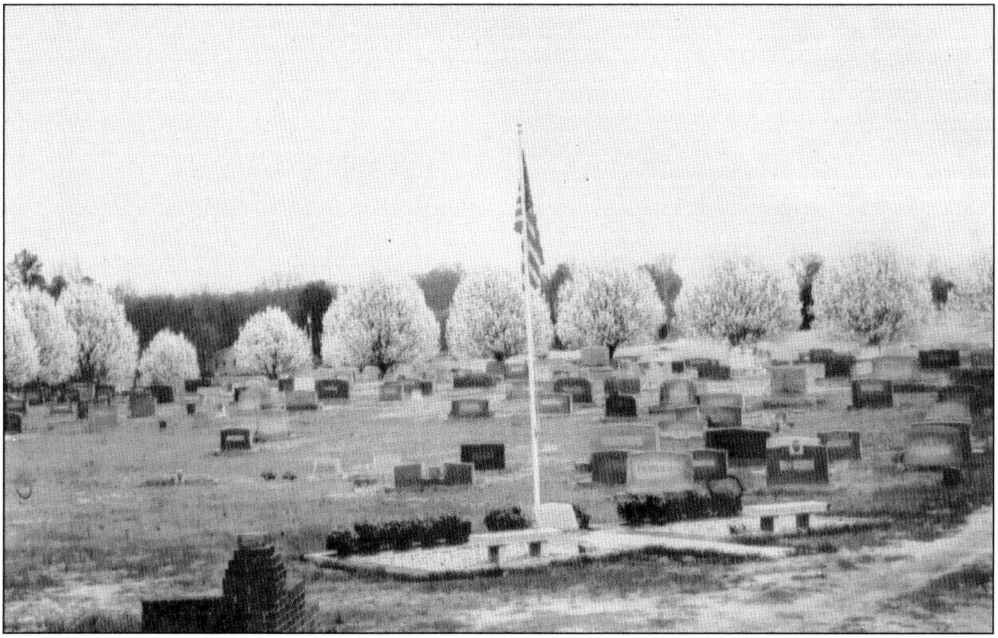

At both Bethel and Corinth Baptist Churches, a special section of the cemetery honors deceased members of the church who were veterans. Flags decorate the markers in the cemetery—especially on Memorial Day. This tradition allows church members and visitors to meet together, gather in the cemetery, and remember those who have served their nation. (Courtesy of Palmer Bailey.)

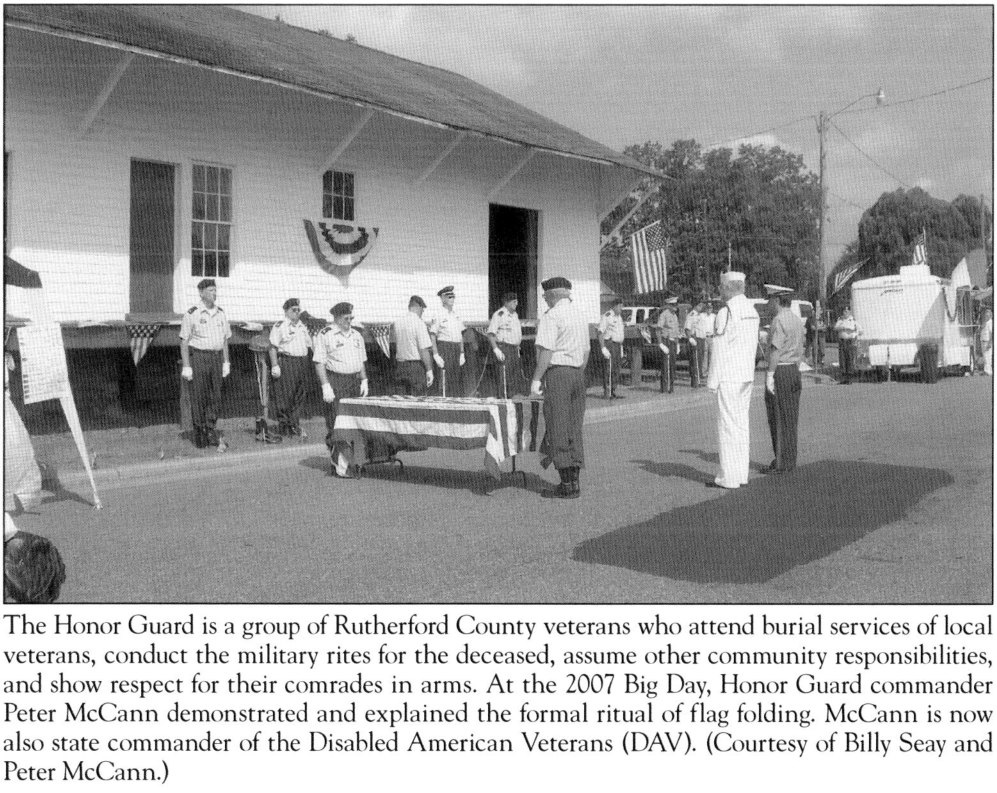

The Honor Guard is a group of Rutherford County veterans who attend burial services of local veterans, conduct the military rites for the deceased, assume other community responsibilities, and show respect for their comrades in arms. At the 2007 Big Day, Honor Guard commander Peter McCann demonstrated and explained the formal ritual of flag folding. McCann is now also state commander of the Disabled American Veterans (DAV). (Courtesy of Billy Seay and Peter McCann.)

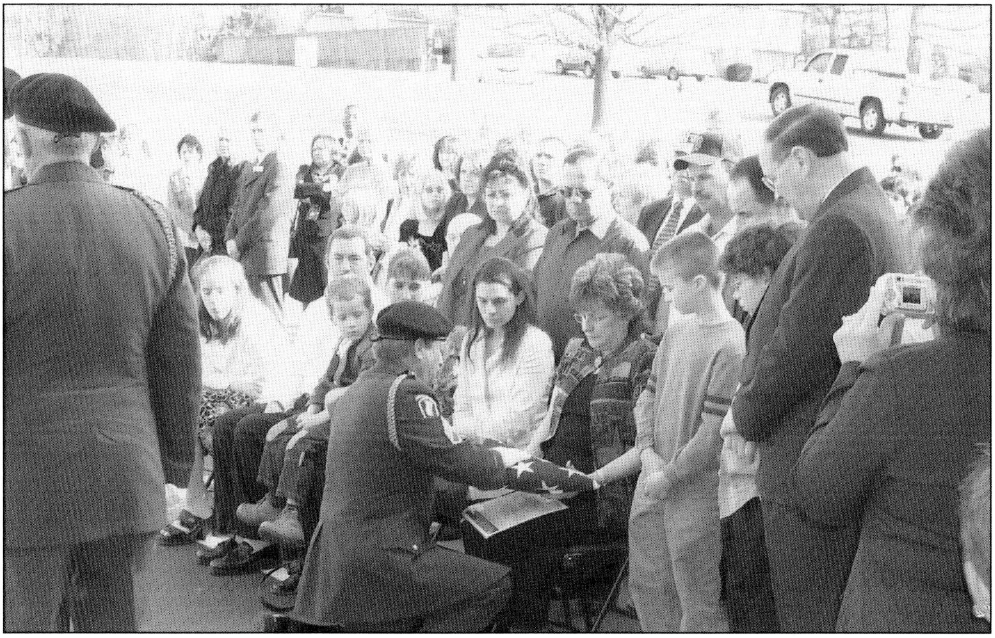

Here Honor Guard commander Peter McCann, a Colfax Township resident, presents the American flag to Eileen Daigle, widow of Vietnam veteran Ron Daigle, who died on February 12, 2005. Between its organization in October 2004 and June 2010, the Honor Guard conducted 576 funerals, averaging 115 ceremonies per year—all without compensation. (Courtesy of Billy Seay and Peter McCann.)

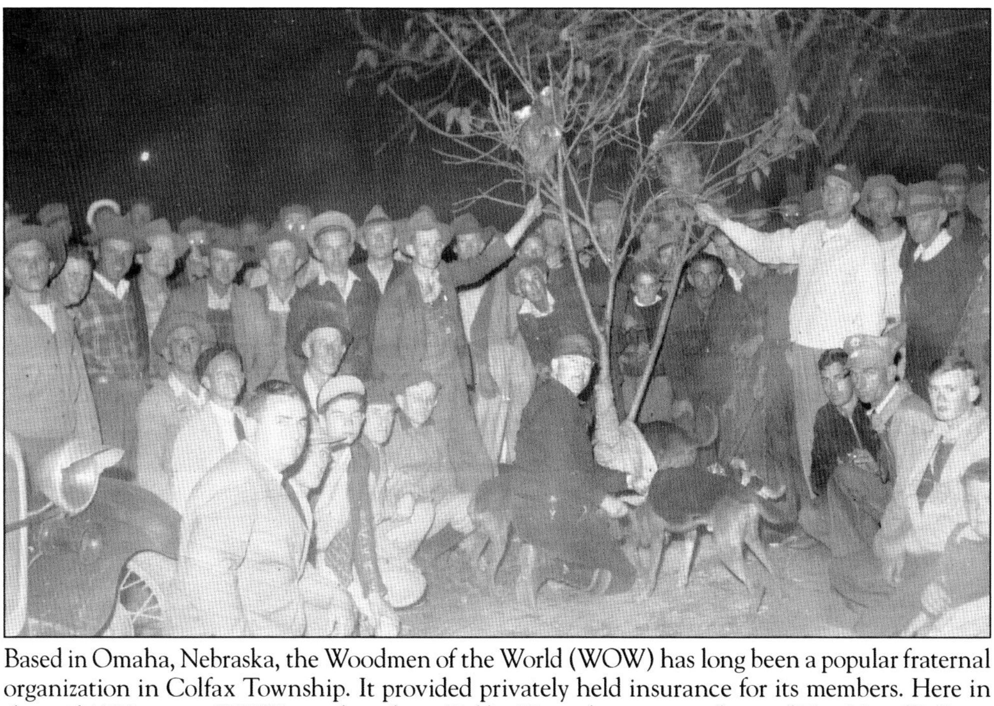

Based in Omaha, Nebraska, the Woodmen of the World (WOW) has long been a popular fraternal organization in Colfax Township. It provided privately held insurance for its members. Here in the mid-1930s, some WOW members from Colfax Township meet in front of Van Harrill's Store after a possum hunt—one example of their activities. (Courtesy of Colfax Museum.)

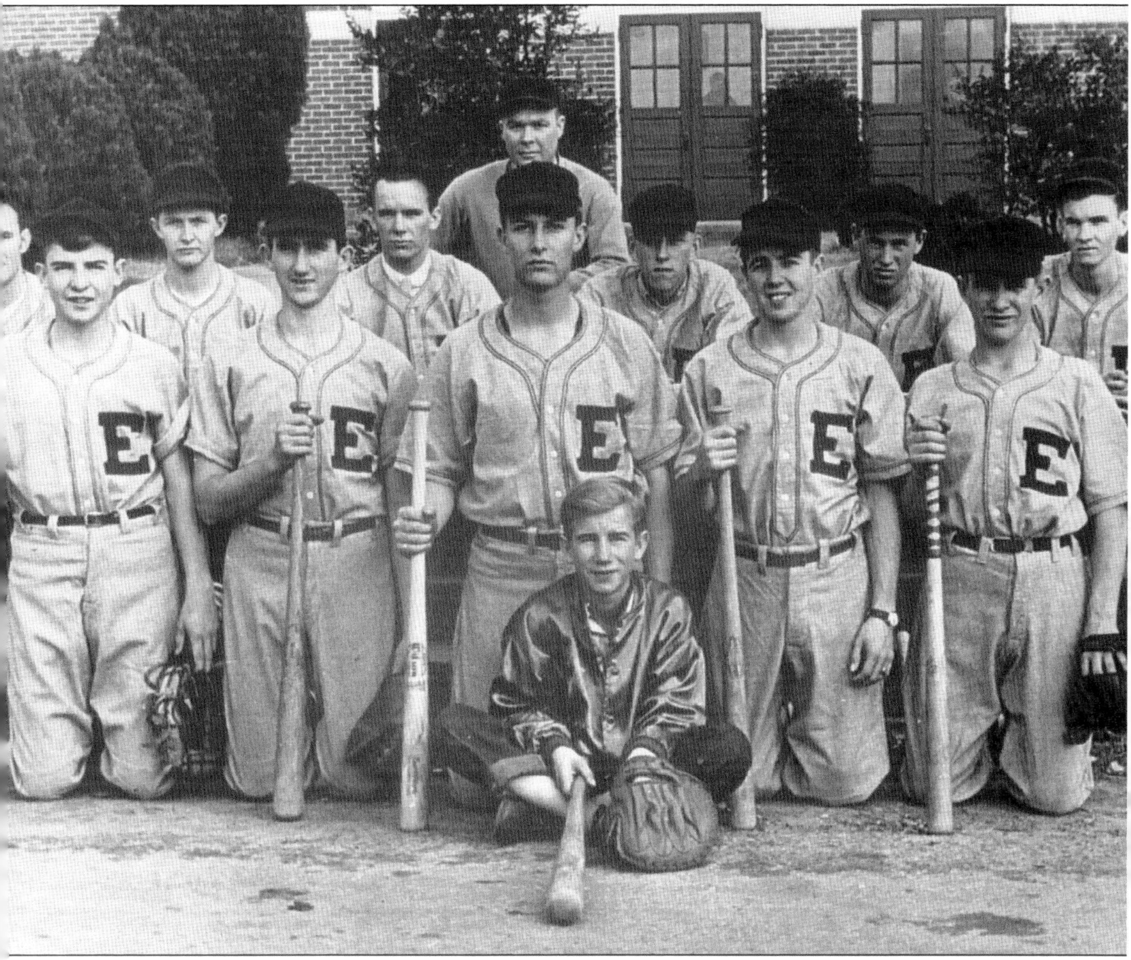

Baseball was popular in Colfax Township. This 1949 photograph shows the Ellenboro High School baseball team. From left to right, the members shown here are (seated) Dean Jolley; (second row) Zeno Daves, Donald Hope, Bobby Culbreth, Lowell Bushong, and Kenneth Daves; (third row) George Tisdale, Lewis Brooks, Weldon Walker, Palmer Bailey, Bobby Biggerstaff, and Martin Beam. Coach Ervin Smart stands behind them. (Courtesy of Palmer Bailey.)

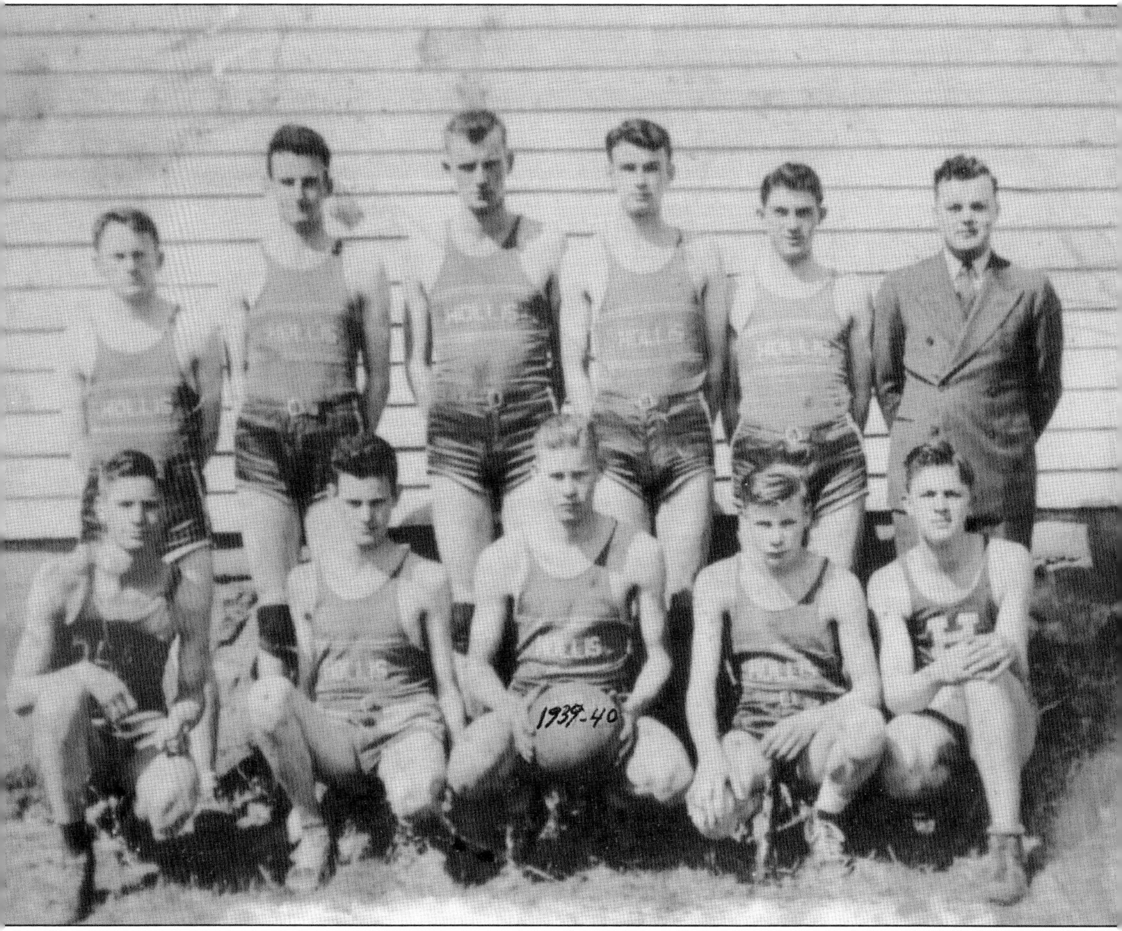

Students from the Duncans Creek, Colfax, and Logan Store Townships and from Sunshine could attend Hollis High School. The sports programs there were a source of pride and entertainment for area residents. This photograph shows the 1939–1940 Hollis basketball team—the North Carolina state champions. Seen here from left to right are (first row) Virgil Canipe, John Crowe Jr., William Canipe, Clifford Jenkins, and Gene Blanton; (second row) Bob Withrow, Norris Crowe, Martin Martin, Fred Gettys, Hyatt Melton, and coach S. P. Teague. (Courtesy of Joe Price.)

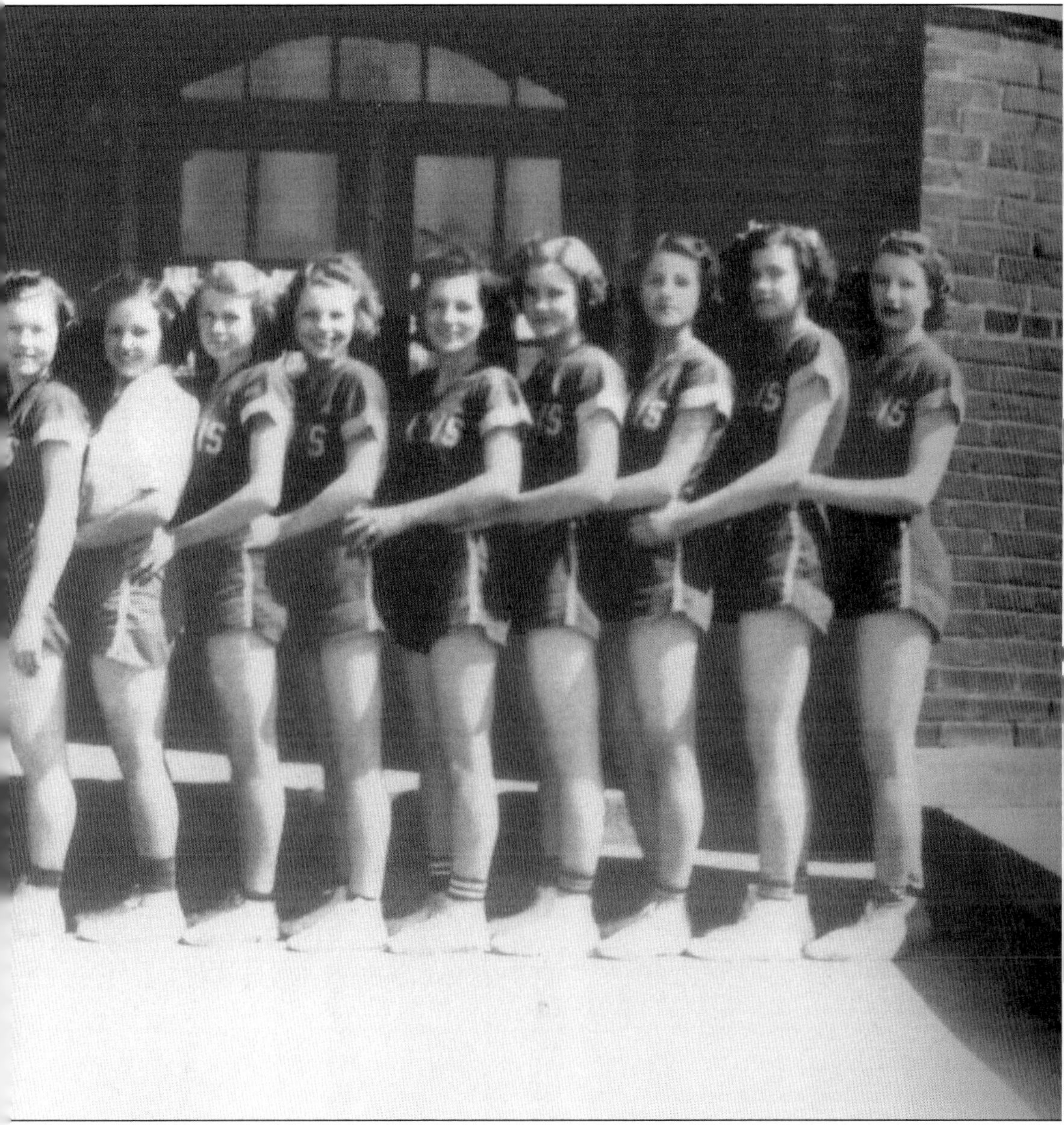

This photograph shows the 1939 Hollis High School girls' basketball team. Seen here from left to right are Nell Waters (Edwards), Gertrude Black, Frances McFarland, Nell Daves (Price Burns), Buna Daves (Edwards), Sadie Bradley, Maude Whitener, Tewie Bradley, and Inez Hunt. (Courtesy of Anita Price Davis.)

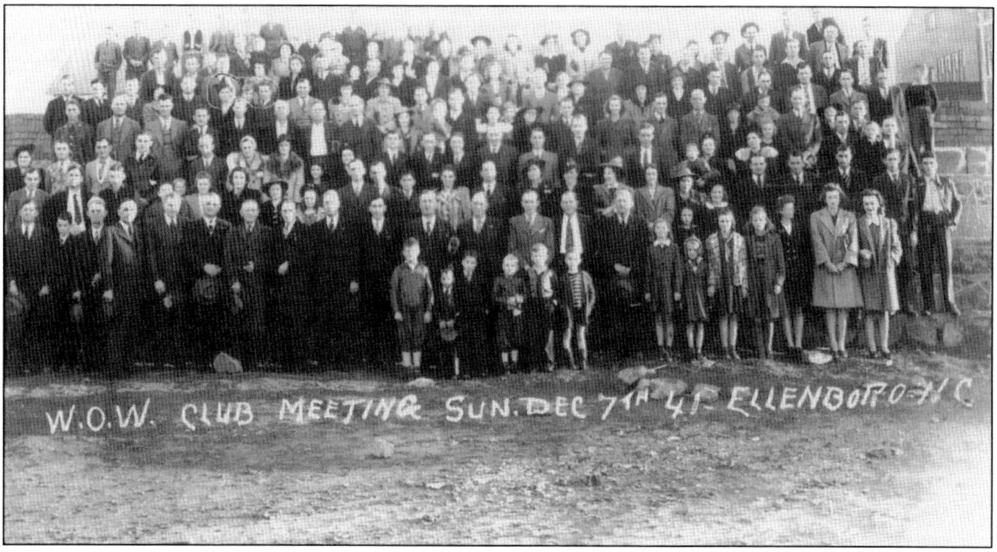

On December 7, 1941, members of the Colfax Woodmen of the World met on the steps of the Ellenboro School playground for a photograph after church. The members were unaware of the imminent Japanese attack on Pearl Harbor. (Courtesy of Jerrell Bedford.)

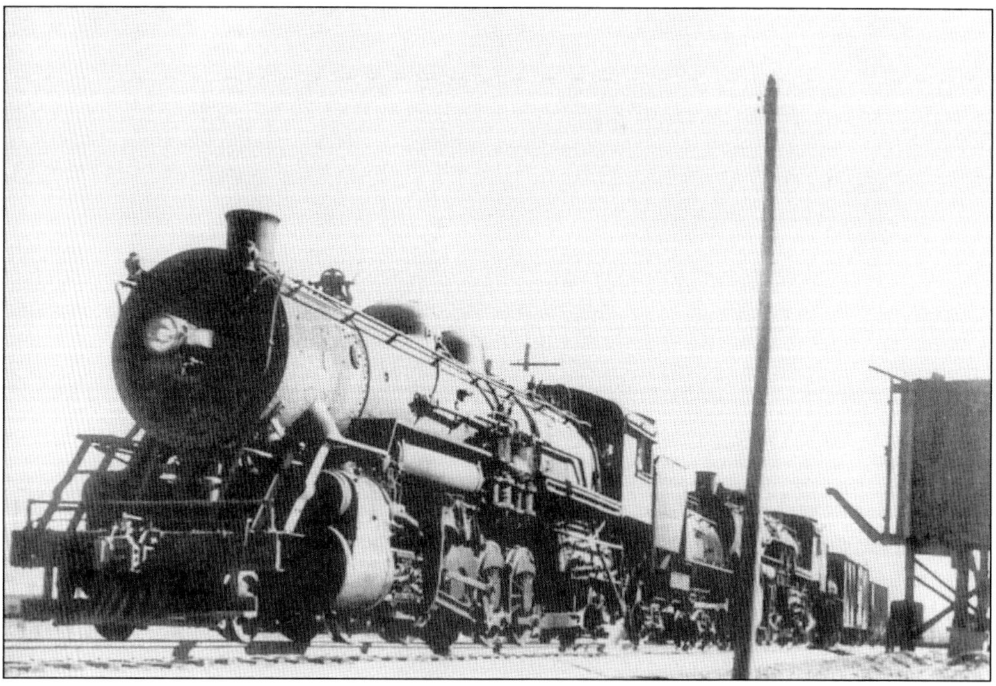

Buses and trains traversed Colfax Township. Here the Seaboard Air Line Railway 2401 (2-10-2) and a westbound freight (1936/1937) are preparing to take on water at the Ellenboro tank. The pump pond at Still Head Creek behind the old Bethel Baptist Church furnished the tank's water. Seaboard removed the tank in the early 1950s. (Courtesy of Paul Price.)

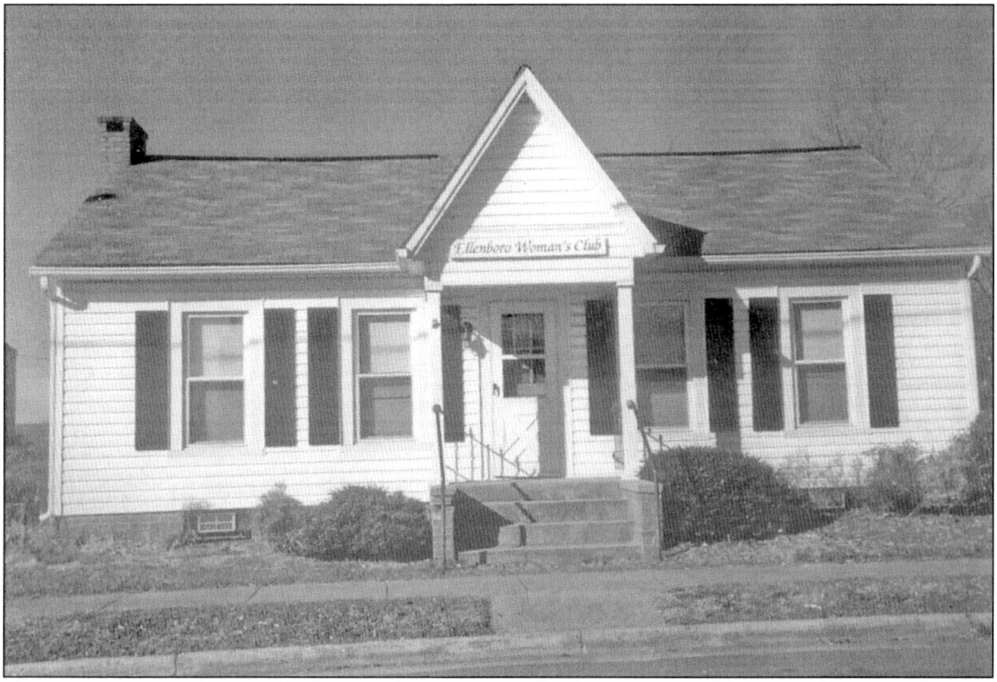

"Aunt" Kate Harrill donated land in 1925 for the construction of the Ellenboro Club House, intended as the meeting place for the Ellenboro Woman's Club. Many families, organizations (including the Home Demonstration Club and the Woodmen of the World), and individuals rented the structure for parties, reunions, showers, meetings, and even the Ellenboro Teen Club (1959–1960). Renting the structure to others provided income for the Ellenboro Woman's Club. (Courtesy of James M. Walker.)

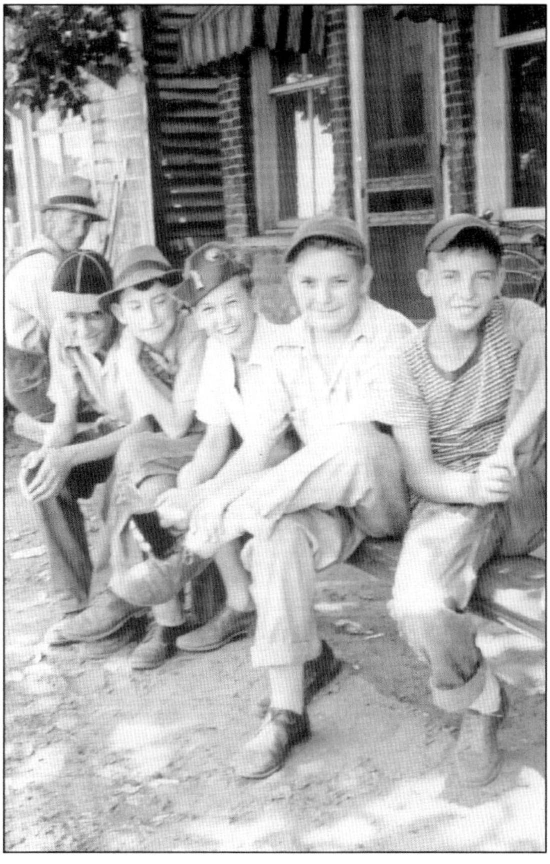

Groups of young people sometimes met informally at various locales. Here a group of boys in the early 1940s loaf in front of Grady Hamrick's store. From left to right, they are Donald Black, Claude Helton, Hank Martin, Vito Crisco Hamrick, and Zeno Daves. The man at left is Oliver Limerick. (Courtesy of Paul Price.)

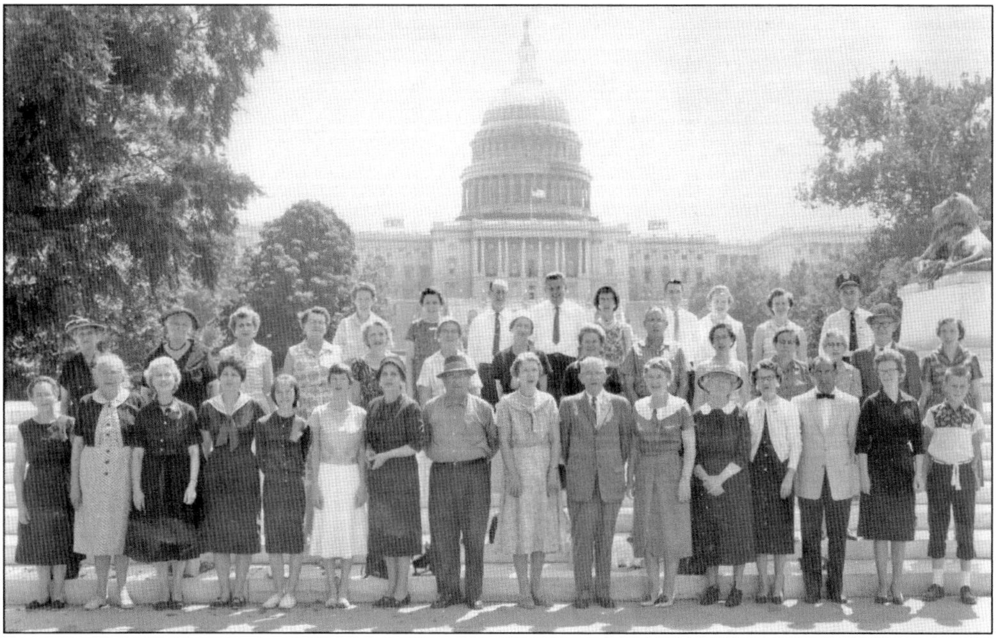

A. B. Bushong offered trips—typically to Washington, D.C.—for area residents during vacation periods. These excursions were often the first opportunity that many Colfax citizens had to visit the nation's capital. Daisy Price Whisnant is at far left and Frances Gettys Bailey is fourth from left in the first row. Bushong is wearing a hat near the center of the first row. (Courtesy of Lowell Bushong.)

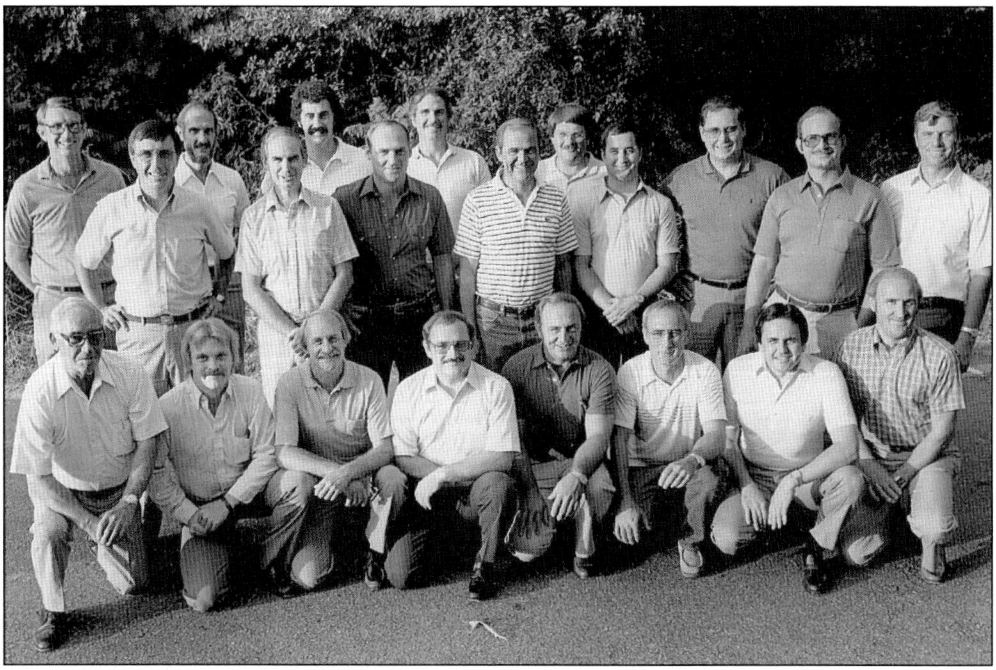

Pictured here are many of the Boy Scouts who gained the rank of Eagle Scout under the guidance of C. A. Kennedy, shown kneeling at far left in the first row. They had gathered on this occasion in Kennedy's honor. (Courtesy of Wilbur Wright.)

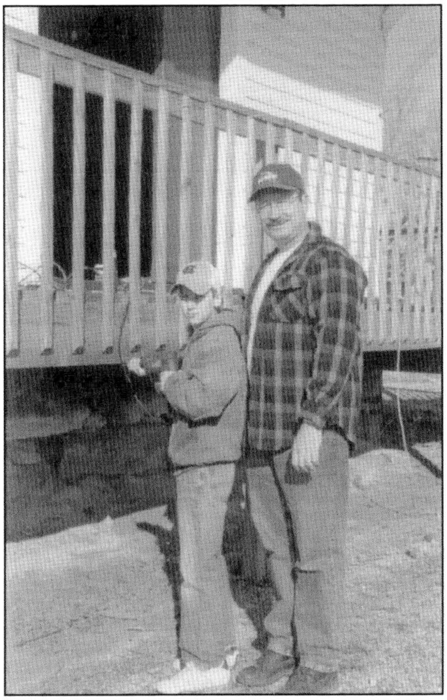

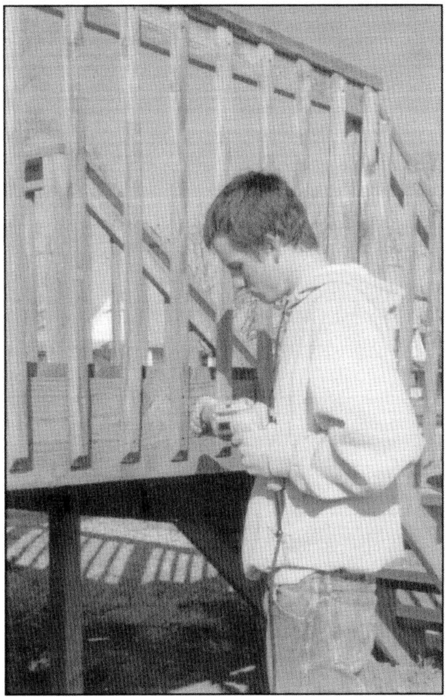

Members of Colfax Boy Scout Troop No. 126 are seen here helping in the renovation of the Colfax Museum in 2008. Working around the depot are (above left) Ethan Parker and Scoutmaster Tommy Tisdale and (above right) Hunter Parker. (Courtesy of James M. Walker.)

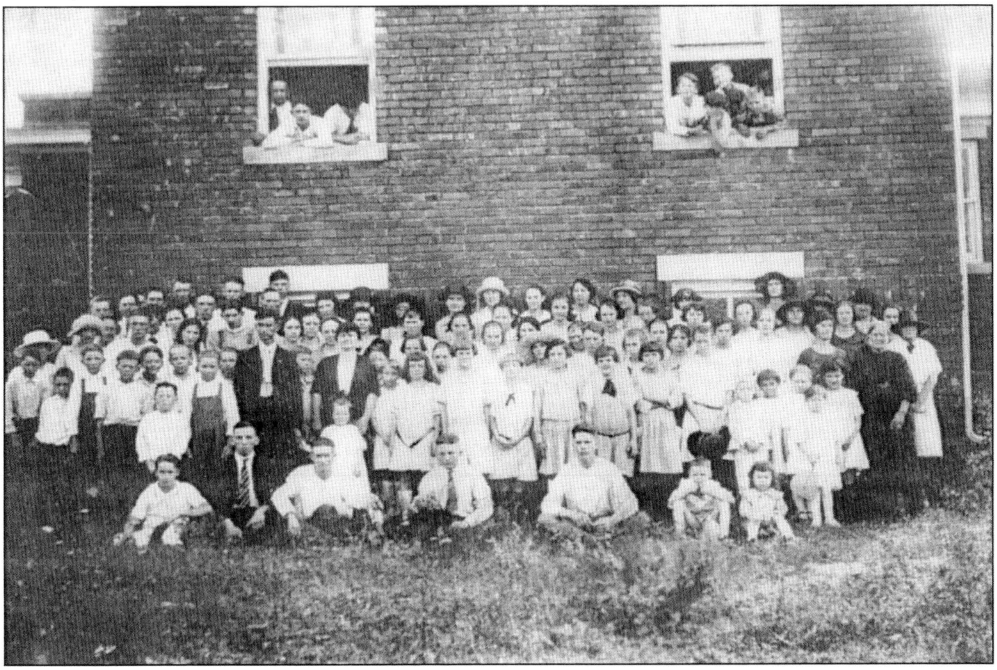

Shape-note singing was an early form of music notation for untrained singers and choirs. Singing schools taught the method to church and civic groups. Bethel Baptist Church hosted this 1930s singing school. Notice that attendees included seniors and the very young. Zeb Daves (third from left, first row) and his brother Fay (fourth from left, first row) both attended. (Courtesy of Susan Daves McGee.)

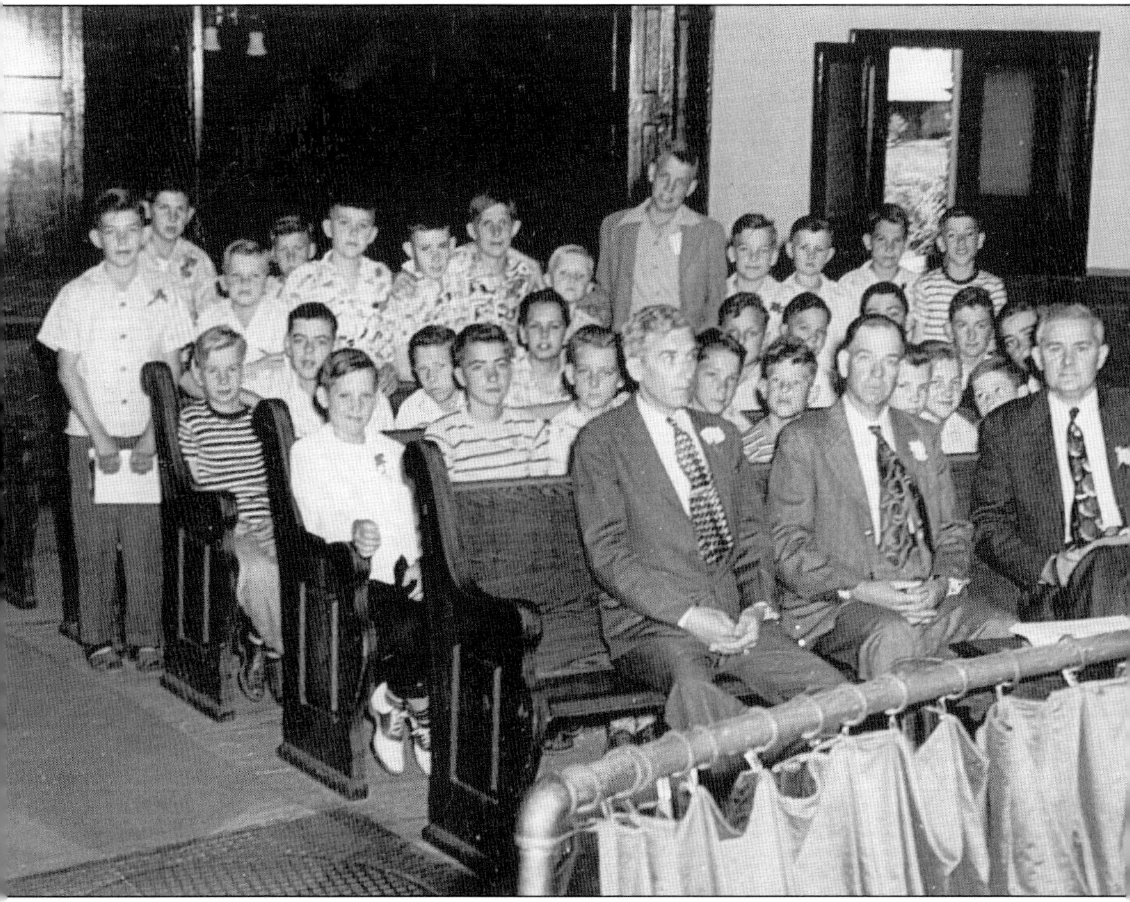

This 1949 photograph shows the boys' Sunday school class at Bethel Baptist Church. From left to right, the teachers are (first row) Rev. C. F. Laughlin, Laxton Burns, and Delbert Byars. The students are (second row) Don Edwards, Francis Jolley, Roy Greene, Bobby Owens, Horace Billingsley, Book Jenkins, Max Wilson, Ronnie Smart, and James Burns; (third row) Dean Jolley, Donald Hamrick, Edward Jenkins, Bobby Joe Hamrick, Clyde Jones, Kenneth Burns, Charles Burns, and Claude Helton; (fourth row) Bobby Sellars, Bob Billingsley, Donald Byars, Lowell Hamrick, Kenneth Daves, Jimmy Daves, Larry Glover, Donald Sellars, Everette Wilson, Jerry Daves, and Wallace Billingsley; (fifth row) George Raines and Morris Wilson. (Courtesy of Colfax Museum.)

Six

PEOPLE

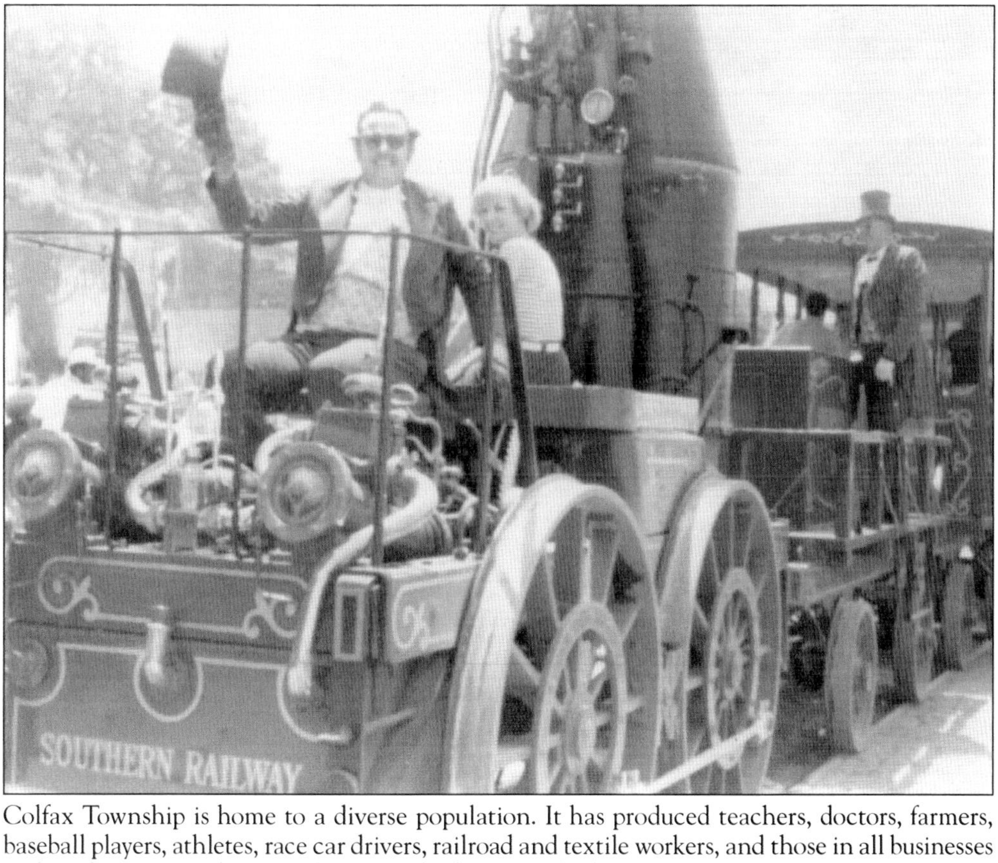

Colfax Township is home to a diverse population. It has produced teachers, doctors, farmers, baseball players, athletes, race car drivers, railroad and textile workers, and those in all businesses and professions. In the township, everybody is somebody. Seen here is the Southern Railway replica of the 1830 *Best Friend of Charleston*, the first regularly scheduled passenger train in the United States. When Ivey Ray Mauney saw the train, he became interested in its restoration. Here engineer Mauney drives the train for public relations for Southern Railway with his wife, Evelyn "Polly," whom he jokingly called his "first" (and only) wife. (Courtesy of Ivey Ray Mauney.)

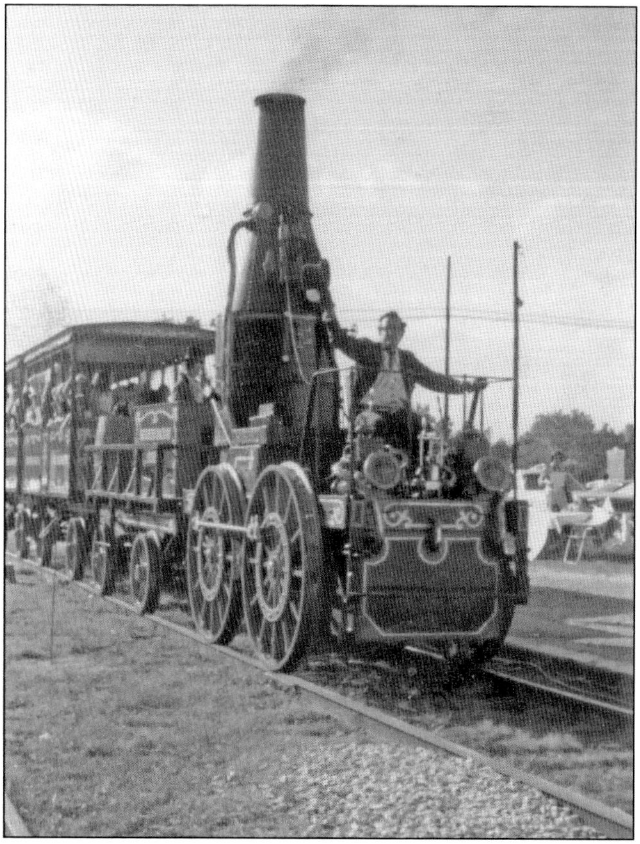

I. Ray Mauney traveled to Washington in 1976 for President Carter's inauguration. While passing the reviewing stand, he blew the whistle, and President Carter rose and saluted. *The Best Friend of Charleston* is now in a museum in Atlanta. (Courtesy of Ivey Ray Mauney.)

John Bynum Bubalee Griffin Walker Jr. lived his entire life in Colfax Township. He delighted in helping others. He was a friend to all in both the white and black communities. Walker was a railway worker, a grave digger, construction worker, and a baseball player in the Negro Leagues. (Courtesy of Colfax Museum.)

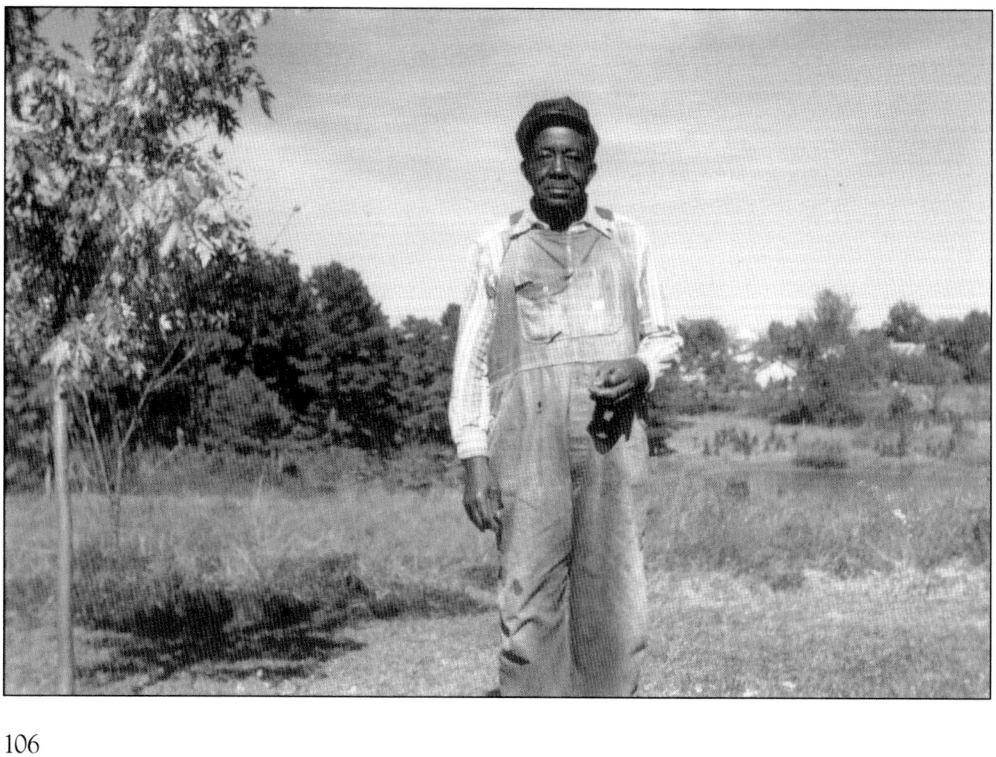

Confederate soldier John Greene fought throughout the Civil War without suffering a wound. He returned to Colfax as the constable. In 1898, Constable Greene cornered a fugitive, and in the ensuing gunfight, he killed the combatant but was mortally wounded and died within the hour. Greene is one of three county law enforcement officers to die in the line of duty. His grave is in Bethel Baptist Church Cemetery. (Courtesy of Polly Condrey.)

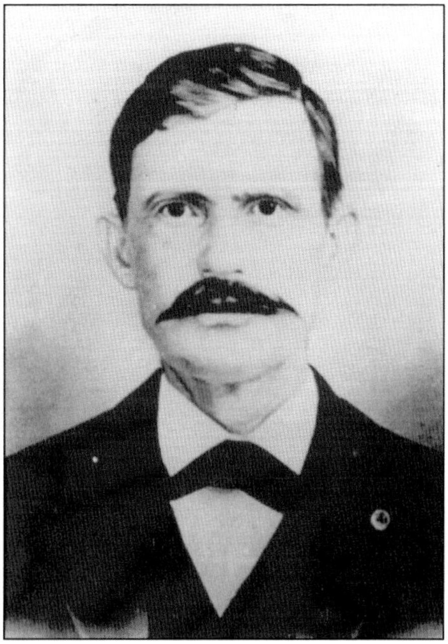

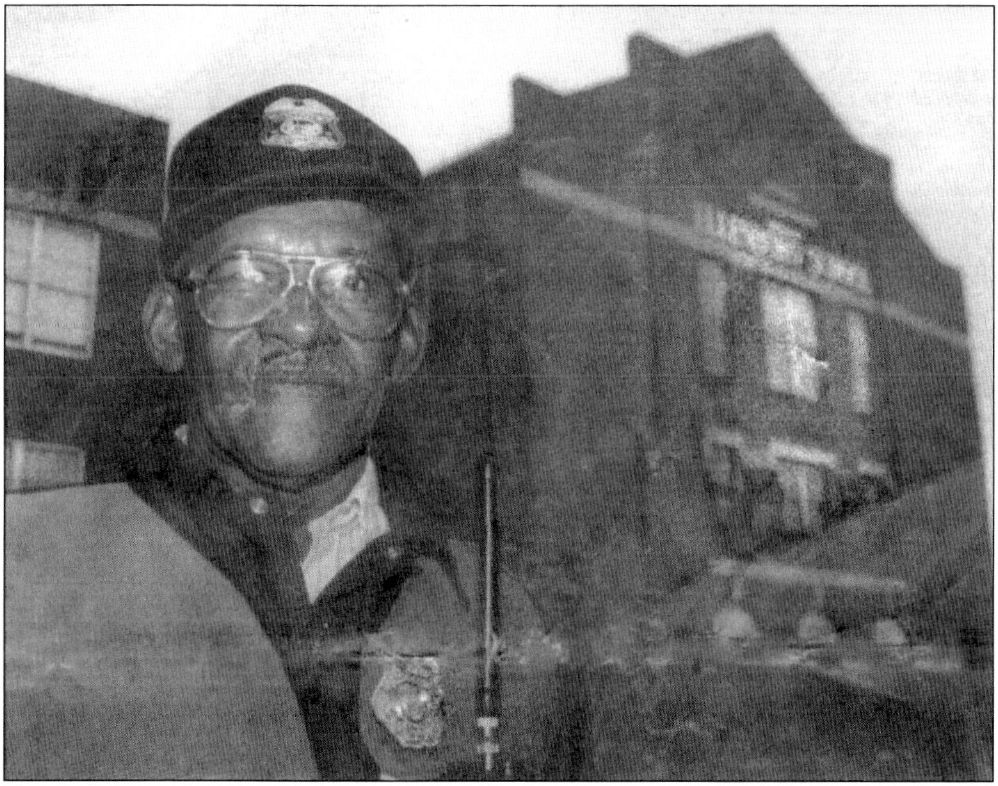

Jesse Ben Logan was a well-known resident of Colfax Township. He worked as janitor at Ellenboro School (in background), helped direct traffic for special events, and was always present for the annual Lewis family performance in the Ellenboro School auditorium. He often rode his bicycle along local streets and roads. (Courtesy of Hattie Logan.)

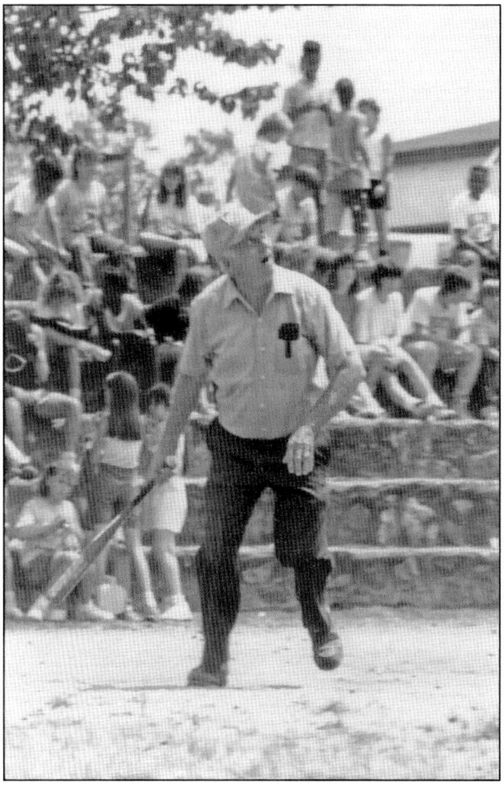

A familiar merchant in Hopewell Community was Richard B. "Bud" McFarland. Here Bud takes a break from his Hopewell Grocery. (Courtesy of Brenda McFarland Toney and Joyce Waters McFarland.)

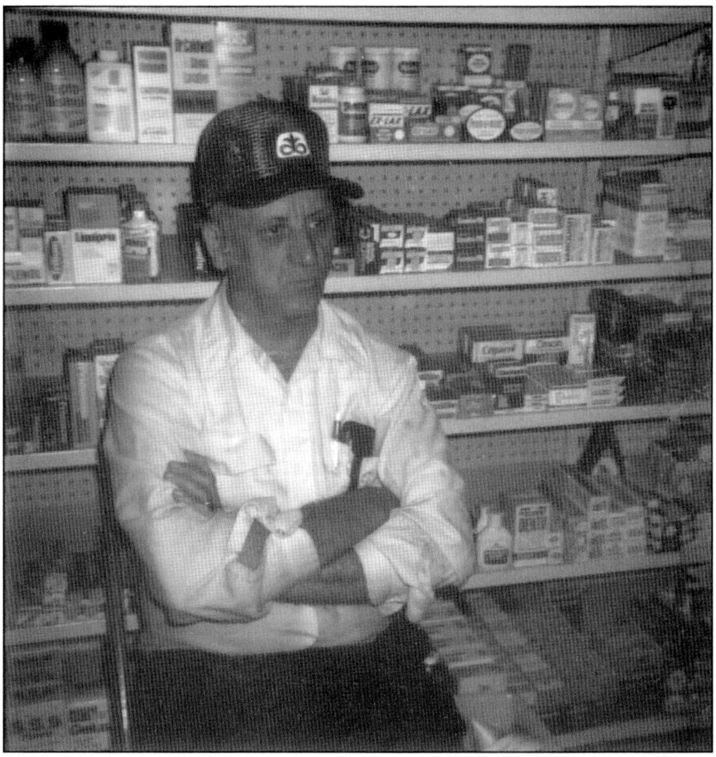

Here Richard B. "Bud" McFarland is in familiar surroundings: his store in Hopewell. (Courtesy of Brenda McFarland Toney and Joyce Waters McFarland.)

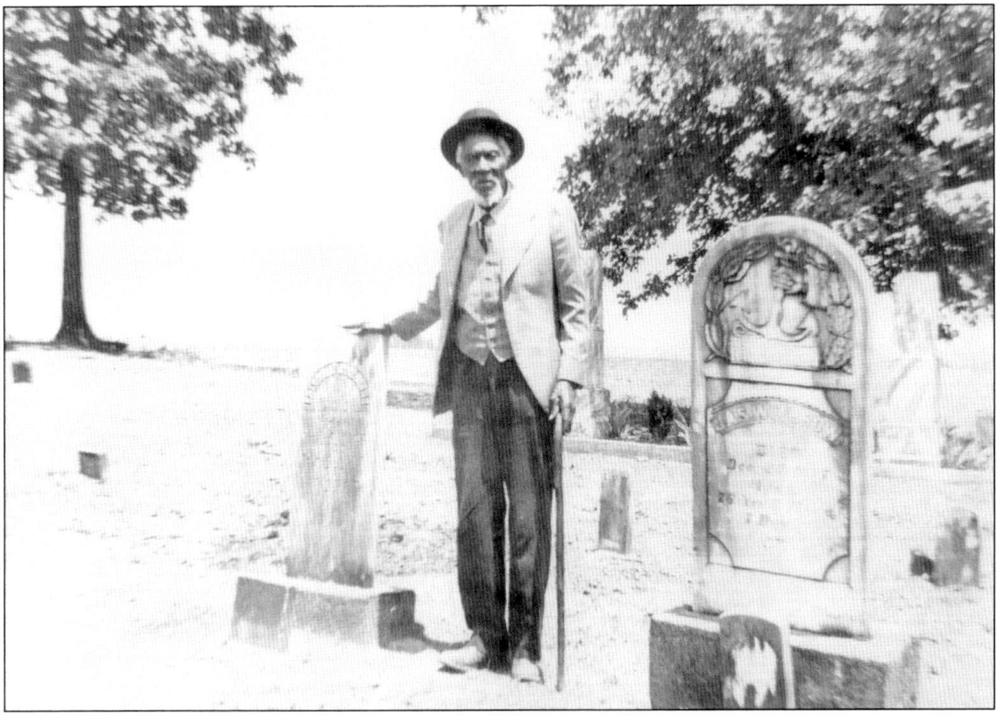

Ervin Withrow stands between the graves of Rev. James Withrow (a circuit-riding Methodist minister) and James's wife, Eraxina Wells Withrow. Ervin was born a slave to James Withrow in the Hollis community in 1845. Withrow lived into his 90s and often recounted his Civil War stories. (Courtesy of Scott Withrow.)

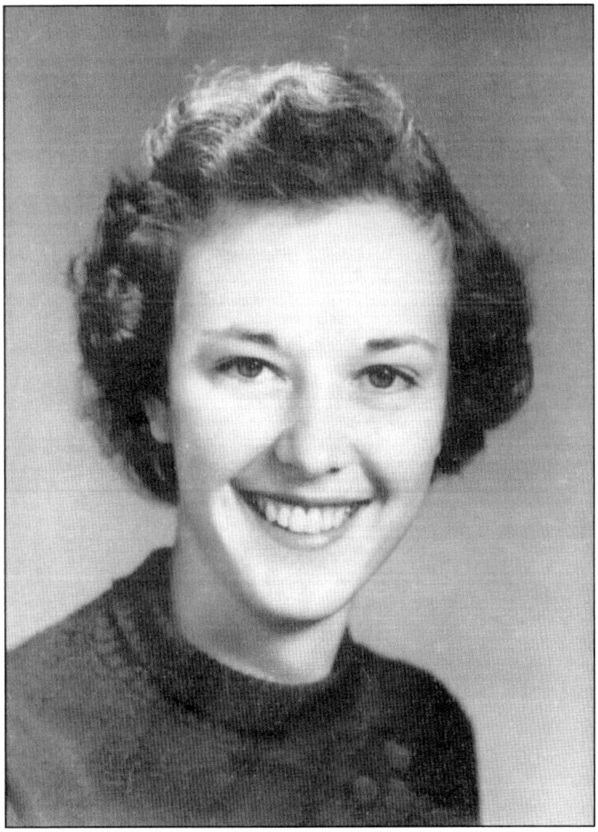

Betty Rhyne Owens (1937–1956) was the daughter of Elizabeth Rhyne, a longtime resident of Colfax Township. After she and Bobby Owens married at Fort Hood, Texas, they were coming home for Easter when they were involved in a fiery car crash. Betty died immediately, but Bobby lived for a week longer. Before his death, he asked for orchids for the arrangements for his beloved wife. (Courtesy of Jim Rhyne.)

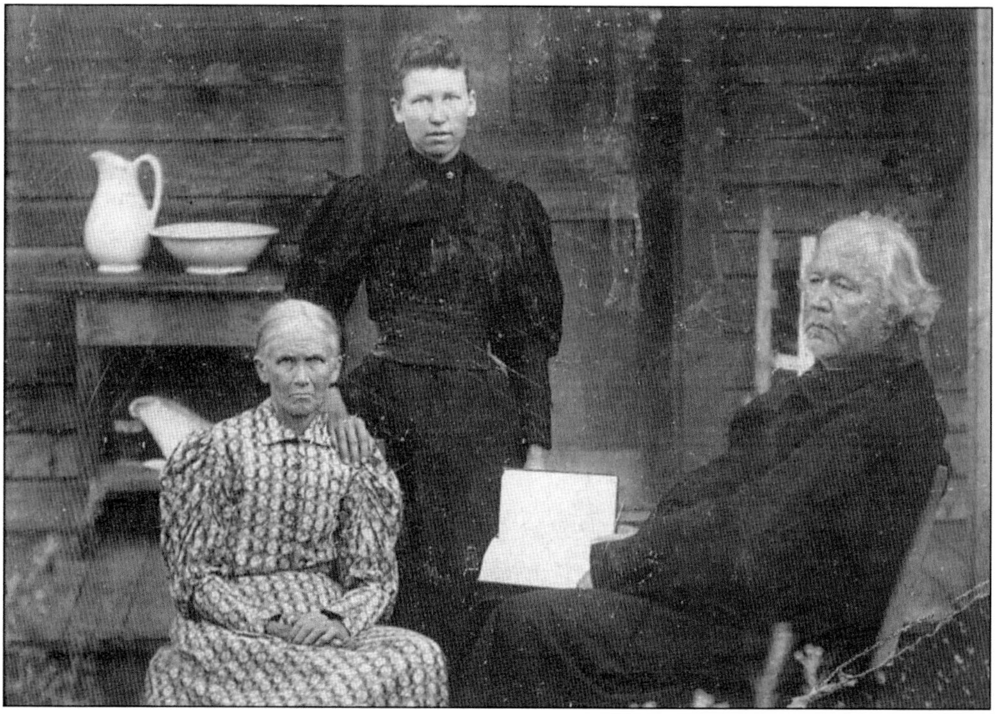

Dr. James Oliver Martin (right) was born in 1828 in what is now Colfax Township. He—and later his son Frank (born in 1862)—served as doctors in and around Colfax. In the 1894 typhoid fever epidemic, both doctors treated fever victims; Frank died from the disease. Both men's graves are in Salem Cemetery. James is the great-great-grandfather of Colfax resident Hank Martin. (Courtesy of Hank Martin.)

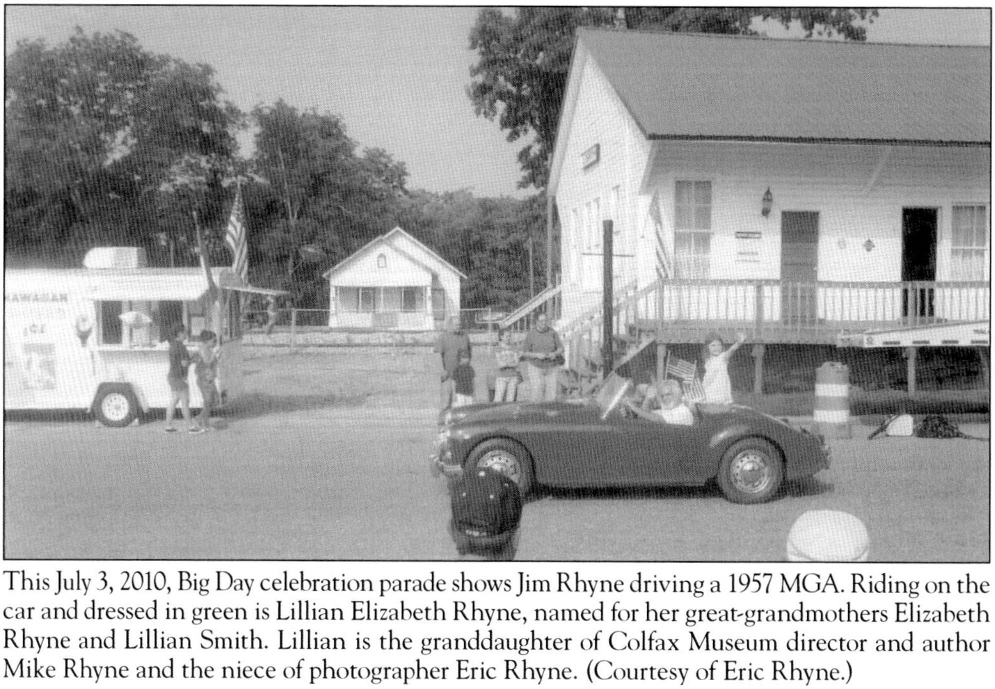

This July 3, 2010, Big Day celebration parade shows Jim Rhyne driving a 1957 MGA. Riding on the car and dressed in green is Lillian Elizabeth Rhyne, named for her great-grandmothers Elizabeth Rhyne and Lillian Smith. Lillian is the granddaughter of Colfax Museum director and author Mike Rhyne and the niece of photographer Eric Rhyne. (Courtesy of Eric Rhyne.)

This photograph shows some residents of Colfax Township. From left to right, they are (first row) Helen Helton and Reese Hamrick; (second row) Dorothy Helton and Lowell Hamrick. They are gathered near the Luther and Oma Jane Helton house in the mid-1950s. (Courtesy of Paul Price.)

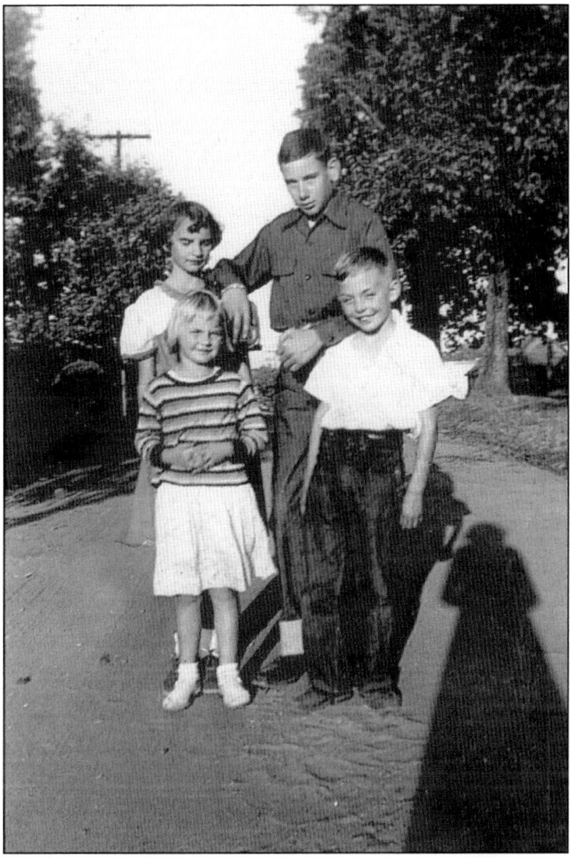

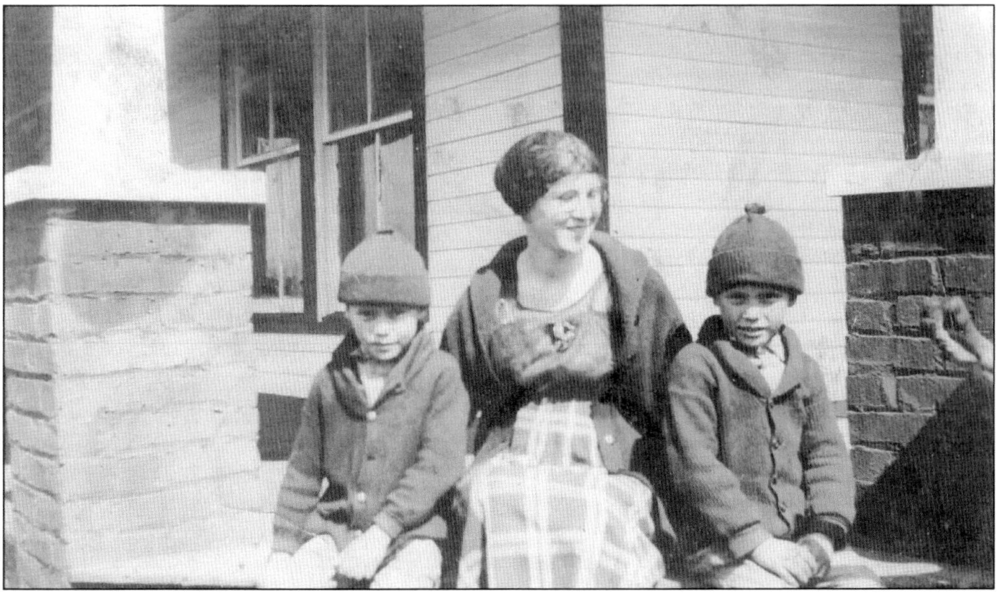

This photograph on the steps of the Oak Grove School shows Edmund Blanton (left) and his twin, Everett Blanton. They sit with their teacher, Gertrude Ledbetter. The Oak Grove School building has also served as a private residence. (Courtesy of Mae Blanton.)

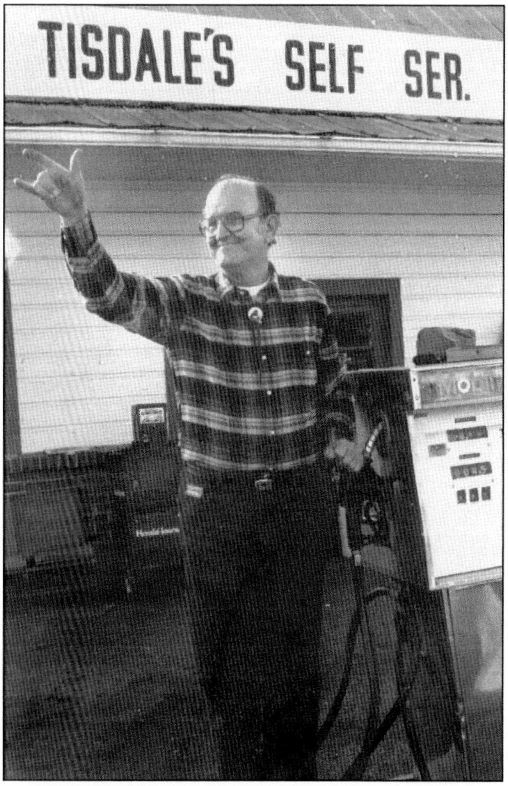

Thomas Tisdale was a local merchant like his father, T. P. Tisdale. Other Tisdale stores were located on Piney Mountain Road and in the drugstore building, pictured earlier. Here Thomas (the self-proclaimed "prettiest man in Ellenboro") stands near the pumps of the Highway 74 store, which also served as the Queen City Trailways Bus Station. (Courtesy of Colfax Museum.)

Thomas Tisdale married Jean Green. The author of *Dear Companion* and *Forward through the Ages: Bethel Baptist Church*, Jean Green Tisdale served Bethel Baptist Church in many capacities—organist, pianist, teacher, and Girls in Action leader, among others. The Tisdales and their store were fixtures in the community. (Courtesy of Colfax Museum.)

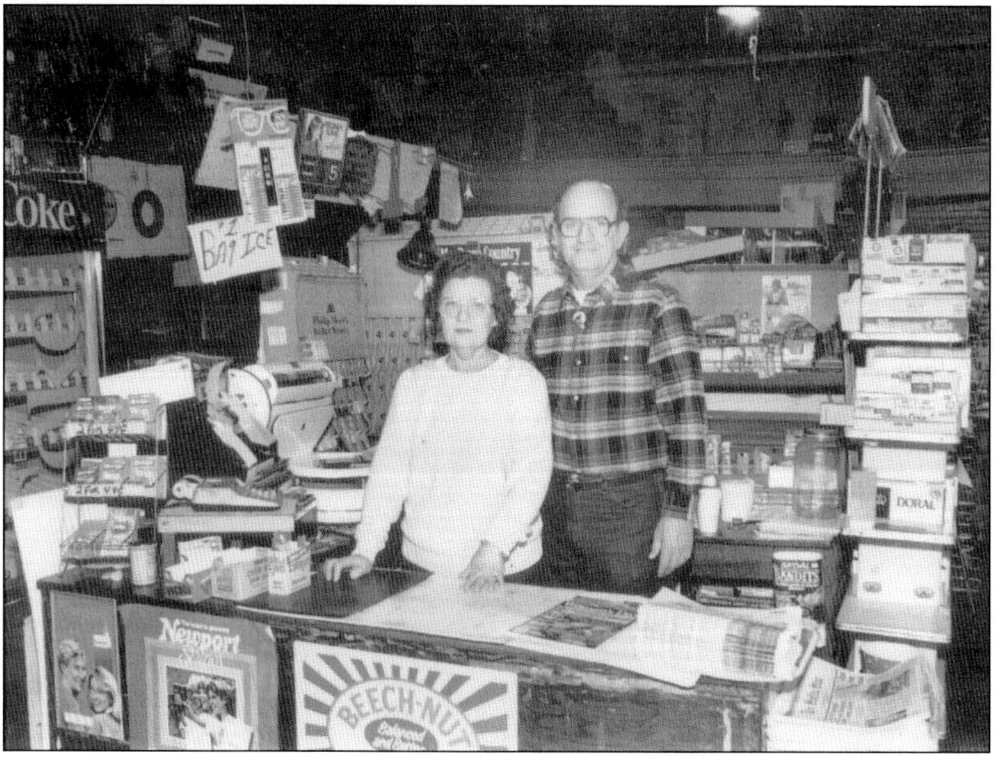

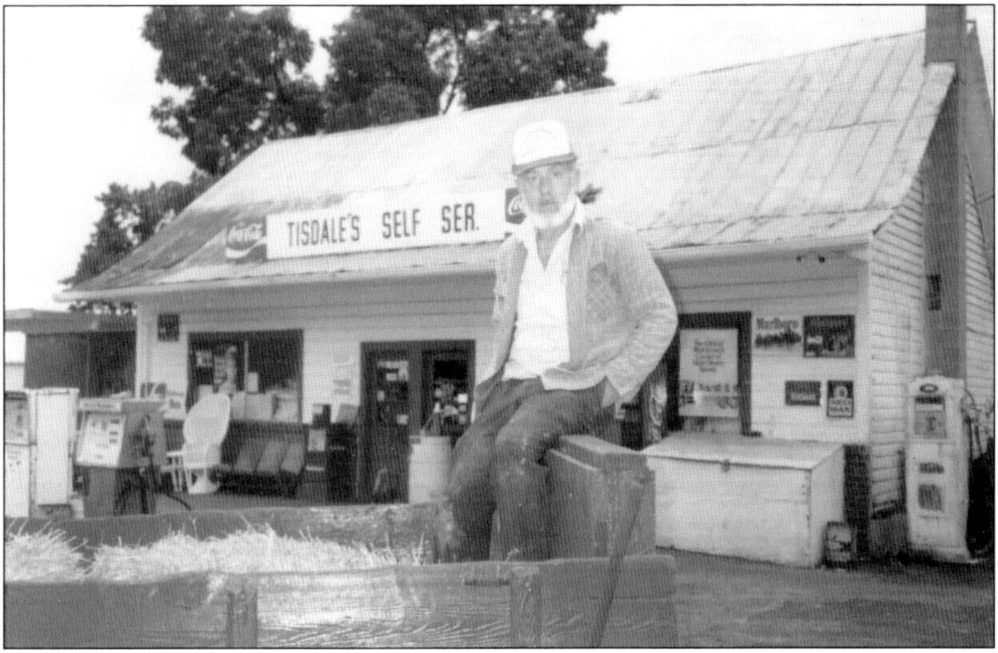

Well-known Colfax resident Luther Gillikin sits on a wagon in front of Thomas Tisdale's store on Highway 74. Gillikin has worked as a deputy sheriff, a textile worker, a general "fix-all" person, and employee of the Town of Ellenboro and Concord Water. His wife is Linda Jones Gillikin. (Courtesy of Colfax Museum.)

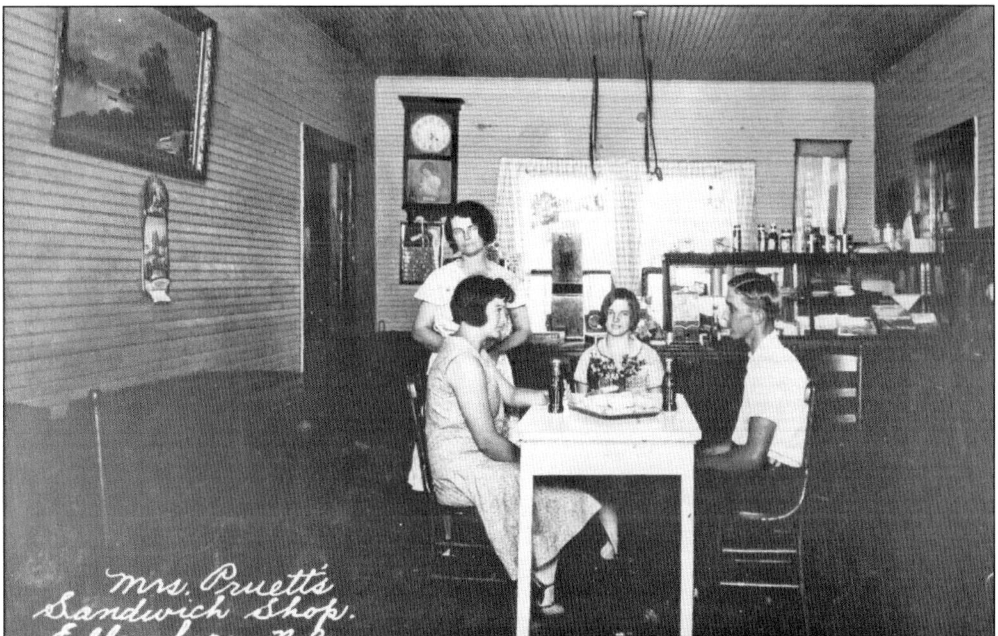

Beulah Pruette (standing) owned a popular sandwich shop in Colfax Township. Restaurants were not plentiful in the area during the 1930s, when she operated the business. The shop was on a hill near the present Needmore Store on Highway 74. (Courtesy of Mary Pruette and Robert Watkins.)

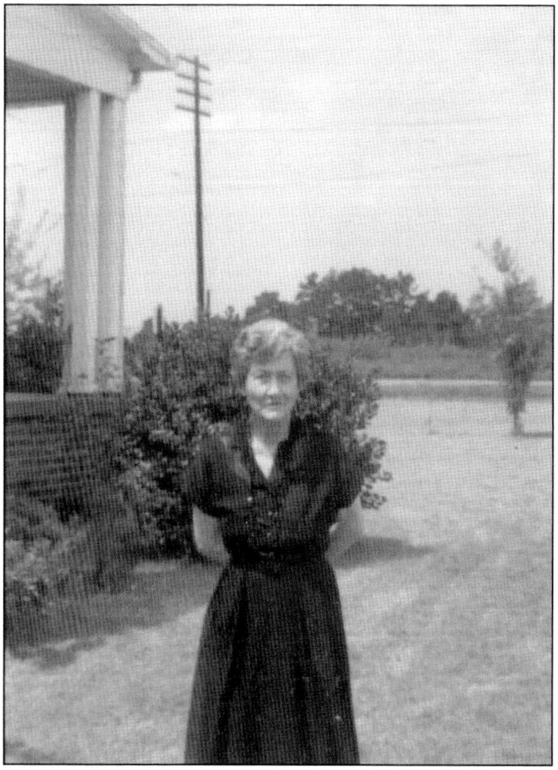

Cleo Burns served Colfax Township as an adult educator, art instructor, and as a public schoolteacher—often in one-room schools. During her 37 years of teaching, she taught all grades. Cleo Burns painted the baptismal river scene in the sanctuary of the Bethel Baptist Church and influenced many people across the county and state. (Courtesy of Anita Price Davis.)

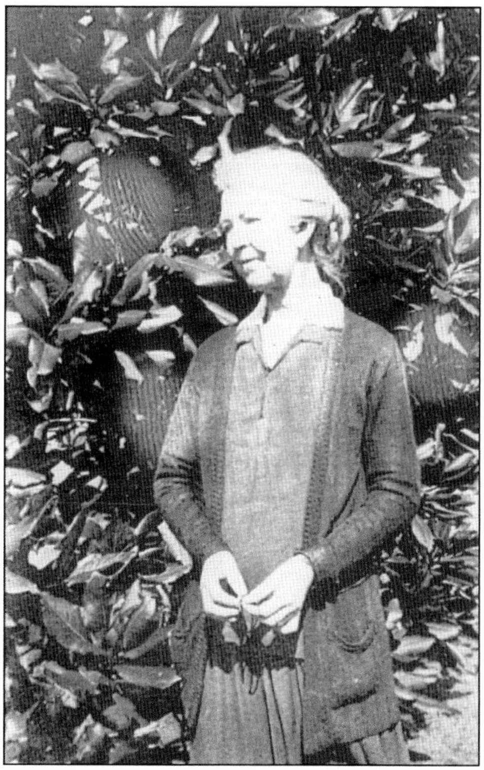

Mary Elizabeth Byers Griffin was a lifelong educator who taught all around the county, often in one-room schools. She and Cleo Burns were contemporaries and friends; they often taught together. While teaching at Cliffside, Mary Elizabeth met and married school principal William F. Griffin. Mary Elizabeth lived in the Byers House in Ellenboro from 1925 to 1955. (Courtesy of Pat Rhyne.)

Thomas E. Crowe (1908–1953) was serving as principal of Ellenboro School when he died suddenly on April 11, 1953. His widow, Rachel Price Crowe (1907–1991), continued to teach until her retirement from Ellenboro School. (Courtesy of Frank Wall.)

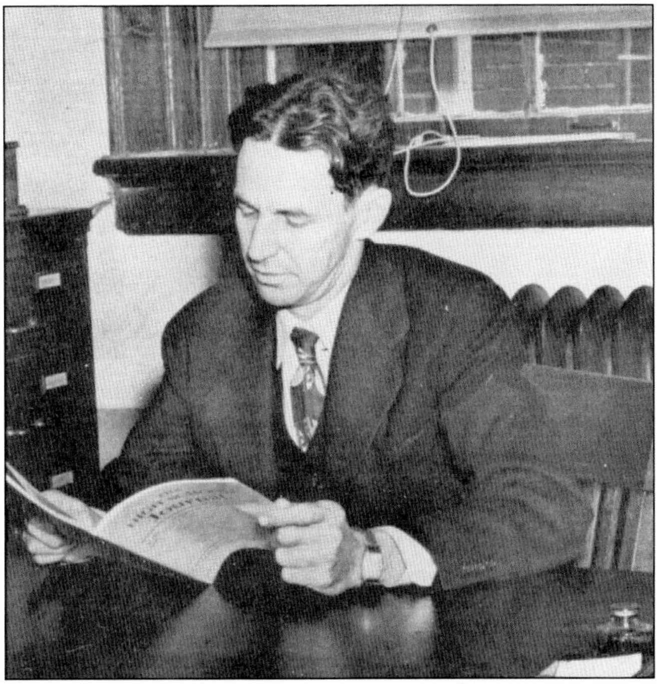

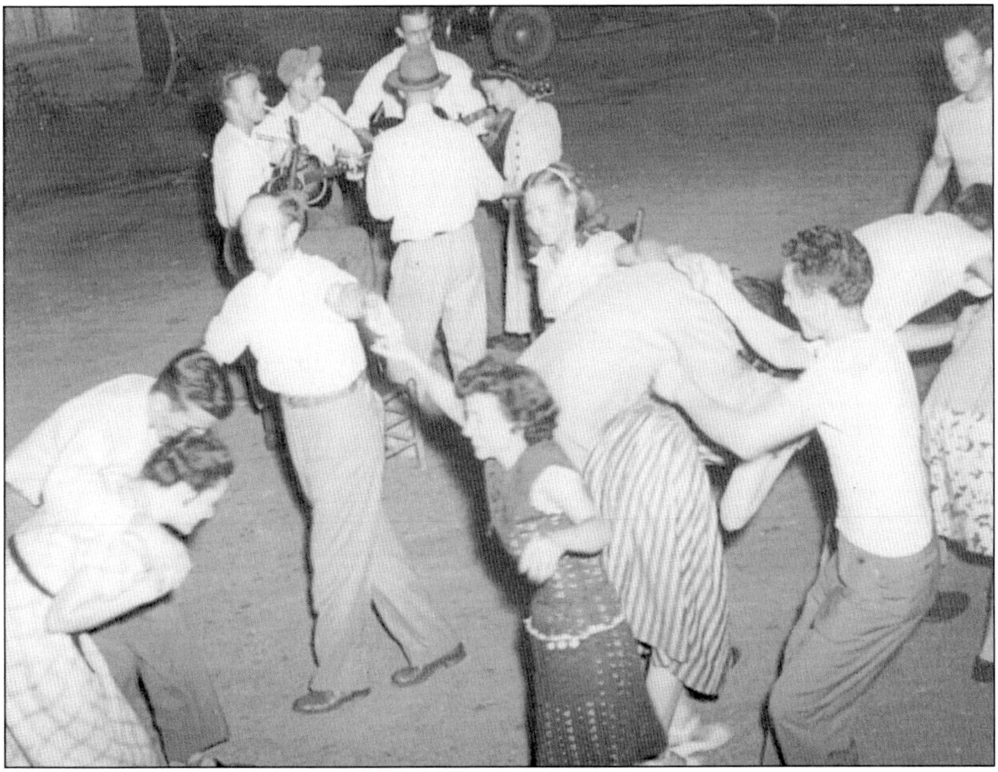

Street dances were popular forms of entertainment in Ellenboro in the late 1930s and early 1940s. Here teacher Peggy Wilson (center, dark dress), husband Hudson Wilson, and others promenade in the street. (Courtesy of Colfax Museum.)

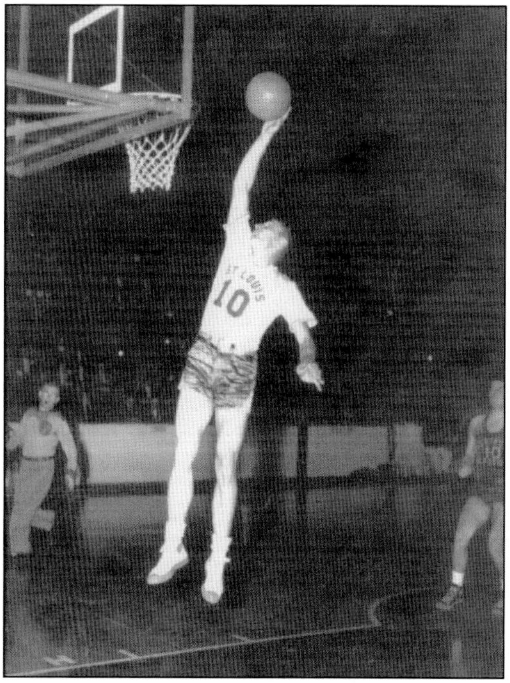

Belus Smawley (1918–2003) from Colfax Township was one of the first basketball players to perfect the jump shot. Smawley played for Appalachian State University, where he later coached. He played professionally in leagues that were the predecessors of today's NBA and on such teams as the St. Louis Bombers, the Syracuse Nationals, and the Baltimore Bullets. Smawley averaged 12.7 points per game. (Courtesy of Palmer Bailey.)

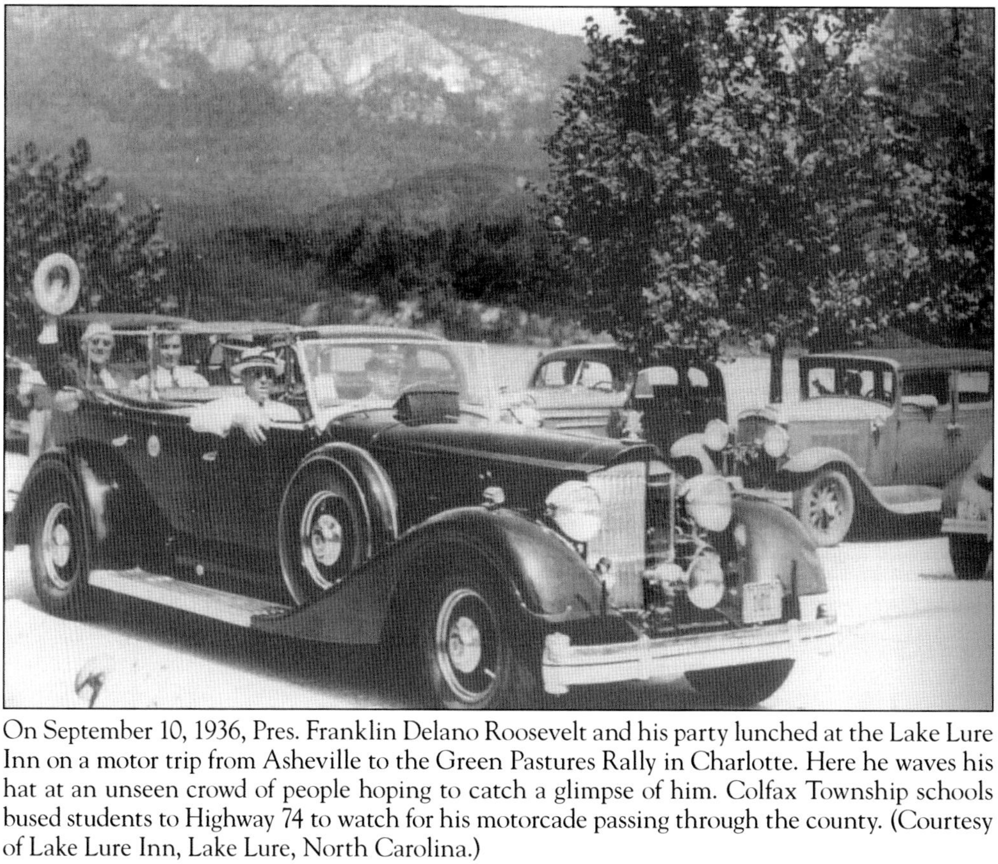

On September 10, 1936, Pres. Franklin Delano Roosevelt and his party lunched at the Lake Lure Inn on a motor trip from Asheville to the Green Pastures Rally in Charlotte. Here he waves his hat at an unseen crowd of people hoping to catch a glimpse of him. Colfax Township schools bused students to Highway 74 to watch for his motorcade passing through the county. (Courtesy of Lake Lure Inn, Lake Lure, North Carolina.)

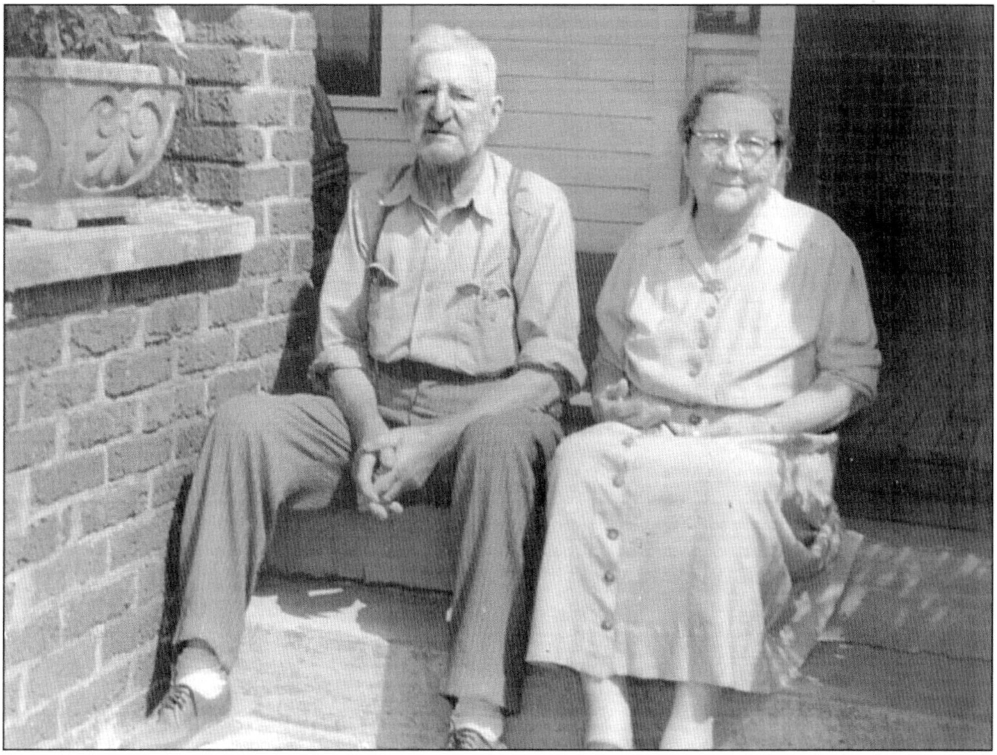

Mart and Margaret "Madge" Wright sit on the steps of their home in Colfax Township sometime before 1960. Mart was a farmer and a conductor for the Seaboard Railway; Madge was a homemaker. (Courtesy of Charles "Bass" Wright.)

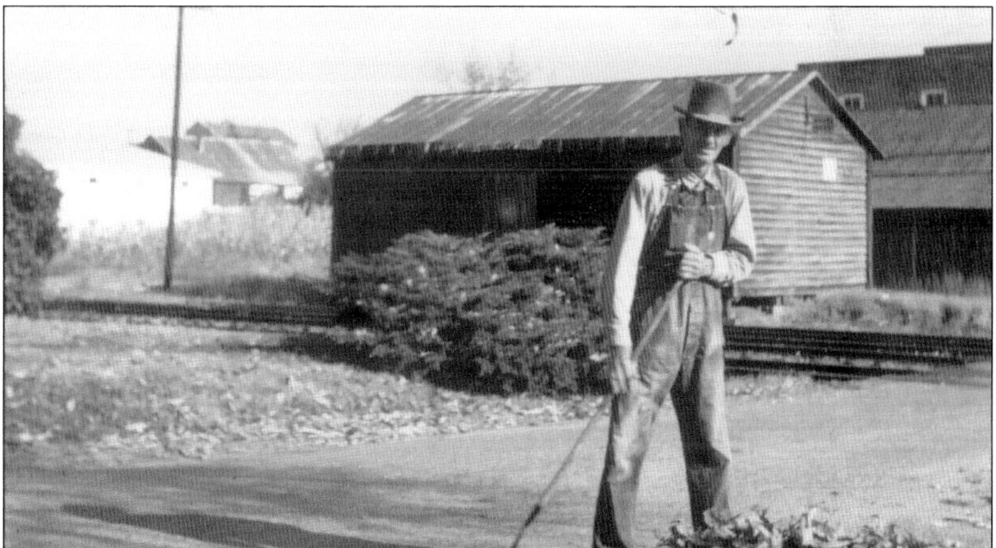

Captured in a typical activity, farmer William Luther Helton (1904–1995) is raking leaves near the railroad tracks and his Ellenboro home. The husband of Oma Jane Helton, Luther was the father of Dan William, Claude Gordon, Dorothy Jane, Helen Diane, and Joyce Yvonne. For many years, he helped care for the potato houses begun by A. B. Bushong. (Courtesy of Scott Withrow.)

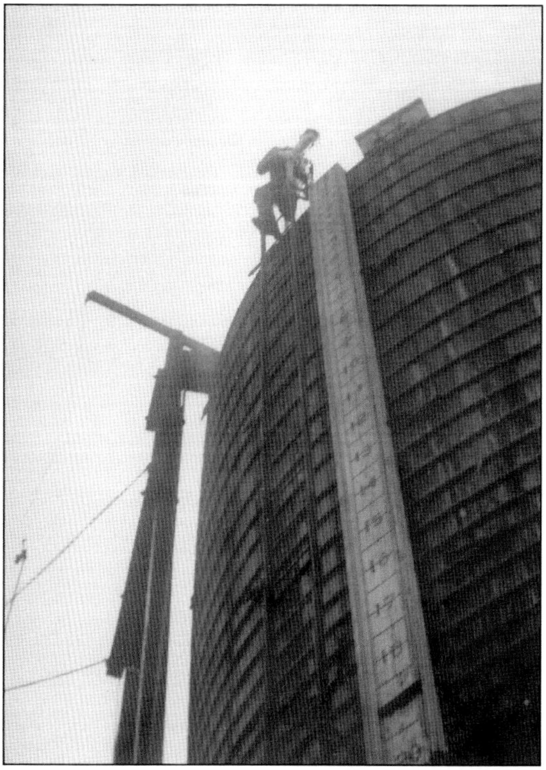

Shown in the 1930s, Dewitt Lowery stands atop the Seaboard Air Line Railway water tank, which was across the tracks from the present Ellenboro Fire Department. Dewitt served as mayor of Ellenboro from 1970 to 1982, worked for the North Carolina State Department of Transportation, and was among many World War II veterans who lived in Colfax Township. (Courtesy of Ruby Lowery.)

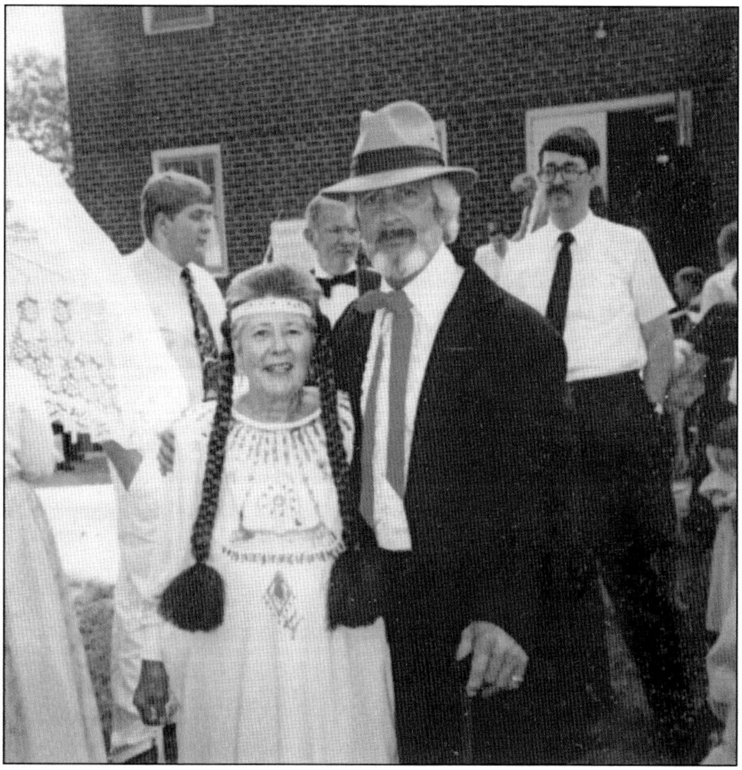

Theodora Russell and Jim Rhyne stand in front of Oak Grove Church in 1992—the church's bicentennial. That year the memorial committee asked attendees of the event to dress in period attire. Here Jim appears as a riverboat gambler with Theodora as Pocahontas. Jim served as Ellenboro mayor from 2005 to 2008. (Courtesy of Pat Rhyne.)

Here Wilbur Wright shows the fish that he and Jerry "Coot" Daves caught in a local stream in the early 1950s. Wilbur later attended Appalachian State University, taught at Chase High, and served Isothermal Community College as teacher, director of the evening school, dean of student affairs, and registrar. He was also Ellenboro's mayor in 1989. (Courtesy of Paul Price.)

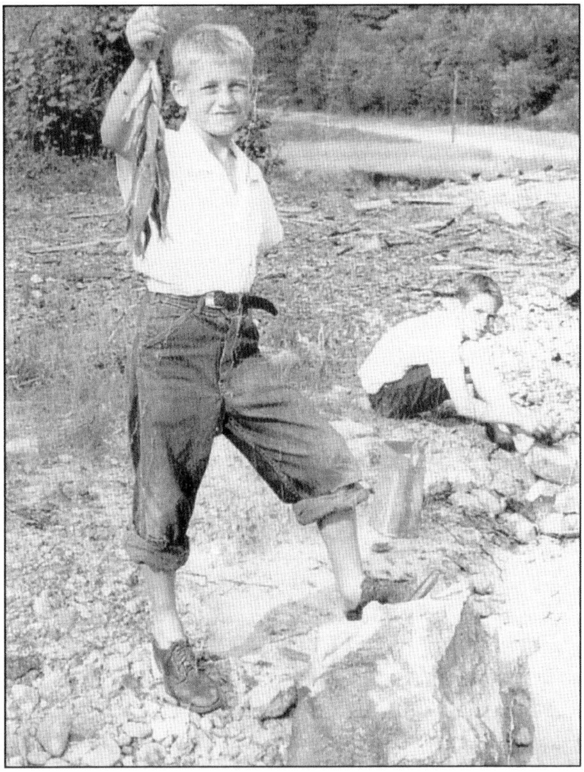

In the mid-1940s, Hank Martin fishes at a local pond. After graduation from Ellenboro High School in 1952, Hank made a career in the U.S. Navy. He returned to Colfax Township after 20 years in the military with a full retirement. Hank has been particularly supportive of the Colfax Museum. This photograph was a prizewinner in a *Charlotte Observer* contest. (Courtesy of Paul Price.)

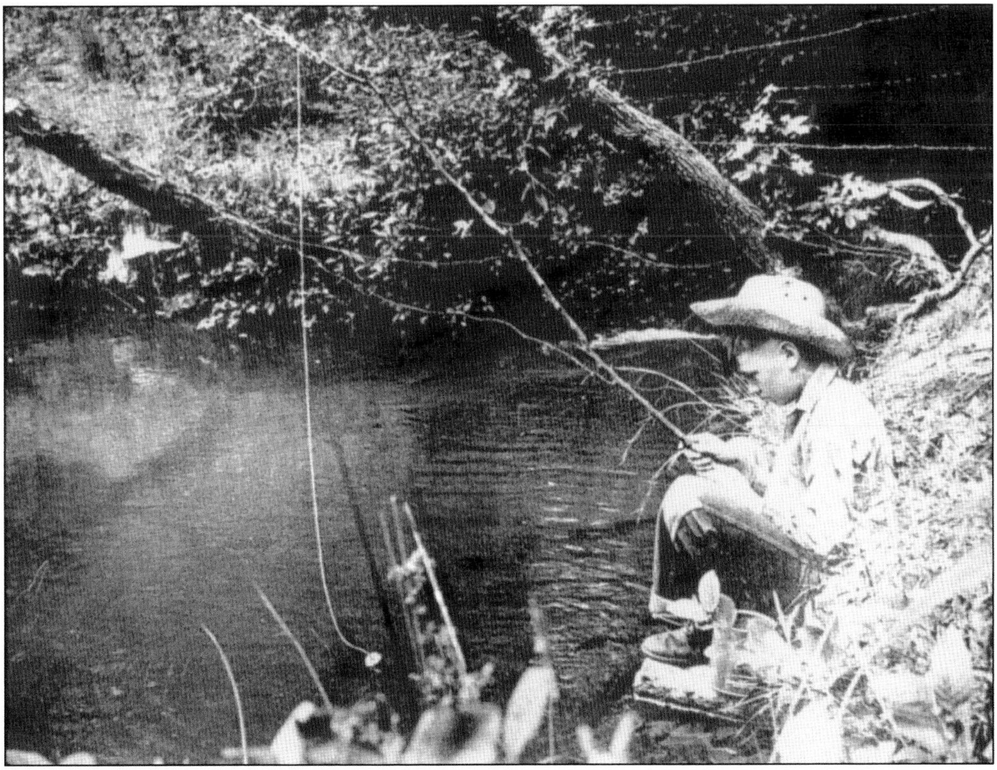

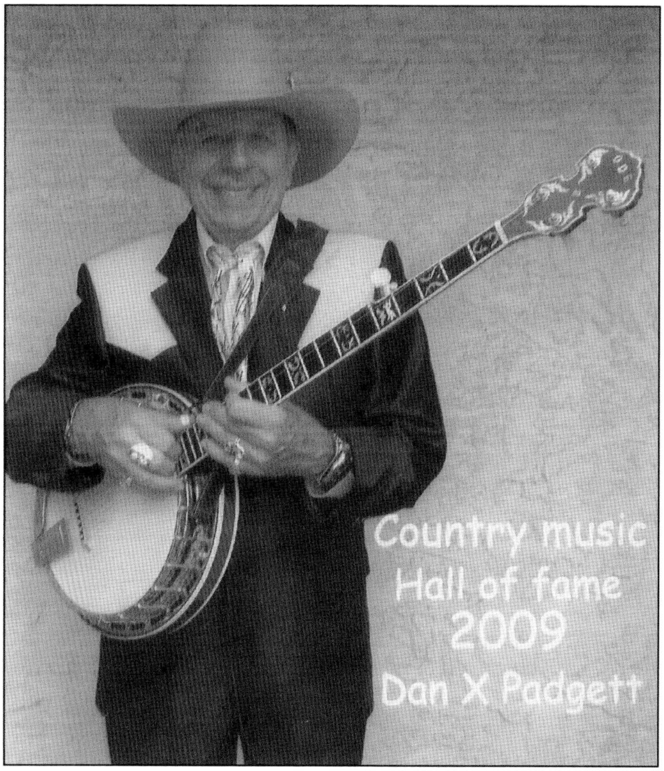

Dan X. Padgett is a local musician who has taught 11 instruments for the past 40 years in his own music studios in Spartanburg, Race Path, and Shelby. He performed on all of Lester Flatt and Earl Scruggs's television shows, played with Bill Monroe, and was a regular on channels 7 and 13. He performed at the fiddler's convention and on the Grand Ole Opry for three years. Padgett received induction into the Country Music Hall of Fame in 2009. (Courtesy of Dan X. Padgett.)

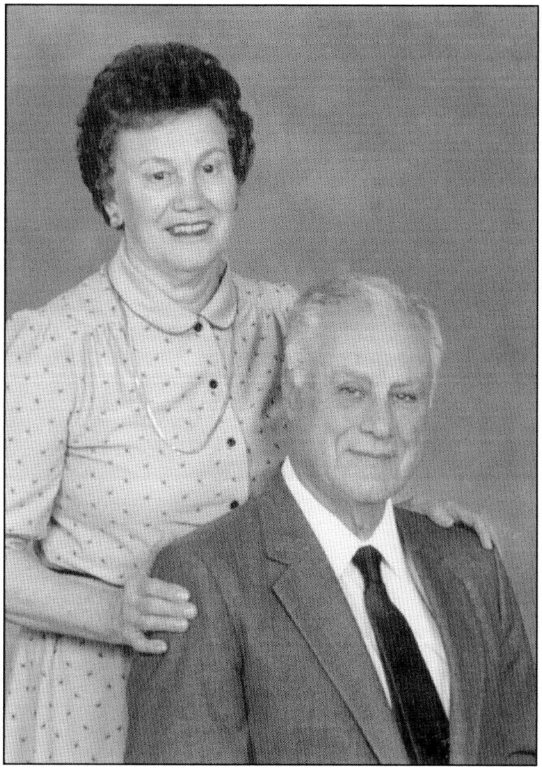

Mike Davis (1918–2006), a native of Tennessee and a 1942 college graduate, served in the 19th Photographic Technical Unit during World War II. Davis taught and coached at Cool Springs from 1949 to 1953. After Thomas E. Crowe's death, Davis served as Ellenboro's principal until 1977. Here Mike poses with his wife, Ruth (1921–2010). They had two sons, Michael and Tim. (Courtesy of Michael Davis.)

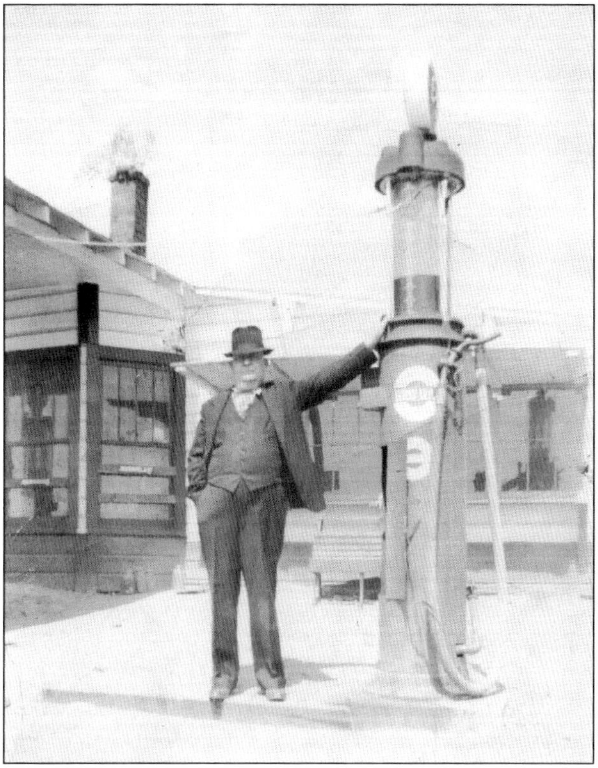

Born in Hopewell on February 22, 1887, Plato Rollins Price lived in Colfax Township for most of his life and operated a store on Highway 74/20 at the Cleveland/Rutherford county line for 40 years. Here he stands in front of his original county line station. Price was the father of Edward Rollins Price, Arthur Fred Price, Ruth Price Grindstaff, Falls Price, Roy Price, and Jessie Price. He was the grandfather of Anita Price Davis, Jeanne Price, Carolyn Grindstaff Barbee, and others. He died on November 4, 1976. (Courtesy of Carolyn Grindstaff Barbee.)

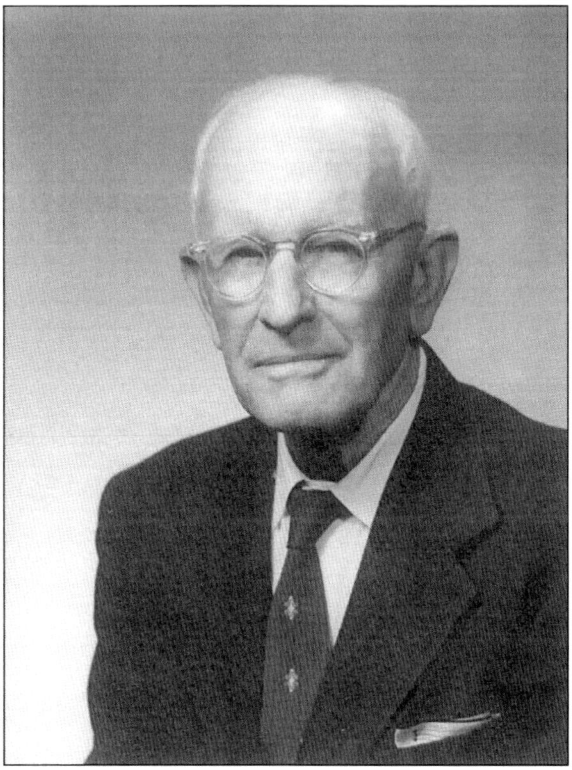

Orus Reid Coffield (1876–1965) was a member of the North Carolina State House of Representatives (1913), the Knights of Pythias, and the Methodist church, and was a Master Mason. A Colfax resident from 1908, he was an agent-operator with the Seaboard Railroad for 52 years, Ellenboro agent for the G. B. Harrill Insurance Company, member of the school board for 45 years, and Ellenboro mayor (off and on) for 40 years. (Courtesy of Harriet Stewart Coffield.)

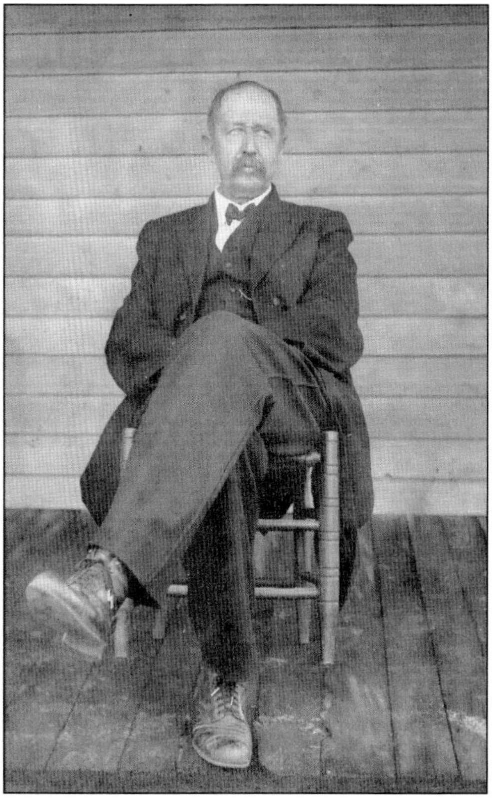

Rev. Zachariah Dobbins Harrill (1851–1935) was a well-known name in Colfax Township. Harrill was a Baptist minister and lived on Railroad Street in Ellenboro. A farmer, he preached at Piney Knob Baptist Church and other area churches. Harrill is buried in the cemetery of Bethel Baptist Church. (Courtesy of Scott Withrow.)

Here Wallace Billingsley poses in a Cliffside Railroad steam engine at a commemorative celebration in 1987. Wallace worked as section foreman for CSX. Before 1983, he worked with Seaboard Air Line Railway. (Courtesy of Scott Withrow.)

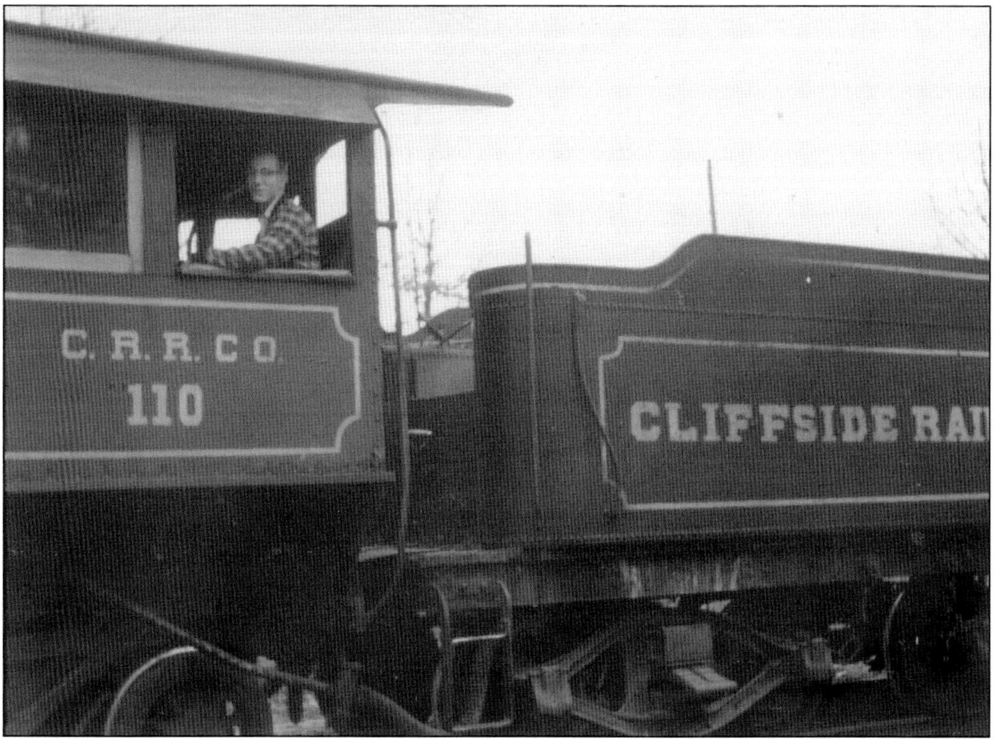

Bonnie (1917–1987) and Annie (1920–1987) Melton, who worked at the Doncaster-Tanner Company in Rutherfordton, lived on the east side of Highway 74/20 in Ellenboro, North Carolina. Known for their many acts of kindness in the community, the sisters served as Girls Auxiliary leaders for Bethel Baptist Church. Their father was Thomas A. Melton (1888–1956), who ran a local coal and ice company. (Courtesy of Scott Withrow.)

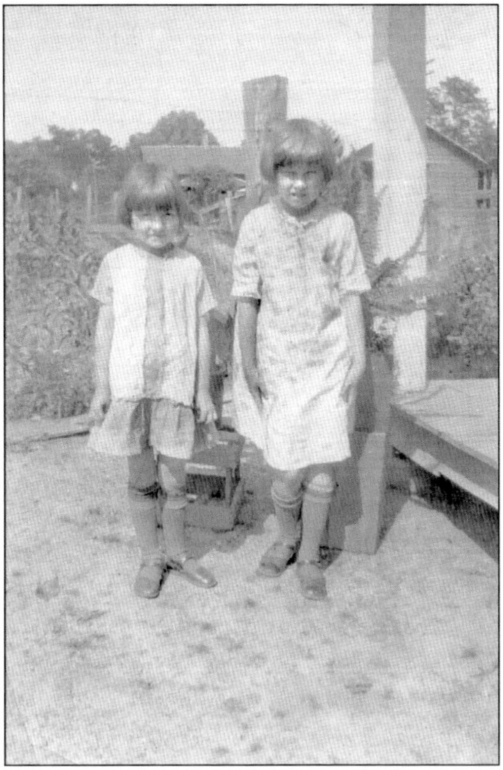

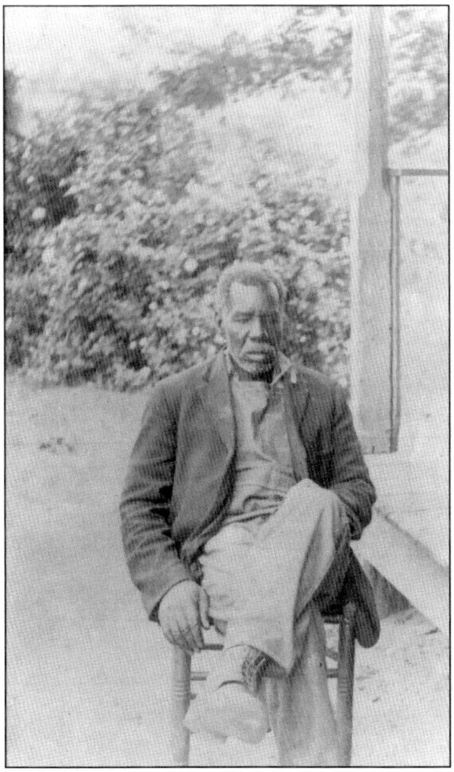

Dock Webb was a descendent of slaves and a member of the Webb family of Concord Community. Dock Webb was a farmhand for the Hamrick family, south of Ellenboro. He wore a size 17 shoe. (Courtesy of Scott Withrow.)

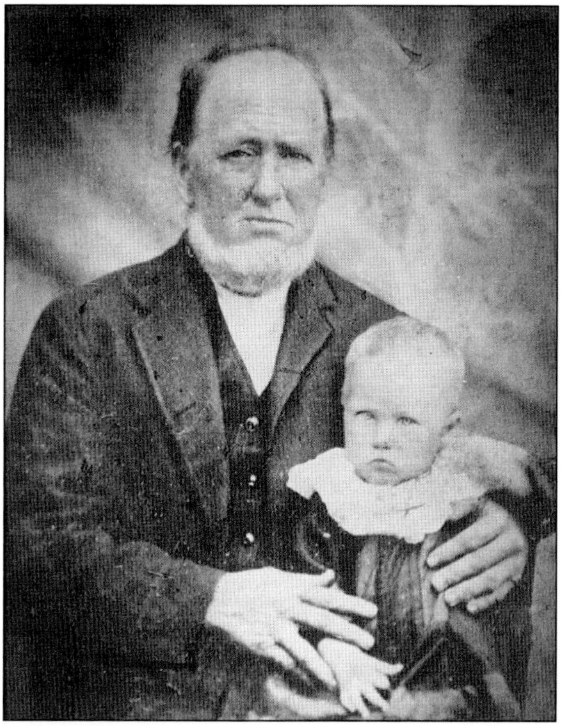

Burwell Benson Byers (1828–1898) was born in the area that is now eastern Colfax Township. Byers had a store on Short Road before the Civil War. B. B. became the first mayor of Ellenboro after the incorporation of the town in 1889. His granddaughter Ida Byers Matheny (1883–1976) is shown in this 1885 photograph. His grave is in the Byers plot in Oak Grove Methodist Church Cemetery. (Courtesy of Mike Rhyne.)

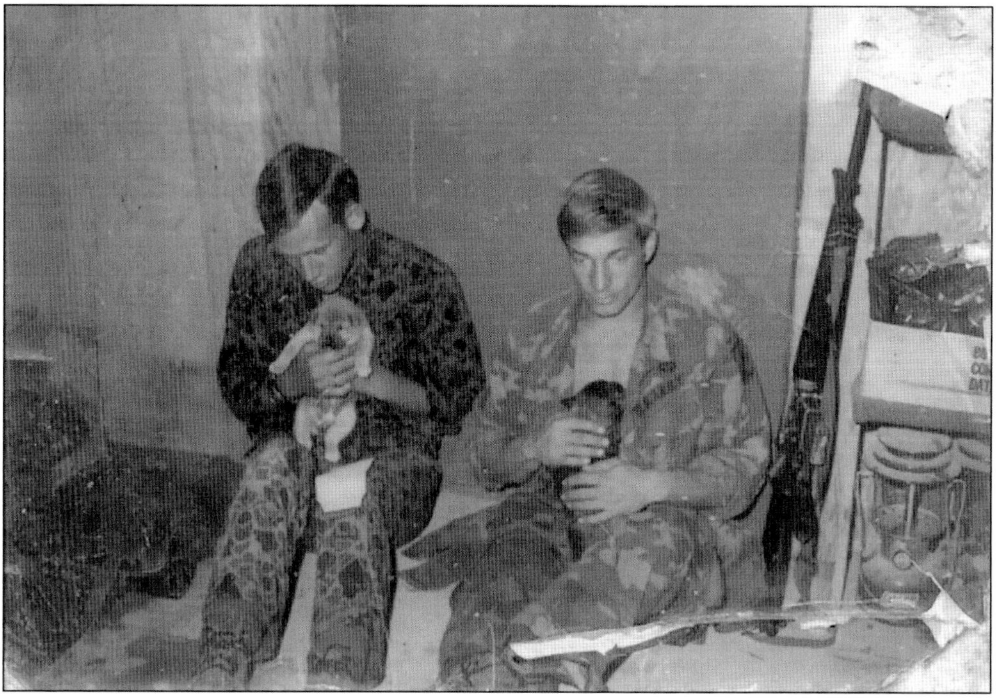

Peter McCann is a Vietnam veteran, commander and local organizer of the Honor Guard, and state commander of the DAV. Despite the suffering he witnessed and endured during the war, Peter remained compassionate. Here he sits—rifle ready—and comforts a pup he found in the area around An Loc. (Courtesy of Peter McCann.)

This 1944 image shows Henry K. Bailey (1888–1972) and wife Una Bridges Bailey (1898–1973) in their yard. Henry was a World War I veteran, a farmer, and a Southern Railroad construction worker. He helped in the construction of Camp Croft in Spartanburg, South Carolina, and Fort Bragg. The Bailey children are Bobby K., Palmer D., Emogene, Sally Jo, Rachel, and Freddie. (Courtesy of Palmer Bailey.)

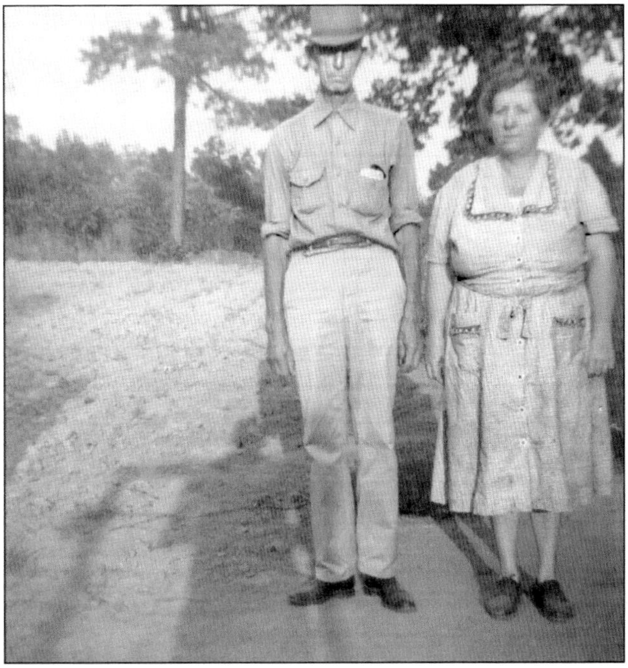

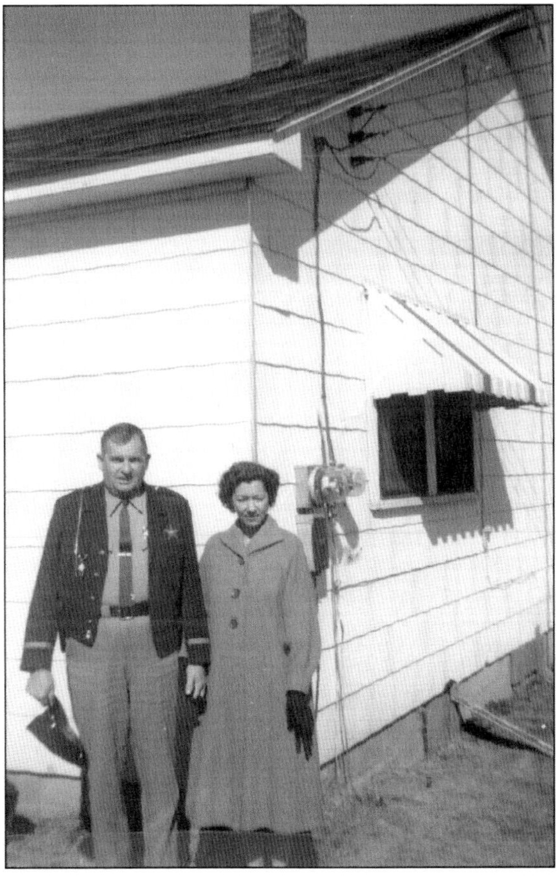

Born in Hopewell in 1915, Columbus Hubert Melton was a Rutherford County deputy sheriff. He served with Sheriff Damon Huskey from 1959 until 1975, except for four years when Huskey did not serve. Melton was buried in the Hopewell United Methodist Church Cemetery in 2003. His survivors include his wife, Annabel Hardin Melton, his daughter, Judith Melton Harrill, and his son, Gary Melton of Hopewell. (Courtesy of Judith Melton Harrill.)

INDEX